The
KNITTING
BOOK

The KNITTING BOOK

Introduction by Una Stubbs

100 IDÉES

CONRAN OCTOPUS

First published in 1988 by
Conran Octopus Limited
37 Shelton Street
London WC2H 9HN

This paperback edition published
in 1993 by Conran Octopus Limited

The editors would like to thank Penny Hill, Marilyn Wilson,
Frances Kennett and Beryl Miller, and Pingouin and 3
Suisses yarns for their assistance.

ISBN 1 85029 475 5

British Library Cataloguing in Publication Data
Knitting for all the family.
1. Clothing. Knitting – Patterns
i. 100 Idées
646.4'07

Typeset by SX Composing Limited
Printed in China

ACKNOWLEDGMENTS

2 E. Novick/A. de Chabaneix-A. Luntz
10-11 G. de Chabaneix/I. Garcon
12-19 G. de Chabaneix/C. de Chabaneix
20-23 D. Burgi/A. de Chabaneix-Luntz
24-27 G. de Chabaneix/C. de Chabaneix
28-31 M. Duffas/I. Garcon
32-39 G. de Chabaneix/I. Garcon
42-47 G. de Chabaneix/C. de Chabaneix

48-49 G. de Chabaneix/C. de Chabaneix
50-59 G. de Chabaneix/C. de Chabaneix
61-63 G. de Chabaneix/I. Garcon
64-71 G. de Chabaneix/A. de Chabaneix
72-73 J. Tisne/A. Luntz
74-79 G. de Chabaneix/C. de Chabaneix
80-85 G. de Chabaneix/I. Garcon
86-87 G. de Chabaneix/C. de Chabaneix
89-91 M. Duffas/J. Schoumacher

92-101 G. de Chabaneix/C. de Chabaneix
102-105 B. Maltaverne/C. Lebeau
106-113 D. Burgi/A. de Chabaneix-A. Luntz
115-117 G. de Chabaneix/C. de Chabaneix
118-125 J. Tisne/J. Schoumacher
126-127 G. de Chabaneix/A. Luntz
129-133 P. Degrandy/A. de Chabaneix-A. Luntz
136-138 O. Bucourt/J. Schoumacher
141-142 E. Novick/A. Luntz

144-149 O. Bucourt/A. de Chabaneix-A. Luntz
152-157 Y. Duronsoy/J. Schoumacher
158-160 G. de Chabaneix/A. Luntz
164-169 J. Tisne/J. Schoumacher
170-171 E.Novick/A. de Chabaneix-A. Luntz
175-178 O. Bucourt/A. de Chabaneix-A. Luntz
181 G. de Chabaneix/A. Luntz
183 C. Streeter
184-187 D. Burgi/I. Garcon
188-191 B. Maltaverne/C. Lebeau

CONTENTS

1

2

3

4

INTRODUCTION

This book makes knitting fun, absorbing, easy and rewarding. I love the fact that it includes both simple classic styles and more ornate ones. It is the first time I have read a knitting book where you could choose to make a woolly for a baby, or anyone right up to grandpa. With its huge range of designs and practical diagrams, THE KNITTING BOOK makes creating these beautiful garments temptingly simple. Although I am only a novice knitter, I feel I could even tackle an aran sweater with the enlargements of the actual patterns of stitches to guide me. But I think I will start with a small jumper for a friend's youngest child, and if it is successful, then perhaps I'll try an identical one, a couple of sizes larger for her oldest child. The patterns for the family are particularly valuable being sized from small children through to adults.

I come from a family of knitters, as do most people of my age and background. If your mother or relations didn't knit, then you didn't have a sweater. I well remember the evenings spent around the fire with my father, sister and brother listening to the radio, or the family picnic outings, and there was always the gentle clicking of my mother and gran's needles. Where ever we went they knitted, they had to or we wouldn't be warm.

We each had one sweater which, when worn out or grown out of, was unravelled, the wool carefully washed and hung on the line in skeins to remove the corrugations, then reknitted with some extra wool that was often a very poor match. It was a never-ending job, but I believe knitting kept the women and the family tranquil, no matter how hard those times were.

My sister and I were first taught to add a couple of rows and though our childish attempts looked clumsy and uneven, mingling with mother's fine work, the rows were left there importantly. My mother knew full well that my soppy old dad would treasure his daughters' knobbly efforts stretched around his tum. We were then encouraged to knit for our teddies, then for ourselves. By the time we were teenagers we were sent to choose our own wools, but the patterns we could select from seemed to be deathly dull with extremely starchy instructions. We longed to have bought sweaters which were by then all the rage. When I eventually started work and bought my own clothes, a hand-knitted sweater was sadly for many years looked down on with disdain by all.

I am so happy that this is no longer the case. Thanks to books like this one, youngsters will be encouraged to learn the joys of knitting, choosing needles and wools – there is such a wide range included here – and then with pride pass on the skills to their children. I seriously think that knitting provides endless pleasure – I long to get clicking.

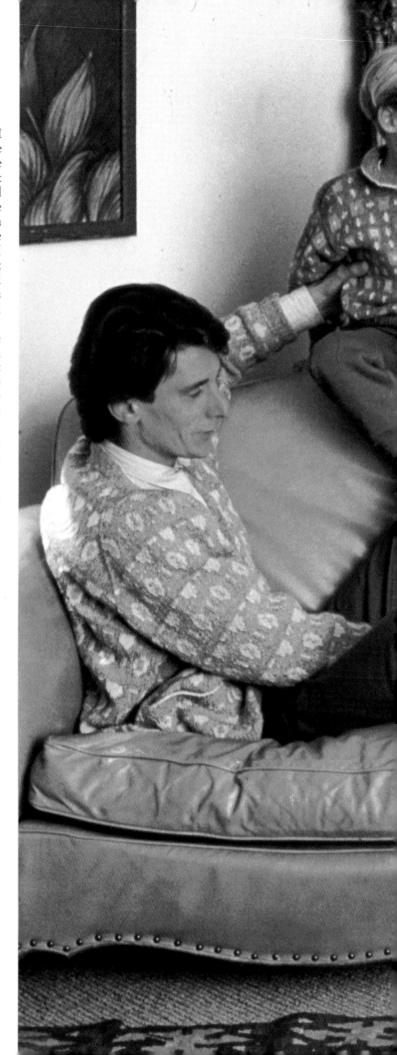

6

BASIC ESSENTIALS

One of the pleasures of knitting is that although the basic skills of casting on and off, knit and purl stitches are simple to learn, they lead on to an almost infinite variety of patterns and textures. It is assumed that people using this book will have mastered the basics and are ready to try more complex types of pattern. If any of the designs include techniques with which you are unfamiliar, the following instructions are intended to show how they should be tackled. They also include details of the finishing touches which make all the difference to the appearance of a knitted garment.

Abbreviations

The standard abbreviations used in this book are listed below, any further abbreviations are explained within the patterns which contain them.

k = knit
p = purl
st(s) = stitches
st st = stocking stitch
rev st st = reverse stocking stitch
p side = right side
m st = moss stitch
g st = garter stitch
rep = repeat
beg = beginning
patt = pattern
yfd = yarn forward
yrn = yarn round needle
tog = together
SKPO = slip 1, k 1, pass slipped st over
tbl = through back of loop (or loops)
rem = remaining
cont = continue
foll(s) = follow(s)(ing)
alt = alternate
kfb (or pfb) = knit (or purl) into front and back of next stitch
inc = increase
dec = decrease
cm = centimetres

Tension

The correct tension is given for each pattern. It is easy to rush ahead and start the main pattern without knitting a tension sample first, but a high proportion of failures or at best not-very-successful garments have turned out that way because the knitter did not first make a tension sample.

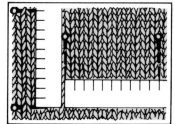

With each design, therefore, we state the correct tension and suggest the number of stitches on which the sample should be worked. Cast on that number and work in the pattern (or stocking stitch if this is the basic stitch used in the design). Knit until the sample measures at least 12cm (5in) and then cast off and measure the tension.

If the tension is not exactly right, make another sample using larger or smaller needles as necessary to obtain the correct tension. If you have more stitches to 10cm (4in) than stated, you are working too tightly and should try larger needles; if you have fewer stitches, you are working too loosely and should use smaller needles. Use needles which will produce the correct tension for the main parts of the garment, as given, and remember to make corresponding alterations in the needle size(s) given for any other parts, such as cuffs and waistband.

Although all this can be time-consuming and irritating, especially if you are full of enthusiasm to start on your new project, it is infinitely better than wasting both time and money knitting to the wrong tension.

Sides

The first row worked is always the right side unless otherwise stated.

'Front of work' refers to the side on which you are actually knitting and 'back' to the side of the work which is away from you: these should not be confused with the terms 'right side' and 'wrong side' of work.

Swiss darning

Swiss darning is a popular and very simple way of decorating knitted garments by covering the knitting stitch-by-stitch with yarns embroidered on in contrast colours. The effect is almost as if the colours had been knitted in with the garment, but it is generally much quicker and easier to work. Some of the patterns in this book, such as the Wisteria Cardigan (see page 20) already include Swiss darning, but you could also use the technique for some of the other designs, as an alternative to knitting. On the Japanese Wave sweater, for example, on page 158, there are several colours which are only used in very restricted areas, such as the tiny crests of the huge wave. You might find that these are easier to Swiss darn than to knit in with the rest of the pattern.

Swiss darning can be worked either horizontally or vertically, whichever fits in most easily with the motif or pattern. If you are working isolated dots, simply carry the yarn across the back of the work as you would if knitting a Fair Isle pattern. Use a blunt-ended wool needle and, if you are using scrap-bag yarns, make sure that they are thick enough to cover the knitted stitches.

Horizontal technique

Thread your needle and bring it out at the bottom right-hand corner of the motif, at the base of the first knitted stitch to be covered. Working from right to left, insert the needle behind the stitch immediately above.

Pull the yarn through, then insert the needle back through the base of the first stitch and

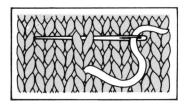

bring it out at the base of the stitch immediately to the left.

Pull the yarn through, covering the first stitch, then work from left to right along the row. When the first row is complete, work back from left to right along the row above.

Vertical technique

This is worked more like chain-stitch embroidery, which Swiss darning closely resembles. Begin at the bottom, as for the horizontal technique, bringing the yarn through at the base of the first stitch and taking the needle from right to left behind the stitch above. Pull the yarn through and then insert the needle vertically behind the first stitch, as shown. Pull the yarn through to cover the first stitch and continue upwards.

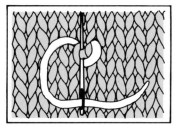

Jacquard knitting

Many of the designs in this book are examples of the technique known as jacquard. The method of working is quite different from traditional Fair Isle in which two or more colours are carried across the row and used when needed. Jacquard designs either have motifs which may be small or large and are isolated against a background colour or else they have large panels or geometric shapes worked in various colours. In all these cases it is necessary to use separate balls of colour for each of the different motifs or shapes and if these are large, a separate ball of the background colour is also needed for the stitches on each side. Join on the balls where necessary by making a single knot into the previous stitch; afterwards these knots can be unpicked and the ends darned in securely.

To avoid using whole balls of the various colours wind off a small ball for each section; it is more convenient to wind them on to strips of cardboard. Cut a slit in the card so that the yarn can be passed through the slit when it is not being used. It will then hang without becoming entangled. All the spare colours are kept on the wrong side of the work and it is essential each time you begin with a new colour to pick it up from underneath the colour previously used so that it passes right around the previous colour. This will avoid holes forming in the work.

The technique requires practice to avoid the edges of the various sections becoming too loose but once the skill has been mastered spectacular results can be obtained. In many of the designs certain very small sections are embroidered on afterwards by the method known as Swiss darning, which is used to add detail to plain stocking stitch. The stitches are knitted in the background colour and are later covered completely with the new colour.

Increases and Decreases
To increase at the beginning of a row either cast on a stitch or work into the front and back of the 1st

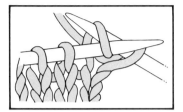

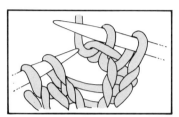

stitch. To increase at the end of a row work into the front and back of the last stitch. In this way it is easier to match the increases at the sides and thus make a neater seam. To decrease at the beginning of a row either cast off a stitch or work SKPO. At the end of a row work the last two stitches together.

Making up
Once you have knitted all the separate sections of a design, you will be longing to wear the finished article and it is very tempting to rush through the making-up stage. This is a mistake, because a lumpy seam can spoil the effect of hours and hours of careful knitting and if you've waited so long, then it's worth waiting just a little longer to get it right.

Blocking and pressing
First check the ball band to see whether or not the yarn can be pressed and if so at what heat. If it can be pressed, then each part of the garment must be blocked and pressed before it is seamed.

Blocking is simply a way of putting the pieces under a very

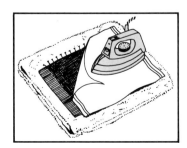

slight tension during pressing. Fold a large towel or blanket to make a thick ironing pad, then lay the piece of knitting right side down on the pad. If there is a measurement diagram, check this as you pin the piece out, pulling it back into shape if it has become distorted. For a back or front, start by pinning at the widest point, which is generally the chest measurement. Push the pins in right up to the head and position them about a centimetre apart all the way around the garment except at ribbed cuffs and hems, which are never pressed.

When the piece is pinned out, cover it with a clean cloth (damp or dry according to the instructions on the ball band): never put the iron directly on the knitting. Press very lightly, lifting the iron up and putting it down on new sections.

Seaming
Always use a blunt-ended wool needle for seaming. There are several ways of joining a seam. The back-stitch seam is ideal for heavily textured fabrics and for shoulder seams, but the flat seam is also useful for heavily textured knitting, ribbed edges and button bands. The invisible seam is best used for vertical joins only (not shoulders) on straight-sided pieces worked in stocking stitch.

Method 1 Back-stitch seam
Place the two pieces to be joined with right sides together and begin sewing at the right-hand end of the seam, securing the end of the yarn with a double stitch. Push the needle through both layers and bring it up to the top again. Push the needle in again at the starting point and

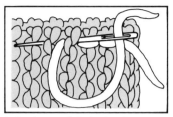

bring it out a little further from the point where you last brought it out to make one back-stitch. Continue backstitching to the end of the seam.

Method 2 Flat seam
Start with right sides together and a double stitch, as for the back-stitch seam. Carefully matching rows or stitches, and pushing the needle through vertically for greater accuracy, join the seam with a running stitch effect.

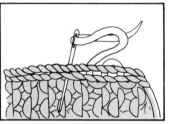

Method 3 Invisible seaming
Place the two pieces right side up and side by side, matching the rows and edge stitches. Secure the end of the yarn at the bottom right-hand edge and pick up the matching stitch on the left-hand edge. Pull the yarn through tightly, then return to the right-hand edge and pick up the stitch on the next row up. Repeat until the seam is complete.

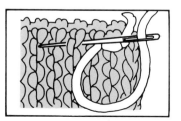 

1
BABY KNITS

GEMINI GEM

Perfectly suited to the dual nature of a Gemini baby (22 May to 22 June), this two-tone outfit with accompanying blanket is completely reversible, a highly practical feature which will no doubt also appeal to those who are not addicted to star gazing and have their feet firmly planted on the ground. Quickly knitted in garter stitch on large needles, this is the ideal design for an inexperienced knitter.

CHECKLIST

JACKET, ROMPERS, HAT AND BOOTEES

Materials
Anny Blatt Soft'Anny: 3 balls apricot No 1129 (**A**) and 3 balls rose No 1113 (**B**). Pair each of needles size 4mm and 5mm; 4 buttons.

Sizes
Three sizes, to fit ages 3 (6-9) months. Actual measurements shown on diagram.

Stitches used
Each garment is worked entirely in g st, k loop = *pick up loop lying between needles and k it through the back.*

Tension
Over g st using 5mm (larger) needles, 14 sts and 28 rows to 10cm (4in). Work a sample on 20 sts.

BLANKET

Materials
Anny Blatt Soft'Anny: 6 balls anis (pale green) No 1669 (**A**) and 6 balls ciel (pale blue) No 1125 (**B**). Pair of needles size 4½mm.

Size
Finished blanket measures 110cm (43½in) square.

Stitch used
Blanket is worked entirely in g st.

Tension
Over g st using 4½mm needles, 15 sts and 30 rows to 10cm (4in). Work a sample on 20 sts.

INSTRUCTIONS

JACKET

Section A (Work entirely in **A**.)
Main part Beg at front edge of left front cast on 24 (26-28) sts using larger needles and work in g st counting 1st row as right side. Work 48 (52-56) rows.✲✲ Using a short length of yarn cast on 26 (28-30) sts for sleeve. Return to main part.

▦ *Next row* K 24 (26-28) then onto same needle k the sts of sleeve.

▦ *Next row* (wrong side) K 30 (32-34), turn leaving rem 20 (22-24) sts of main part unworked. Cont on the 30 (32-34) sts for sleeve and dec 1 st at both ends of every foll 6th row 3 (2-1) times then every foll 8th row 2 (3-4) times. Cont on rem 20 (22-24) sts until sleeve measures 15(16-17)cm, 5⅞(6¼-6¾)in, from beg. Cast off loosely.

▦ **Back** Fold sleeve in half and pick up and k 4 sts along the

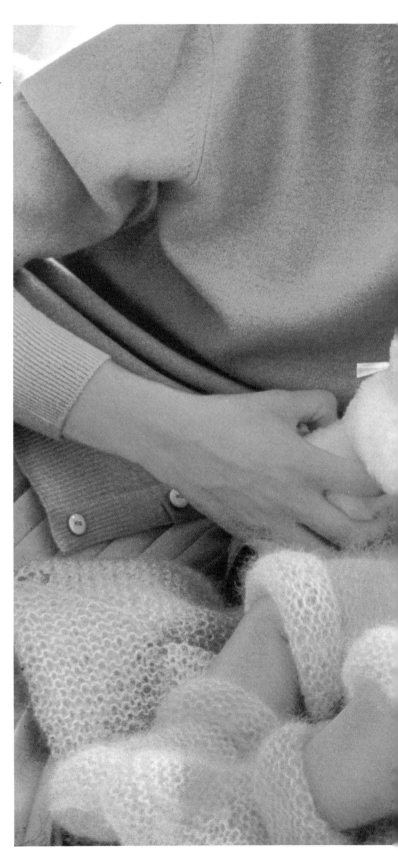

outer 4 sts of those cast on for sleeve then onto same needle with wrong side facing k the 20 (22-24) sts of main part which were left unworked.** Cont on 24 (26-28) sts and work 68 (74-80) rows. Now work exactly as for left sleeve from ** to **. You now have 24 (26-28) sts for right front. Cont on these sts and work 48 (52-56) rows. Cast off loosely.

▨ **Yoke** With right side facing and using larger needles, pick up and k 26 (28-30) sts along upper edge of right front, 22 (24-26) sts along upper edge of right sleeve, 36 (38-40) sts along upper edge of back, 22 (24-26) sts along upper edge of left sleeve and 26 (28-30) sts along upper edge of left front. 132 (142-152) sts. Cont in g st across all sts; k 1 row then begin shaping.
▨ *1st row* K 26 (28-30), SKTPO, k 16 (18-20), k 3 tog, k 36 (38-40), SKTPO, k 16 (18-20), k 3 tog, k 26 (28-30).
▨ *2nd and alt rows* K.
▨ *3rd row* K 26 (28-30), SKTPO, k 12 (14-16), k 3 tog, k 36 (38-40), SKTPO, k 12 (14-16), k 3 tog, k 26 (28-30). Work double decs in same positions on next 2 alt rows working 4 sts fewer between pairs of decs each time. Work 1 row on rem 100 (110-120) sts. Change to smaller needles and work neck border.
▨ *1st row* K 4 (5-6), [k 2 tog, k 5] 13 (14-15) times, k 2 tog, k 3 (5-7).
▨ *2nd and alt rows* K.
▨ *3rd row* K 3 (4-6), [k 2 tog, k 4] 13 (14-15) times, k 2 tog, k 3 (5-6)
▨ *5th row* K 3 (4-6), [k 2 tog, k 3] 13 (14-15) times, k 2 tog, k 2 (4-5).
▨ *7th row* K 2 (4-5), [k 2 tog, k 2] 13 (14-15) times, k 2 tog, k 2 (3-5). Cont on rem 44 (50-56) sts and work 4 rows without shaping then cast off firmly.

Section B (Working entirely in **B** work each part as for Section A.)

▨ **Finishing** Join sleeve seams of each section. Place one section inside the other so that right sides of each are tog. Sew sections tog along outer edge of sleeves, all around neck and front edges and along lower edge leaving a space at centre back. Turn right side out and neatly close opening.

ROMPERS

Section A (Worked entirely in **A**.)

▨ **Front** For one leg cast on 14 (15-16) sts using larger needles and work in g st counting 1st row as right side. Work 6(7-8)cm, 2⅜(2¾-3⅛)in, ending with a wrong-side row. Inc 1 st at beg of next row then cont on these 15 (16-17) sts until work measures 11(12-13)cm, 4¼(4¾-5⅛)in, from beg, ending at shaped edge. Cut yarn and leave sts on a spare needle. Work second leg in same way but working the inc at opposite edge; cont until you have worked same number of rows ending at straight edge.
▨ *Next row* K 15(16-17), turn, cast on 4(5-5) sts, turn, then beg at shaped edge k 15(16-17) sts of first leg. Cont on these 34(37-39) sts until work measures 26(28-30)cm, 10¼(11-11¾)in, from beg then change to smaller needles and cont until front measures 29(31-33)cm, 11⅜(12¼-13)in, from beg, ending with a wrong-side row. **
▨ **Neck Shaping** *Next row* Cast off 4, k until there are 11 (12-13) sts on right needle, leave these sts of left front on a holder, cast off next 4 (5-5) sts, k until there are 11 (12-13) sts on right needle for right front, cast off rem 4 sts and fasten off. Rejoin yarn to sts of right front and dec 1 st at both ends of every alt row until 3 (2-3) sts rem. Cast off. Complete left front in same way.

▨ **Back** Work as for front to **.
▨ *Next row* Cast off 7 (8-9), k until there are 4 sts on right needle, place these sts onto a safety pin for right shoulder strap, cast off next 12 (13-13) sts, k until there are 4 sts on right needle, cast off rem 7 (8-9) sts and fasten off. Rejoin yarn to second group of 4 sts and using smaller needles cont in g st for left shoulder strap. Work 14(15-16)cm, 5½(5⅞-6¼)in,

then make buttonhole.

▦ *Next row* K 2 tog, yfd, k 2. Work 2 more rows then cast off. Work right shoulder strap in same way.

Section B (Working entirely in **B**, work front and back as for section A.)

▦ **Finishing** Join inner leg and crotch seams of Section A then join side seams. Repeat for Section B. Place one section inside the other with right sides tog. Join sections all around upper edges. Turn right side out and neatly sew the sections tog around lower edge of legs. Oversew the straps of each section tog and buttonhole st around double buttonholes. Sew a button to top of each front, on A section and 2 more on B section so that straps can be fastened through buttons on both sides.

BOOTEES

▦ These are single thickness. Using smaller needles and **A** cast on 29 (31-33) sts for centre of sole and work in g st; work 2 rows without shaping.
▦ *3rd row* K 1, k loop, k 13 (14-15), k loop, k 1, k loop, k 13 (14-15), k loop, k 1.
▦ *4th row* K.
▦ *5th row* K 1, k loop, k 14 (15-16), k loop, k 3, k loop, k 14 (15-16), k loop, k 1. Cont on these 37 (39-41) sts and work 13 (15-17) rows.

▦ **Instep Shaping** *1st row* K 21 (22-23), k 2 tog, turn, thus leaving 14 (15-16) sts unworked.
▦ *2nd row* Slip 1, k 5, k 2 tog, turn leaving 14 (15-16) sts at this edge also. Rep 2nd row twice more, thus taking in 1 st from those at side each time. Change to **B** and rep 2nd row 12 times more. Turn after last row and k to end. Cont on 21 (23-25) sts and work 26 (28-30) rows then cast off loosely.
▦ Fold cast-on edge in half and join with a flat seam. Sew back seam of bootee reversing it for turnover top. If you choose, you

can outline the sole with a row of crochet as folls: using a medium-sized crochet hook and **A**, work a row of d c along the ridge formed by 8th (10th-12th) row of g st from beg.

HAT

Section A (Work entirely in **A**.)

▦ Using larger needles cast on 56 (60-64) sts and work in g st; cont until hat measures 14(15-16)cm, 5½ (5⅞-6¼)in, from beg, then shape top.
▦ *1st row* K 3, [k 2 tog, k 2] 13 (14-15) times, k 1. Work 3 rows without shaping.
▦ *5th row* K 2, [k 2 tog, k 1] 13 (14-15) times, k 2. K 1 row.
▦ *7th row* [K 2 tog] 15 (16-17) times. K 1 row.
▦ *9th row* [K 2 tog] 7 (8-8) times, k 1 (0-1). Cut yarn; thread end through rem sts; draw up tightly and sew securely, then join back seam.

Section B (Working entirely in **B**, work as for Section A.)

▦ **Finishing** Place one hat inside the other with right sides tog and seams level; oversew around cast-on edges leaving a space at back, turn right side out and neatly close opening. Sew the two layers tog with a few sts at top of hat.

BLANKET

▦ **Main Part** Using **A** cast on 136 sts and work in g st for 90cm (35½in).
▦ Cast off.
▦ Work another section in the same way using **B**.

▦ **Border** Using **A** cast on 16 sts and work in g st for 90cm (35½in) then shape corner.
▦ ** *1st row* Count this as right side of work. K 15, turn.
▦ *2nd and alt rows* Slip 1, k to end.
▦ *3rd row* K 14, turn.
▦ *5th row* K 13, turn. Cont working 1 st fewer on every alt row until 27th row has been worked on 2 sts; rep 2nd row.

▦ *29th row* K 3, turn.
▦ *30th row* As 2nd. Work 1 more st before turning on every alt row until you are working across the full 16 sts. Cont in g st across all sts for 90cm (35½in) ending at outer edge after a wrong-side row. ** Rep from ** to ** twice more.
▦ Shape last corner as before and when 1 row has been worked on 16 sts cast off.
▦ Make another border using **B**.

▦ **Finishing** Backstitch cast-on and cast-off edges of each border strip. With right sides tog backstitch border worked in **B** around main part worked in **A** and border in **A** around main part in **B**.
▦ Hold the two sections with wrong sides inside and join by oversewing all around outer edges, taking small neat sts between the rows of g st on border.

JACKET
10 (11-12)
7.5 (8-8.5)
25 (27-29)
15 (16-17)
24 (25.5-27)
14 (15.5-17)
24 (26-28.5)

15 (16-17)
ROMPERS
24 (26-28)
back
29 (31-33)
11 (12-13)
10 (10.5-11.5)

24 (26-28)
front
29 (31-33)
11 (12-13)
10 (10.5-11.5)

ROSA MUNDI

Say it with roses: knit a minor labour of love for the one you love. Three shades of pink in a beautifully soft yarn are used for this chic and very feminine little sweater with its intriguingly irregular combination of checks, stripes and panels and a single cable to one side of the neck. The blue spots are embroidered on afterwards, so the pattern is not quite as difficult as it might look. An opening on the left shoulder allows for easy dressing and buttons up for a snug fit. It is heartbreaking when a baby grows out of a pretty garment too soon, so if you are knitting for a child that is still to arrive, and you suspect that it may be large at birth, play safe and choose a larger size.

CHECKLIST

Materials

Anny Blatt Soft'Anny, *one ball in each of the foll colours: rose (pale pink) No 113* (**A**), *vieux rose (mid pink) No 144* (**B**), *and indien (deep pink) No 115* (**C**). *A small amount of blue embroidery cotton is used for the spots. Pair each of needles size 3mm and 3¾mm; a cable needle; 3 small buttons.*

Sizes

Three sizes, to fit ages 3 (6-9 to 12) months. Actual measurements shown on diagram.

Stitches used

Double rib; st st; patt, *worked from charts. Use separate small balls or short lengths of the shades for each different section, joining them on as required and taking care to twist yarns around each other on wrong side when changing colour during a row.*
Cable Panel, *worked on 6 sts in* **B** *as shown on charts.*
  1st row P 1, k 4, p 1.
  2nd row K 1, p 4, k 1.
  3rd and 4th rows As 1st and 2nd.
  5th row P 1, slip next 2 sts on cable needle, leave at back, k 2, then k 2 from cable needle, p 1.
  6th to 10th rows Rep 2nd row once then 1st and 2nd rows twice more. These 10 rows form one patt for this panel. After working this panel ensure that **B** *yarn is taken through to wrong side of work.*
Note *This sweater is worked in one piece beginning at the lower edge of the front and ending at the lower edge of the back; cuffs are worked on afterwards.*

Tension

Over st st using 3¾mm needles, 20 sts and 30 rows to 10cm (4in). Work a sample on 26 sts.

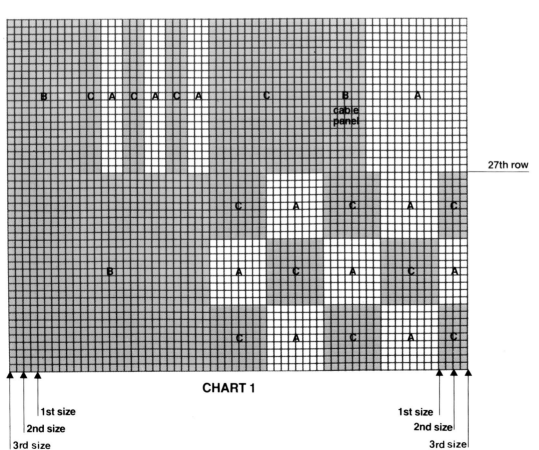

27th row

CHART 1

1st size
2nd size
3rd size

1st size
2nd size
3rd size

INSTRUCTIONS

Main Part With smaller needles and **A**, cast on 54 (58-62) sts and work in rib.
▦ *1st row* (right side) K 2, * p 2, k 2; rep from * to end.
▦ *2nd row* P 2, * k 2, p 2; rep from * to end. Cont in this rib working 4 rows **B** then 4 rows **C** and inc 1 st at both ends of last rib row. 56 (60-64) sts. Change to larger needles and working in st st work patt from Chart No 1, joining small balls of colours as needed.
▦ *1st row* K 0 (2-4) **C**, [8 **A**, 8 **C**] twice, 24 (26-28) **B**. Cont working from chart as now set always twisting yarns around

Key
A = *pale pink*
B = *mid pink*
C = *deep pink*

Begin and end at position indicated according to size. Begin on 1st row of chart and continue until 36 (42-48) rows have been worked then begin sleeve shapings as explained in the instructions.

Centre back

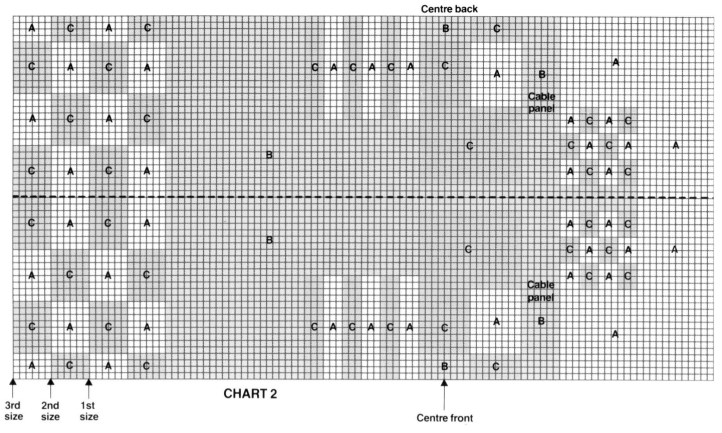

CHART 2

3rd size 2nd size 1st size

Centre front

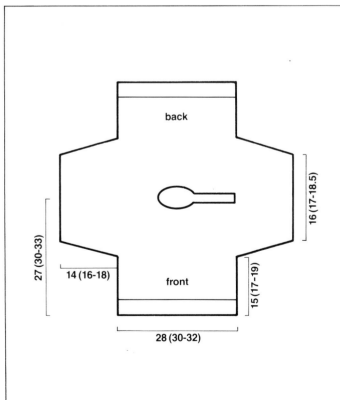

back

front

27 (30-33)

14 (16-18)

28 (30-32)

16 (17-18.5)

15 (17-19)

each other when changing colour. When 27th row has been worked begin next section.

▦ *28th row* P 6 (8-10) **B**, [3 **C**, 3 **A**] 3 times, 16 **C**, 6 **B**, 10 (12-14) **A**. Beg on foll row work cable panel as explained above on the group of 6 sts in **B** and cont in patt as now set until 36 (42-48) rows have been worked from beg of this chart.

▦ **Sleeve Shaping** Cont with colours as set and cast on 4 sts at beg of next 2 (6-8) rows (then 5 sts at beg of next 2 rows for 3rd size only); keep the extra sts added at sides in same colour as side panels. 64 (84-106) sts. Now begin a square in **B** at centre.

▦ *Next row* Using **A**, cast on 4 (5-5) sts, k these sts and next 14 (24-35) sts in **A**, now work the cable panel in **B**, then k 8 **C**, 8 **B**, [3 **A**, 3 **C**] 3 times, 10 (20-31) **B**. Keeping all colours as set cast on 4 (5-5) sts at beg of next row then 5 sts at beg of next 8 (6-4) rows keeping the extra sts added at sides in same colour as side panels. 112 (124-136) sts. Now

work from Chart No 2 beg with 5th (3rd-1st) row of chart; work 12 (14-16) rows.

▦ **Neck Shaping** *17th row of chart* Patt 52 (57-62) and leave these sts of left front on a spare needle, cast off next 8 (10-12) sts, patt to end. Cont on 52 (57-62) sts now rem on needle for right front. Dec 1 st at neck edge on next 2 rows then at same edge on next 3 alt rows. Work 3 rows on rem 47 (52-57) sts; 28th row of chart has now been worked and shoulder level is reached.

▦ Cont on same sts for right back; work 2 rows without shaping thus ending at neck edge then cast on 6 sts at beg of next row. Work 1 row thus ending at neck edge then leave these 53 (58-63) sts on a spare needle.

▦ With wrong side facing return to sts of left front and cont in patt; dec 1 st at neck edge on next 2 rows then at same edge on next 3 alt rows.

▦ *26th row of chart* Cast off 20 sts to form shoulder opening, patt to end. Work 2 rows on rem

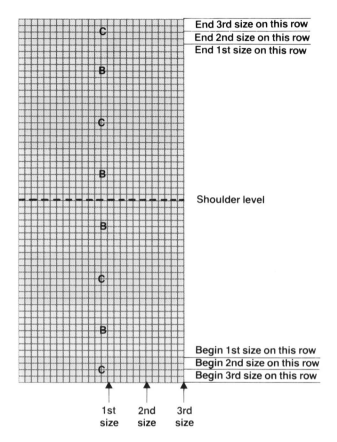

End 3rd size on this row
End 2nd size on this row
End 1st size on this row

Shoulder level

Begin 1st size on this row
Begin 2nd size on this row
Begin 3rd size on this row

| 1st size | 2nd size | 3rd size |

Chart shows full width of sweater including sleeves. Begin and end at the position indicated and on the row indicated according to size being worked. The dotted line across the centre of the chart indicates shoulder level; the neck opening is not shown as this is different for each size and is explained in the instructions.

Cuffs With right side of work facing and using smaller needles and **A**, pick up and k 30 (34-38) sts along outer edge of one sleeve. Beg with 2nd row work in rib as on welt working 4 rows **C**, 4 rows **B** and 2 rows **A**. Cast off in rib. Work other cuff in same way.

Neck and Shoulder Borders With right side of work facing using smaller needles and **B**, pick up and k 26 (28-30) sts around front neck edge and 20 (22-24) sts across back neck. 46 (50-54) sts. Beg with 2nd row work in rib for 6 rows using **B** only; cast off in rib. With right side of work facing using smaller

needles and **B**, pick up and k 26 sts along left front shoulder edge including edge of neck border. Beg with 2nd row work in rib and after working 2 rows make buttonholes.

Next row Beg at neck edge, wrong side facing, rib 2, cast off 2, [rib until there are 6 sts on right needle after previous buttonhole, cast off 2] twice, rib to end. On foll row cast on 2 sts over each buttonhole. Work 2 more rows then cast off in rib. Work similar border on left back but omitting buttonholes.

Finishing Join side and sleeve seams matching patt. Overlap front shoulder border on back border and sew ends to side of shoulder opening. Sew buttons to back border to correspond with buttonholes.

Using blue embroidery cotton form spots on the large **B** section at beg of right front and the small **B** square at centre of neckline working a group of French knots close tog. Work spots in same positions on back.

27 (32-37) sts thus reaching shoulder level then cont for left back and work next 2 rows of chart. Using a short length of **B** cast on 20 sts onto a spare needle; return to sts of left back.

31st row Patt 27 (32-37), then working across 20 sts just cast on, k 0 (0-1) **A**, 2 (3-3) **C**, 3 **A**, 3 **C**, 3 **A**, then with **B** work 1st row of cable panel on next 6 sts, then k 3 (2-1) **C**. Keeping patt correct cast on 6 sts at beg of next row.

33rd row Patt 53 (58-63), turn, cast on 6 (8-10) sts, turn, then patt across sts of right back. 112 (124-136) sts. Cont in patt across all sts and work 19 (21-23) rows thus ending with the 52nd (54th-56th) row of chart.

Sleeve Shaping *1st row* Using **A** cast off 5, k until there are 33 (39-45) sts on right needle, work cable panel in **B**, then k 8 **C**, 8 **B**, [3 **A**, 3 **C**] 3 times, then k rem 34 (40-46) sts. Keeping side sections in **A** and **B** and the stripes and panels as on this row, cast off 5 sts at beg of next 7 (7-5) rows then for 1st size only cast off

4 sts at beg of next 2 rows. 64 (84-106) sts.

Next row Using **A** cast off 4 (4-5), k until there are 10 (20-30) sts on right needle, work cable panel in **B** then k 16 **C**, [3 **A**, 3 **C**] 3 times, k 10 (20-31) **B**. Cont in patt as set and complete sleeve shaping by casting off for 1st size 4 sts at beg of foll row (for 2nd size 4 sts at beg of next 5 rows; for 3rd size 5 sts at beg of next row and 4 sts at beg of next 8 rows). 56 (60-64) sts. Cont with patt as given at top of Chart No 1 and work 9 (15-21) rows without shaping thus ending with a right-side row. Discontinue the cable panel and work all sts in st st, working first 27 rows of chart; as next row is a p row begin at left-hand edge of chart and patt ends on a p row. Change to smaller needles and **C**; k 1 row and dec 1 st at each end; cont on rem 54 (58-62) sts in rib as on front welt beg with 2nd row working 3 rows in **C** then 4 rows **B** and 2 rows **A**. Cast off in rib using **A**.

FAIR ISLE TRIO

An eye-catching trio of sweaters makes a wonderful gift for three young triplets, cousins or friends. All have the same basic shape, but each one has a different colour pattern. The sweater with the blue collar, which uses only four colours, instead of the eight used in each of the others, would make a relatively simple introduction to Fair Isle knitting for a beginner moving on to this more complicated technique. The fine mohair yarn is used double stranded throughout, for extra warmth without weight.

CHECKLIST

Materials
STYLE 1
For Style 1, with yellow collar, in centre of picture, Welcomme Super Mohair, *one ball in each of the foll colours: azalée (bright pink) No 136* (**A**) *begonia (deep pink) No 130* (**B**), *cobalt (bright blue) No 131* (**C**), *bleu de perse (sea-green) No 111* (**D**), *emeraude (deep green) No 155* (**E**), *feu (bright red) No 129* (**F**), *giroselle (yellow) No 128* (**G**), *and pacific (deep blue) No 153* (**H**). *Pair each of needles size 4mm and 5mm; 2 small buttons.*

STYLE 2
For style 2, with pink collar, left of picture: yarns, needles and buttons as above.

STYLE 3
For Style 3, with blue collar, right of picture: one ball each of colours **B**, **C**, **D** *and* **G**, *plus needles and buttons as for Style 1.*

Sizes
Three sizes, to fit ages 3 (6-9) months. Actual measurements shown on diagram.

Stitches used
Single rib; st st; patt, *worked from charts as explained below.*
Note *Yarn is used double throughout: take each ball and wind it into two equal balls then rewind these into a double stranded ball which will be easier to use.*

Tension
Over patt using 5mm needles and yarn double, 18 sts and 20 rows to 10cm (4in). Work a sample on 23 sts as for 2nd size on Style 3.

INSTRUCTIONS

STYLE 1

▦ **Back** With smaller needles and **E** (wound into a double-stranded ball as described above), cast on 39 (43-47) sts and work in rib.
▦ ✳✳ *1st row* (right side) P 1, ✳ k 1, p 1; rep from ✳ to end.
▦ *2nd row* K 1, ✳ p 1, k 1; rep from ✳ to end. Rep these 2 rows 1 (2-3) times more then 1st row again; 5 (7-9) rows worked. ✳✳
▦ *Inc row* P 4 (6-8), [inc in next st, p 9] 3 times, inc in next st, p 4 (6-8). 43 (47-51) sts. Change to larger needles and working in st st work patt from Chart No 1.
▦ *1st row* K 1 **B**, ✳ 3 **E**, 1 **B**; rep from ✳ to last 2 sts, 2 **E**.
▦ *2nd row* P 1 **E**, ✳ 3 **B**, 1 **E**; rep from ✳ to last 2 sts, 2 **B**.

▦ *3rd row* K in **B**.
▦ *4th row* P in **H**.
▦ *5th row* K 4 **H**, ✳ 1 **G**, 5 **H**; rep from ✳ to last 3 (1-5) sts, 1 **G**, 2 (0-4) **H**. Cont in patt from this chart; always begin each k row at right-hand edge of chart. As the various patts have different numbers of sts for the patt rep they will end at different positions on the chart so make a note of the position where the k row ends and begin the p row at same position. Cont in patt without shaping until 46 (50-54) rows have been worked.
▦ **Neck Shaping** For 1st and 2nd sizes work rem rows in patt; for 3rd size work in **A**.
▦ *Next row* K 12 (13-14) and leave these sts for right back, cast off next 19 (21-23) sts, k to end. Cont on 12 (13-14) sts now rem at end of needle for left back; p 1 row then cast off sts for shoulder edge. Rejoin yarn to neck edge of right back sts, p to end. Cast off these sts.

▦ **Front** Work as for back until 29th row of chart has been worked, then make front opening.
▦ *30th row* Using **A**, p 20 (22-24) and leave these sts of right front on a spare needle, cast off 3, p to end. Cont on 20 (22-24) sts now rem on needle for left front taking care to keep patt correct. Work 11 (15-19) rows thus ending at the opening edge.
▦ **Neck Shaping** Cast off 4 (5-6) sts at beg of next row, 2 sts at same edge on next alt row and 1 st on next 2 alt rows; you have now worked a total of 48 (52-56) rows in patt, reaching same position as on back. Cast off rem 12 (13-14) sts for shoulder edge. With right side facing rejoin yarn to sts of right front and cont in patt for 10 (14-18) rows thus ending at the opening edge. Work neck shaping as for left front, p 1 row on rem 12 (13-14) sts then cast off.

▦ **Sleeves** With smaller needles and **E** cast on 23 (27-29) sts and work as for back welt from ✳✳ to ✳✳.
▦ *Inc row* P 2 (4-2), [inc in next st,

warm, light and bright

p 5 (5-4)] 3 (3-5) times, inc in next st, p 2 (4-1). 27 (31-35) sts. Change to larger needles and working in st st work patt from Chart No 2; on the first 4 rows the patt will fit in same way as on back. Cont in patt and inc 1 st at both ends of next row, then every foll 6th row 1 (2-3) times, then every foll 4th row 4 (3-2) times, working extra sts into patt. Cont on 39 (43-47) sts until 33 (35-37) rows have been worked in patt. Cast off all sts.

▨ **Front Borders** With right side of work facing and using smaller needles and **A**, pick up and k 13 (17-21) sts along front edge of right front and work in rib beg with 2nd row. If sweater is for a boy work 4 rows in rib then cast off in rib. If for a girl work 1 row then make buttonholes.
▨ *Next row* Beg at lower edge, right side facing, rib 3 (5-5), yrn, p 2 tog, rib 4 (6-10), yrn, p 2 tog, rib 2. Work 2 more rows in rib then cast off in rib. Pick up same number of sts along front edge of left front. If sweater is for a girl work 4 rows in rib beg with 2nd row then cast off in rib. If for a boy rep 2nd rib row then make buttonholes.
▨ *Next row* Beg at upper edge, right side facing, rib 2, p 2 tog, yrn, rib 4 (6-10), p 2 tog, yrn, rib 3 (5-5). Rib 2 more rows then cast off in rib.

▨ **Finishing and Collar** Join shoulder seams. With right side of work facing and using smaller needles and **G**, beg half-way across right front border pick up and k 14 (15-16) sts along right front neck edge, 25 (27-29) sts across back neck and 14 (15-16) sts along left front neck edge ending half-way across left front border. Beg with 1st row as this is right side of collar, work 5(5.5-6) cm, 2(2⅛-2⅜)in, in rib then cast off loosely in rib.
▨ On each side edge mark a point 10.5(12-13)cm, 4⅛(4¾-5⅛in), down from shoulder seam for armholes and sew cast-off edge of sleeves between markers. Join side and sleeve seams.
▨ Slip-st edges of front borders

to base of opening overlapping buttonhole border on the button border. Sew on buttons to correspond with buttonholes.

STYLE 2

▨ **Back** With smaller needles and **E** cast on 39 (43-47) sts and work as given for Style 1 until the inc row has been worked. Change to larger needles and working in st st work patt from Chart No 3.
▨ *1st row* K 3 **E**, * 1 **B**, 3 **E**; rep from * to end.
▨ *2nd row* P 1 **B**, * 1 **E**, 3 **B**; rep from * to last 2 sts, 1 **E**, 1 **B**.
▨ *3rd row* K in **B**.
▨ *4th row* P in **H**. Now begin the bird motifs arranged as foll:
▨ *5th row* K 5 (7-9) **H**, * 2 **G**, 1 **H**, 2 **G**, 11 **H**; * rep from * to * once, 2 **G**, 1 **H**, 2 **G**, 1 (3-5) **H**. Cont as now set until motifs are completed then cont working from chart; begin each k row at right-hand edge of chart and mark on chart the position where rows end so that p row can begin at same position. Cont without shaping until 46 (50-54) rows have been worked in patt. Working rem rows in patt work neck shaping as for Style 1.

▨ **Front** Work as for back until 29th row of chart has been worked. Cont in patt and work front opening on foll row, as given for Style 1; cont working correct patt from Chart No 3 and complete as for front of Style 1.

▨ **Sleeves** With smaller needles and **E** cast on 23 (27-29) sts and work as for sleeves of Style 1 until the inc row has been worked. Change to larger needles and working in st st work patt from Chart No 3, working as for back until 4th row has been worked.
▨ Work 5th row as on back but working the sts from * to * once. Cont in patt but inc 1 st at both ends of next row, then every foll 6th row 1 (2-3) times then every foll 4th row 4 (3-2) times working extra sts into patt. Cont on 39 (43-47) sts until 33 (35-37) rows have been worked in patt. Cast off all sts.

▨ **Front Borders** Work front borders as for Style 1 but using **D**, work collar as for Style 1 but using **A**, make up as for Style 1.

STYLE 3

▨ **Back** With smaller needles and **C** cast on 39 (43-47) sts and work as given for Style 1 until the inc row has been worked. Change to larger needles and working in st st work patt from Chart No 4.
▨ *1st row* K 1 **C**, * 1 **B**, 1 **C**; rep from * to end.
▨ *2nd row* P in **B**.
▨ *3rd row* * K 2 **B**, 1 **G**; rep from * to last 1 (2-0) sts, 1 (2-0) **B**.
▨ *4th row* P 1 (2-0) **G**, * 1 **B**, 2 **G**; rep from * to end. Cont in patt as now set always beg each k row at right-hand edge of chart and mark the position where row ends then begin p row at this position.
▨ Cont without shaping until 46 (50-54) rows have been worked from chart then work neck

shaping as for Style 1 but working in patt.

▨ **Front** Work as for back until 29th row of chart has been worked. Using **B**, work front opening as for Style 1 and cont working correct patt; complete as for front of Style 1.

▨ **Sleeves** With smaller needles and **C** cast on 23 (27-29) sts and work as for sleeves of Style 1 until the inc row has been worked. Change to larger needles and working in st st work patt from Chart No 4.
▨ *1st row* K 1 **C**, * 1 **B**, 1 **C**; rep from * to end.
▨ *2nd row* P in **B**.
▨ *3rd row* * K 2 **B**, 1 **G**; rep from * to last 0 (1-2) sts, k 0 (1-2) **B**.
▨ *4th row* P 0 (1-2) **G**, * 1 **B**, 2 **G**; rep from * to end. Cont working from this chart and complete as for sleeves of Style 1. Work front borders as for Style 1 but using **D**, work collar as for Style 1 but using **C**, make up as for Style 1.

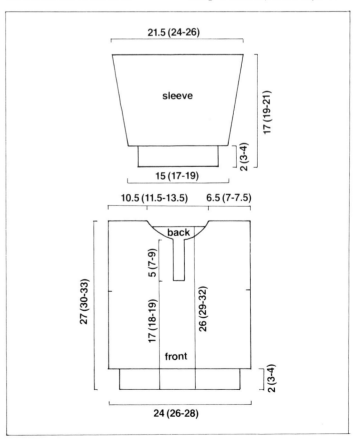

On each chart begin reading knit rows from right-hand edge; as the various patt panels have a different number of sts in the patt repeat they will end at different positions on the chart so mark where the knit row ends and begin the purl row at this position. For Style 2 the bird arrangement is explained in the instructions.

KEY

F
A
E
D
G
B
H
C

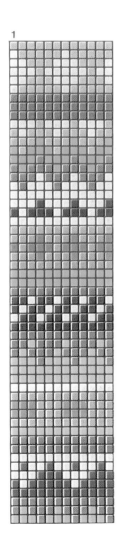

1

2

3

4

SLEEPY PIXIE LAYETTE

One of the delights of knitting for babies is that you can sometimes afford to pamper them with luxury yarns, like the alpaca and soft baby yarns used here. This heart-melting pixie with the mischievous eyes can happily be taken on an outing when the temperature drops. Indoors you can take off his edge-to-edge cardigan and his long pixie hat to reveal a cable sweater with buttoned front opening.

CHECKLIST

Materials

Georges Picaud Alpaga: *for cardigan, one (2-2) balls grey No 99 (**A**) and one (2-2) balls turquoise blue No 90 (**B**); for sweater, 2 balls (all sizes) grey No 99; for hat, one ball (all sizes) turquoise blue No 90, and for socks, one ball turquoise blue No 90. Georges Picaud* Layette for *the trousers: 2 balls (all sizes) sky blue No 3 (**C**). Pair each of needles size 3mm, 3¼mm and 3¾mm; two double-pointed needles size 4mm for cardigan; a cable needle; 3 buttons for sweater; elastic thread for trousers.*

Sizes

Three sizes, to fit ages 3 (6-9) months. Actual measurements of cardigan, sweater and trousers shown on diagram. Socks, in one size only, fit a baby up to 6 months.

Stitches used

Two-colour patt, *worked on double-pointed needles as foll:*

    1st row *(right side)* With **A**, k 1, * slip 1 pw keeping yarn at back, k 1; rep from * to end. Return to opposite edge of work.

    2nd row *(right side)* With **B**, p 1, * k 1, p 1; rep from * to end.

    3rd row *(wrong side)* With **A**, slip 1 pw, * p 1, then slip 1 pw keeping yarn at front; rep from * to end. Return to opposite edge.

    4th row *(wrong side)* With **B**, p 1, * k 1, p 1; rep from * to end.

These 4 rows form one patt.

    Cable 4 back = *slip next 2 sts on cable needle, leave at back, k 2, then k 2 from cable needle. For arrangement of cables on each design see instructions.*

Tensions

*Over two-colour patt using 4mm needles, 23 sts and 46 rows to 10cm (4in). Work a sample on 29 sts casting on with **B**; k 1 row then work in patt as given above; it is essential to work a sample of this patt so that you become familiar with it before beg garment. Over cable patt on sweater using 3¾mm needles, 34 sts and 34 rows to 10cm (4in); work a sample on 40 sts as given for 1st size on back. Over double rib using quality Layette and 3¼mm needles, 34 sts and 34 rows measured unstretched to 10cm (4in); work a sample on 38 sts.*

INSTRUCTIONS

CARDIGAN

▦ **Back** With double-pointed 4mm needles and **B** cast on 57 (63-69) sts and k 1 row. Join on **A** and work in two-colour patt. Cont without shaping until work measures 23(26-29)cm, 9(10¼-11⅜)in, from beg, ending with a 4th patt row.

▦ **Neck Shaping** *1st row* Patt 20 (22-24) and leave these sts of right back on a spare needle, cast off next 17 (19-21) sts loosely, patt to end. Cont on 20 (22-24) sts now rem on needle for left back; keep patt correct changing ends as usual. Dec 1 st at neck

edge on next 2 rows then at same edge on next alt row. Work 1 row then cast off rem 17 (19-21) sts for shoulder edge. Rejoin yarn to sts of right back at outer edge in order to work 2nd patt row; complete as for left back reversing shapings.

■ **Right Front** With double-pointed 4mm needles and **B** cast on 29 (33-37) sts and k 1 row. Join on **A** and work in patt. Cont without shaping until work

measures 20.5(23.5-26.5)cm, 8(9¼-10½)in, from beg, ending with a 4th patt row. **

■ **Neck Shaping** *1st row* Cast off 6 (7-8), patt to end. Keeping patt correct dec 1 st at neck edge on next 2 (3-4) rows then at same edge on next 4 alt rows. Cont on rem 17 (19-21) sts until work matches back to shoulder edge. Cast off loosely.

■ **Left Front** Work as for right front to **.

■ **Neck Shaping** *1st row* Patt 23 (26-29) then cast off rem 6 (7-8) sts and fasten off. Return to opposite edge in order to work 2nd patt row and complete as for right front reversing shapings.

■ **Sleeves** With double-pointed 4mm needles and **B** cast on 35 (39-41) sts and k 1 row. Jon on **A** and work in patt. Inc 1 st at both ends of every foll 8th row 6 (8-10) times, then every foll 6th row twice for 1st size only, working extra sts into patt. Cont on 51 (55-61) sts until work measures 15(17-19)cm, 5⅞(6¾-7½)in, from beg, ending with a 2nd or 4th patt row. Cast off loosely.

■ **Front Facings** With right side of work facing and using 3¼mm needles and **B**, pick up and k 63 (72-81) sts along front edge of right front. K 1 row on wrong side then beg with another k row work 3 rows in st st. Cast off. Work similar facing on left front.

■ **Finishing and Neck Edging** Join shoulder seams. With right side facing and using 3¼mm needles and **B**, pick up and k 20 (22-24) sts along right front neck edge leaving facing free, then 21 (23-25) sts across back neck and 20 (22-24) sts along left front neck edge leaving facing free. K 1 row then cast off. On each side edge mark a point 11(12-13)cm, 4¼(4¾-5⅛)in, down from shoulder seam for armholes and sew cast-off edge of sleeves between marked points. Join side and sleeve seams. Fold in facings along front edges to wrong side and slip-st in place.

SWEATER

■ **Back** With 3mm needles cast on 69 (75-83) sts and work in single rib.
■ *1st row* (right side) P 1, * k 1, p 1; rep from * to end.
■ *2nd row* K 1, * p 1, k 1; rep from * to end. Rep these 2 rows twice more then 1st row again.
■ *Inc row* Rib 4 (1-5), [inc in next st, rib 5] 10 (12-12) times, inc in next st, rib 4 (1-5). 80 (88-96) sts.

Change to 3¾mm needles and work in cable patt.
■ *1st row* P 6 (2-6), * k 4, p 4; * rep from * to * ending k 4, p 6 (2-6).
■ *2nd row* K 6 (2-6), * p 4, k 4; * rep from * to * ending p 4, k 6 (2-6). Rep these 2 rows once.
■ *5th row* P 6 (2-6), * cable 4 back, p 4; * rep from * to * ending cable 4 back, p 6 (2-6).
■ *6th to 8th rows* Rep 2nd row once then 1st and 2nd rows again. These 8 rows form one patt. Cont in patt until work measures 22(25-28)cm, 8⅝(9¾-11)in, from beg, ending with a wrong-side row.
■ **Neck Shaping** *Next row* Patt 28 (31-33) and leave these sts of right back on needle, cast off next 24 (26-30) sts, patt to end. Cont on 28 (31-33) sts now rem at end of needle for left back. Dec 1 st at neck edge on next row, cast off 4 sts at beg of foll row then work 1 row without shaping. Cast off rem 23 (26-28) sts for shoulder edge. Rejoin yarn to neck edge of right back sts, cast off 4, patt to end. Dec 1 st at neck edge on next row, work 1 row then cast off rem 23 (26-28) sts.

■ **Front** Work as for back until front measures 14(16-18)cm, 5½(6¼-7⅛)in, from beg, ending with a wrong-side row.
■ **Front Opening** *Next row* Patt 38 (42-46) and leave these sts of left front on a spare needle, cast off next 4 sts, patt to end. Cont on 38 (42-46) sts now rem on needle for right front, without shaping, until work measures 20(23-26)cm, 7⅞(9-10¼)in, from beg, ending at the opening edge.
■ **Neck Shaping** Cast off 8 (9-11) sts at beg of next row, 3 sts at same edge on next alt row, 2 sts on next alt row and 1 st on next 2 alt rows. Work 1 row on rem 23 (26-28) sts then cast off for shoulder edge. Rejoin yarn with wrong side facing to sts of left front and cont in patt until you have worked 1 row fewer than on right front to beg of neck. Work neck shaping as for right front and after last dec row work 2 rows straight then cast off rem 23 (26-28) sts.

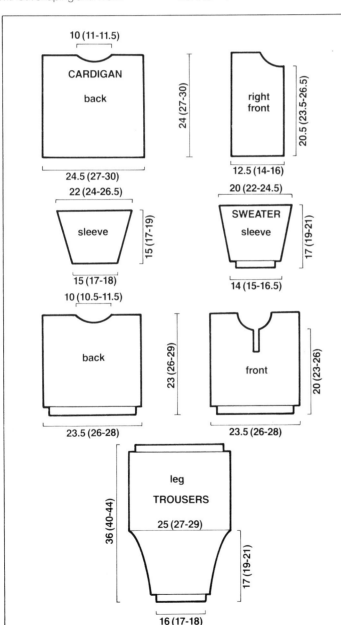

10 (11-11.5)
CARDIGAN back
24 (27-30)
24.5 (27-30)

right front
20.5 (23.5-26.5)
12.5 (14-16)

22 (24-26.5)
sleeve
15 (17-19)
15 (17-18)

20 (22-24.5)
SWEATER sleeve
17 (19-21)
14 (15-16.5)

10 (10.5-11.5)
back
23 (26-29)
23.5 (26-28)

front
20 (23-26)
23.5 (26-28)

leg TROUSERS
36 (40-44)
25 (27-29)
17 (19-21)
16 (17-18)

Sleeves With 3mm needles cast on 37 (39-43) sts and work 7 rows in rib as on back welt.

Inc row Rib 3 (1-3), [inc in next st, rib 2] 10 (12-12) times, inc in next st, rib 3 (1-3). 48 (52-56) sts. Change to 3¾mm needles and patt.

1st row P 2 (4-2), * k 4 to form a cable, p 4; * rep from * to * ending k 4 to form a cable, p 2 (4-2). Cont in patt as now set for 4 more rows, then inc 1 st at both ends of next row, then every foll 6th row 2 (1-0) times, then every foll 4th row 7 (10-13) times, working extra sts into cable patt. Cont on 68 (76-84) sts until work measures 17(19-21)cm, 6¾(7½-8¼)in, from beg. Cast off.

Finishing and Borders Join shoulder seams matching patt. With right side of work facing and using 3mm needles, pick up and k 15 (16-18) sts along right front neck edge, 31 (33-37) sts across back neck and 15 (16-18) sts along left front neck edge. 61 (65-73) sts. Beg with 2nd row work in rib for 5 rows then cast off loosely in rib. If sweater is for a boy, with right side facing and using 3mm needles, pick up and k 29 (33-37) sts along left front edge of opening including edge of neck border. Beg with 2nd row work in rib and after working 2 rows make buttonholes.

Next row Beg at lower edge, wrong side facing, rib 8, [yrn, p 2 tog, rib 6 (8-10) twice, yrn, p 2 tog, rib 3. Work 2 more rows in rib then cast off in rib. Work similar border on right front omitting buttonholes. If sweater is for a girl the buttonholes should be made in right front border; the row begins at neck edge and should be read in reverse.

On each side edge mark a point 10 (11-12)cm, 4(4¼-4¾)in, down from shoulder seam for armholes and sew cast-off edge of sleeves between marked points. Join side and sleeve seams. Sew lower edges of front borders to base of opening, overlapping buttonhole border on the other border. Sew on buttons to correspond.

TROUSERS

Right Leg With 3mm needles and **C** cast on 45 (49-53) sts and work in single rib as given for sweater welt for 7 rows.

Inc row Rib 2 (4-6), [inc in next st, rib 3] 10 times, inc in next st, rib 2 (4-6). 56 (60-64) sts. Change to 3¼mm needles and work in double rib (cable at centre front).

1st row P 2 (0-2), [k 2, p 2] 2 (3-3) times, k 4 for a cable, [p 2, k 2] 10 (11-11) times, p 2 (0-2).

2nd row K 2 (0-2), [p 2, k 2] 10 (11-11) times, p 4, [k 2, p 2] 2 (3-3) times, k 2 (0-2). Rep these 2 rows twice more.

7th row Rib 10 (12-14), cable 4 back, rib 42 (44-46).

8th row As 2nd. These 8 rows form one patt. ** Cont in patt but inc 1 st at both ends of next row, then every foll 4th row 7 (9-11) times then every alt row 6 times, then cast on 2 sts at beg of next 2 rows, working extra sts at sides in double rib. Work 1 row on these 88 (96-104) sts thus ending with a 4th patt row. For all sizes there is a p 2 rib at beg and end of right-side rows. ** Cut yarn and leave sts on a spare needle.

Left Leg Work as for right leg for first 8 rows then change to 3¼mm needles and patt which is the reverse of right leg.

1st row P 2 (0-2), [k 2, p 2] 10 (11-11) times, k 4 for a cable, [p 2, k 2] 2 (3-3) times, p 2 (0-2). Cont in patt as now set until 8th row has been worked then cont as for right leg from ** to **. Join legs.

5th row of patt Cast on 1 and k this st, [p 2, k 2] 14 (15-16) times, p 2, k 4, [p 2, k 2] 6 (7-8) times, p 2, turn and cast on 2 sts, turn, then working sts of right leg [p 2, k 2] 6 (7-8) times, p 2, k 4, [p 2, k 2] 14 (15-16) times, p 2, turn and cast on 1 st. 180 (196-212) sts. Cont in patt as now set across all sts until work measures 34(38-42)cm, 13⅜(15-16½)in, from beg, ending with a right-side row.

Dec row For 1st size p 4, [p 2 tog, p 6, p 2 tog, p 7] 10 times, p 2 tog, p 4 (for 2nd size p 1, [p 2 tog, p 6] 24 times, p 2 tog, p 1; for 3rd size p 7, [p 2 tog, p 5] 29 times, p rem 2 sts).

All sizes Cont on rem 159 (171-183) sts; change to 3mm needles and work 8 rows in single rib. Cast off in rib.

Finishing Join inner leg seams. Join centre back seam. Insert 3 rows of elastic thread through waistband on wrong side securing ends in back seam.

HAT

With 3mm needles cast on 105 (113-123) sts and work in rib as on sweater for 8 rows but working 1 inc in centre of last row. Change to 3¼mm needles and work in patt on 106 (114-124) sts.

1st row P 9 (9-10), * k 4, p 17 (19-21); * rep from * to * 3 times more, k 4, p 9 (9-10).

2nd row K 9 (9-10), * p 4, k 17 (19-21); * rep from * to * 3 times more, p 4, k 9 (9-10). Rep these 2 rows twice more.

7th row P 9 (9-10), * cable 4 back, p 17 (19-21); * rep from * to * 3 times more, cable 4 back, p 9 (9-10).

8th row As 2nd. These 8 rows form one patt. Cont in patt until work measures 12cm (4¾in) from beg, ending with a right-side row, then begin shaping.

1st dec row K 7 (7-8), k 2 tog, * p 4, SKPO, k 13 (15-17), k 2 tog; * rep from * to * 3 times more, p 4, SKPO, k 7 (7-8). 96 (104-114) sts. Work 9 rows in patt having 8 (8-9) sts in rev st st at each side and 15 (17-19) sts between cables.

2nd dec row K 6 (6-7), k 2 tog, * p 4, SKPO, k 11 (13-15), k 2 tog; * rep from * to * 3 times more, p 4, SKPO, k 6 (6-7). 86 (94-104) sts. Cont working decs before and after the cables on every foll 10th row 5 (5-6) times more. Work 9 rows on rem 36 (44-44) sts.

For 1st size only, cont as foll:

** *Next row* K 2 tog, * p 4, SKTPO;* rep from * to * 3 times more, p 4, k 2 tog. Work 9 rows on rem 36 sts.

Next row P 1, [p 3 tog, p 2 tog] 5 times. Cut yarn, thread end through rem sts, draw up but do not close yet.

For 2nd and 3rd sizes, cont as foll:

Next row K 2, * p 4, SKPO, k 1, k 2 tog; * rep from * to * 3 times more, p 4, k 2. Work 9 rows on rem 26 sts then complete as for 1st size from ** to end.

Finishing Make large tassel and sew the end of yarn at top of hat firmly to top of tassel. Backstitch seam of hat.

SOCKS

Beg at upper edge cast on 48 sts using 3mm needles and work in patt.

1st row [K 1, p 1] 11 times, k 4, [p 1, k 1] 11 times.

2nd row [P 1, k 1] 11 times, p 4, [k 1, p 1] 11 times. Rep these 2 rows twice more.

7th row Rib 22, cable 4 back, rib 22.

8th row As 2nd. These 8 rows form one patt. Cont in patt until work measures 9cm (3½in) from beg, ending with a wrong-side row then divide for heel.

Next row Cut yarn, slip 13 sts onto a holder, rejoin yarn, rib 9, work the 4 sts of cable, rib 9, turn and place rem 13 sts on a holder. Cont on centre 22 sts for instep keeping cable correct and work 5cm (2in) ending with a wrong-side row. Cut yarn.

With right side facing rejoin yarn to first group of 13 sts at side, rib these sts, pick up and k 20 sts along side of instep, then working sts of instep p 2 tog, k 2 tog, [p 1, k 1] 3 times, p 2 tog, [k 1, p 1] 3 times, k 2 tog, p 2 tog, then pick up and k 20 sts along other side of instep, then rib 13 sts at other side of heel. Cont on these 83 sts working in rib across all sts for 9 rows then shape toe as foll:

1st row P 2 tog, rib 38, k 3 tog, rib 38, p 2 tog.

2nd row K 1, * p 1, k 1; rep from * to end.

3rd row K 2 tog, rib 36, p 3 tog, rib 36, k 2 tog.

4th row P 1, * k 1, p 1; rep from * to end. Cont to dec 1 st at each end and work double dec in centre on next row and next 3 alt rows. Cast off rem 59 sts. Fold this edge in half and sew. Join seam under foot and along leg.

STRAWBERRY RIPE

Lyrically charming and as fresh and innocent as a nursery rhyme, this little set in soft cotton includes two jackets, one embroidered with a cherry motif and one with strawberries, each with bootees to match. The cherry jacket, knitted in a ridge pattern, fastens at the front, while the strawberry jacket is knitted in reverse stocking stitch and fastens at the back, though both jackets are knitted to the same basic style and can be worn the other way around. Both jackets have a garter stitch lower border and a tubular neck border through which a crocheted or twisted silk cord is threaded.

CHECKLIST

Materials

DMC Cotonia: 6 balls in ecru – 2 for each jacket and one ball for each pair of bootees. DMC coton perlé for the embroidery: for the cherry jacket and bootees, one skein each of 321, 816, 950 and 993; for the strawberry jacket and bootees, one skein each of 350, 352, 816, 817, 891 and 993. Pair of needles size 3mm; 16 buttons – 6 for each jacket and 2 for each pair of bootees.
Note: *The quality originally used had a matt finish. This has now been withdrawn and we have substituted Cotonia which has a sheen.*

Sizes

Jackets are in three sizes to fit ages 3 (6-9 months). Bootees are in one size to fit a baby up to 6 months.

Stitches used

For the cherry jacket: g st; st st, patt, worked on any number of sts as foll: beg with a k row work 5 rows in st st.
    6th row (wrong side) K all sts. These 6 rows form one patt.
    Tubular rib, for neck border, as foll:
    1st row * K 1, yarn to front, slip 1 pw, yarn to back; * rep from * to *.
    All rows are alike and work forms a tube with an opening at the ends through which a cord can be passed.
For the strawberry jacket: g st; st st; rev st st; tubular rib as for cherry jacket.

Tension

For both jackets (cherry jacket over patt, strawberry jacket over rev st st), using 3mm needles, 28 sts and 40 rows to 10cm (4in). Work a sample on 34 sts. It is also advisable to work a sample of tubular rib in order to become familiar with it: cast on an even number of sts and k 1 row then work as given above.

INSTRUCTIONS

CHERRY JACKET

▨ **Main Part** This is worked in one piece from side to side. Beg with left front cast on 40 (46-52) sts and work at once in patt; front border is worked later. Cont until 36 (42-48) rows have been worked then work 4 rows in st st.
▨ ** *5th row of patt* K 30 (34-38) and leave these sts of main part on a holder, k rem 10 (12-14) sts.
▨ *6th row* K 10 (12-14), turn and cast on 30 (34-38) sts for left sleeve. Cont in patt on these 40 (46-52) sts and work 11 (13-15) complete patts then work 4 rows in st st.

STRAWBERRY MOTIFS

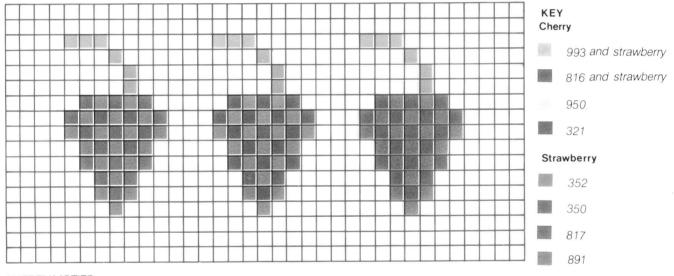

KEY
Cherry

	993 and strawberry
	816 and strawberry
	950
	321

Strawberry

	352
	350
	817
	891

CHERRY MOTIFS

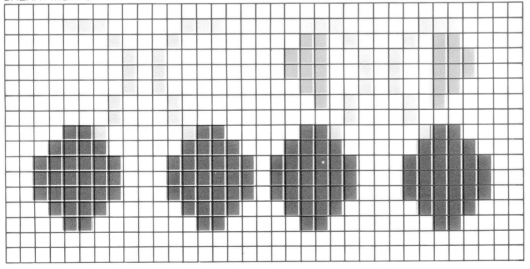

▦ *5th row of patt* Cast off 30 (34-38) sts to complete sleeve, k to end.

▦ *6th row* K 10 (12-14), then onto same needle k the 30 (34-38) sts of main part which were left on a holder. ✶✶ Cont on 40 (46-52) sts for back and work 13 (15-17) patts then work 4 rows in st st. Now work right sleeve as for left sleeve from ✶✶ to ✶✶. Cont on 40 (46-52) sts which are now on needle for right front and work 6 (7-8) complete patts then work 5 rows in st st. Cast off.

▦ **Yoke** With right side facing pick up and k 21 (24-27) sts along upper edge of right front, 36 (42-48) sts across top of right sleeve, 41 (47-53) sts across top of back, 36 (42-48) sts across top of left sleeve and 21 (24-27) sts across top of left front. 155 (179-203) sts. K 1 row on wrong side. Now work in st st beg with another k row; work 2 rows then begin shaping.

▦ *3rd row* K 5, [k 2 tog, k 10] 12 (14-16) times, k 2 tog, k 4. Cont on rem 142 (164-186) sts and work 3 rows in st st. Note that decs are not intended to form lines but have a random effect.

▦ *7th row* K 10, [k 2 tog, k 9] 12 (14-16) times. Cont on rem 130 (150-170) sts and work 3 rows in st st.

▦ *11th row* K 2, [k 2 tog, k 8] 12 (14-16) times, k 2 tog, k 6. Cont on rem 117 (135-153) sts and work 3 rows in st st.

▦ *15th row* K 5, [k 2 tog, k 7] 11 (13-15) times, k 2 tog, k 11. Cont on rem 105 (121-137) sts and work 3 rows in st st.

▦ *19th row* K 3 (4-5), [k 2 tog, k 5] 14 (16-18) times, k 2 tog, k 2 (3-4). P 1 row on rem 90 (104-118) sts then work in tubular rib for 12 rows. Cast off in k.

▦ **Borders** With right side facing pick up and k 60 (66-72) sts along front edge of right front including yoke, working into the upper side of the tubular rib section leaving the underside free. Work in g st and after working 3 rows make buttonholes.

▦ *4th row* Beg at lower edge k 4, [yfd, k 2 tog, k 7 (8-9)] 6 times, k 2.

Work 2 more rows in g st then cast off loosely. Work border on left front in same way but working into underside of tubular rib section and omitting buttonholes.

▦ With right side facing pick up and k 104 (120-136) sts all around lower edge of jacket. Work 6 rows in g st then cast off loosely. With right side facing pick up and k 36 (40-44) sts along lower edge of one sleeve; work 6 rows in g st then cast off loosely. Work other cuff in same way. Join sleeve seams. Embroider cherry motifs around yoke using Swiss darning method explained on page 6.

▦ Using 2 strands of ecru and 2 strands of 2 other colours make a twisted cord (see below) about 61(66-71)cm, 26(28-30)in, long and insert this through the tubular rib section at top of yoke to tie at front. Sew on buttons to correspond with buttonholes.

▦ **Twisted Cord** For each length of cord, decide how long you wish the finished cord to be and cut strands of yarn about three times this length, using half the number of strands that the finished cord is to have. Hold the strands with the ends level and, using a separate strand of yarn, tie them tightly together near one end. Slip this tied end over a hook and twist the strands tightly together starting at the other end. When a very tight twist is formed place one finger at the centre and bring the ends together. Remove your finger and the strands will twist into a cord. Tie both ends firmly together and cut off the original tie. An alternative method of making a cord is to make a length of crochet chain, using a large crochet hook and working with several strands of yarn together. For a neater cord, work back along the chain making a row of slip-sts along each side.

Note It is dangerous ever to tighten a cord around a baby's neck, so adjust the tie to a comfortable length for the neck and then sew very securely and firmly at each edge, leaving the

ends loose to tie in a bow.

▦ **Right Bootee** Beg with centre of sole cast on 40 sts and work in g st shaping sides and centre.

▦ *1st row* K.

▦ *2nd row* K 1, yfd, k 18, [yfd, k 1] twice, yfd, k 18, yfd, k 1.

▦ *3rd and alt rows* K but working the yfd loops tbl to avoid a hole.

▦ *4th row* K 2, yfd, k 18, yfd, k 3, yfd, k 2, yfd, k 18, yfd, k 2.

▦ *6th row* K 3, yfd, k 18, [yfd, k 4] twice, yfd, k 18, yfd, k 3.

▦ *8th row* K 4, yfd, k 18, yfd, k 6, yfd, k 5, yfd, k 18, yfd, k 4.

▦ *10th row* K 5, yfd, k 18, [yfd, k 7] twice, yfd, k 18, yfd, k 5.

▦ *12th row* K 24, yfd, k 9, yfd, k 8, yfd, k 24.

▦ *13th row* As 3rd. Cont on these 68 sts and work 11 rows in g st.

▦ **Instep** *1st row* K 38, k 2 tog, turn thus leaving 28 sts unworked.

▦ *2nd row* Slip 1, p 8, p 2 tog, turn. There are 28 sts at this edge also.

▦ *3rd row* Slip 1, k 8, k 2 tog, turn.

▦ *4th row* Slip 1, p 8, p 2 tog, turn. Rep 3rd and 4th rows 8 times more. Turn as usual after last row and k to end on right side of work.

▦ *Next row* K 18, k 2 tog, k 8, k 2 tog, k 18. 46 sts.

▦ *Next row* K 9 and leave these sts on a safety pin, cast off 28, k to end. ✶✶ Cont on last group of 9 sts.

▦ *Next row* K 9, turn and cast on 6 sts for button-strap. Work 3 rows in g st on these 15 sts then cast off. For ankle strap cast on 13 sts, take needle with these sts in right hand and with wrong side facing k the other group of 9 sts. Cont on 22 sts and work 3 rows in g st then cast off. Make a buttonhole loop on end of ankle strap. Embroider a cherry motif on instep. Fold cast-on edge of sole in half and sew with a flat seam. Sew back seam of bootee. Sew on button to button-strap.

▦ **Left Bootee** Work as for right bootee to ✶✶; cont on last group of 9 sts.

▦ *Next row* K 9, turn and cast on 13 sts for ankle strap. Work 3 rows in g st on 22 sts then cast off. For button-strap cast on 6 sts, take needle with these sts in right hand and with wrong side facing k the other group of 9 sts. Work 3 rows in g st on these 15 sts then cast off. Complete as for right bootee.

STRAWBERRY JACKET

▦ **Main Part** This is worked in one piece from side to side. Beg with right back cast on 40 (46-52) sts and work in rev st st for 40 (46-52) rows.

▦ ✶✶ *Next row* P 30 (34-38) and leave these sts of main part on a holder, p rem 10 (12-14) sts.

▦ *Next row* K 10 (12-14), turn and cast on 30 (34-38) sts for right sleeve. Cont in patt on these 40 (46-52) sts and work 70 (82-94) rows.

▦ *Next row* Cast off 30 (34-38) sts to complete sleeve, p to end.

▦ *Next row* K 10 (12-14), then onto same needle k sts of main part which were left on holder. ✶✶ Cont on 40 (46-52) sts for front and work 82 (94-106) rows in rev st st. Now work left sleeve as for right sleeve from ✶✶ to ✶✶. Cont on 40 (46-52) sts which are now on needle for left back and work 41 (47-53) rows in rev st st. Cast off.

▦ **Yoke** Pick up same groups of sts as for cherry jacket along upper edge in foll order, left back, left sleeve, front, right sleeve, right back. Work entire yoke as for cherry jacket.

▦ **Borders** Work border on left back as for right front of cherry jacket and border on right back as for left front. Work all other borders as for cherry jacket.

▦ **Finishing** As for cherry jacket but embroider strawberry motifs on yoke.

▦ **Bootees** Work both bootees as for cherry set but embroider a strawberry motif on each instep with stalk pointing to the outside as shown.

PASTEL PERFECTION

A patchwork blanket as soft as a dream and an elegant two-piece to match: what more could a stylish baby ask for? Knitted in a beautifully soft cotton yarn that is kind and gentle to a delicate skin, the outfit washes easily, dries quickly and is perfect for mild weather wear. The striped top has a wide neckline, with the back lapping over the front so that it slips on and off easily, and the plain, short length pants have an elasticated waist. The blanket, also cotton, is made from 25 separate rectangles, joined with narrow strips of white – perhaps it could be a joint family effort?

CHECKLIST

TWO-PIECE
Materials
*Sophie Desroches Coton Mat: for the top, 2 (2-3) balls beige (**A**) and one ball white (**B**); for the trousers, 2 (2-3) balls white. Pair each of needles size 2¼mm, 2¾mm and 3mm; narrow elastic for trousers.*

Sizes
Three sizes, to fit ages 6 (9-12) months. Actual measurements shown on diagram.

Stitches used
Double rib; st st.

Tension
Over st st using 3mm needles, 27 sts and 36 rows to 10cm (4in). Work a sample on 32 sts.

INSTRUCTIONS

TOP

▦ **Front** With 2¼mm needles and **B**, cast on 62 (66-74) sts and work in rib.

▦ *1st row* (right side) K 2, * p 2, k 2; rep from * to end.

▦ *2nd row* P 2, * k 2, p 2; rep from * to end. Rep these 2 rows 4 times more then 1st row again.

▦ *12th row* Rib 13 (9-17), [inc in next st, rib 17 (11-19)] 2 (4-2) times, inc in next st, rib 12 (8-16). 65 (71-77) sts. Change to 3mm needles and beg with a k row work in st st working in striped patt of 2 rows **B**, 10 rows **A** throughout. Cont until 50 (54-58) rows have been worked in st st.

▦ **Armhole Shaping** Cast off 3 sts at beg of next 2 rows, 2 sts at beg of next 2 rows and 1 st at beg of next 4 (6-8) rows. Cont on rem 51 (55-59) sts until work measures 21(23-25)cm, 8¼(9-9¾)in, from beg, ending with a p row.

▦ **Neck Shaping** *1st row* K 21 (22-23) and leave these sts of left front on a spare needle, cast off next 9 (11-13) sts, k to end. Cont on 21 (22-23) sts now rem on needle for right front and work 1 row. Cast off 3 (4-4) sts at beg of next row, 2 sts at same edge on next 2 alt rows and 1 st on next alt row; work 3 rows without shaping. ** Dec 1 st at neck edge on next row and next 2 alt rows then dec at same edge on foll 5 rows. Cast off rem 5 (5-6) sts. Rejoin correct colour to neck edge of left front sts, cast off 3 (4-4), p to end. Cast off 2 sts at same edge on next 2 alt rows and 1 st on next alt row then work 4 rows without shaping. Complete as for right front from ** to end.

▦ **Back** Work as for front until armhole shaping is completed then cont until work measures 25(27-29)cm, 9¾(10⅝-11⅜)in, from beg, ending with a p row.

▦ **Neck Shaping** *1st row* K 22 (23-24) and leave these sts of right back on a spare needle, cast off next 7 (9-11) sts, k to end. Cont on 22 (23-24) sts now rem on needle for left back and work 1 row. Cast off 3 (4-4) sts at beg of next row, 2 sts at same edge on next 2 alt rows and 1 st on next 2 alt rows. Work 5 rows straight then complete as for right front from ** to end. Rejoin correct colour to neck edge of right back sts, cast off 3 (4-4), p to end. Cast off 2 sts at same edge on next 2 alt rows and 1 st on next 2 alt rows; work 6 rows without shaping then complete as for right front from ** to end.

▦ **Sleeves** With 2¼mm needles and **B** cast on 38 (38-42) sts and work in rib as on front welt for 7 rows.

▦ *8th row* Rib 3 (4-3), [inc in next st, rib 7 (4-8)] 4 (6-4) times, inc in next st, rib 2 (3-2). 43 (45-47) sts. Change to 3mm needles and working in st st work striped patt as given for front but inc 1 st at both ends of every foll 6th row 7 (8-9) times. Cont on 57 (61-65) sts until 50 (54-58) rows have been worked in st st.

▦ **Top Shaping** Cast off 3 sts at beg of next 2 rows, 2 sts at beg of next 2 rows, 1 st at beg of next 4 (6-8) rows, 2 sts at beg of next 4 rows, 3 sts at beg of next 2 rows and 4 sts at beg of next 4 rows. Cast off rem 13 (15-17) sts.

▦ **Neck Borders** With right side facing and using 2¼mm needles and **B**, pick up and k 66 (70-74) sts along entire upper edge of front including the groups of sts cast off at end of neck shaping. Beg with 2nd row work in rib for 5 rows then cast off loosely in rib. Work similar border on upper edge of back picking up 74 (78-82) sts.

▦ **Finishing** Lap upper edge of back over front along armhole

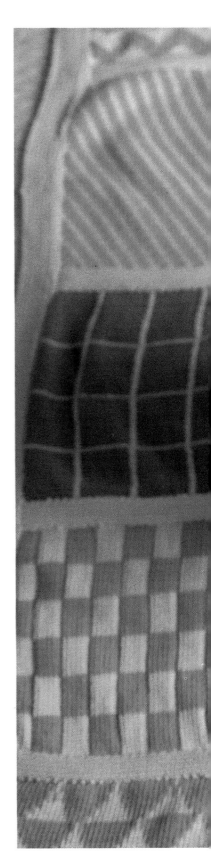

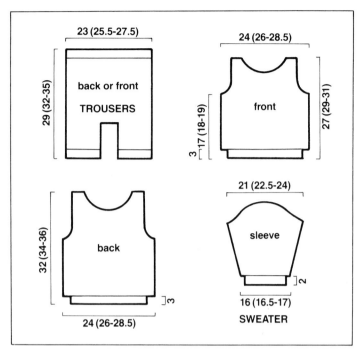

edges for a depth of 5cm (2in) and tack in place. Sew cast-off edges of sleeves to sides of armhole matching stripes and sewing through double thickness where back and front overlap. Remove tackings. Join side and sleeve seams matching stripes.

TROUSERS

Front Beg at waist edge cast on 63 (69-75) sts using 2¾mm needles and **B**. Beg with a k row work in st st for 11 rows then k 1 row on wrong side for fold-line. Change to 3mm needles and beg with another k row cont in st st until work measures 20(22-24)cm, 7⅞(8⅝-9½)in, from beg, ending with a p row.
Next row K 27 (30-33) and leave these sts on a spare needle, cast off 9, k to end. Cont on 27 (30-33) sts now rem on needle for

one leg; cont until work measures 27(30-33)cm, 10⅝(11¾-13)in, from beg, ending with a k row. Change to 2¾mm needles and k 1 row for fold-line then work 7 rows in st st. Cast off loosely. Rejoin yarn to sts for other leg and complete in same way.

Back Work exactly as for front.

Finishing Join side seams then join inner leg and crotch seams making backstitch joins. Cut elastic to baby's waist measurement, overlap ends forming a ring and sew securely. Fold hem section at waist edge to inside enclosing elastic and hold edge in place with a row of herringbone st. Fold up hems on leg edges to inside and slip-st in place.

CHECKLIST

PATCHWORK BLANKET
Materials
*Sophie Desroches Coton Mat: 8 balls white (**A**) and 3 balls each in beige (**B**), green (**C**) and yellow (**D**). Pair each of needles size 2¾mm and 3mm.*

Size
Finished measurements 86cm × 96cm (33⅞in × 37¾in).

Stitches used
Single rib; st st; patts, as explained below.

Tension
Over st st and using 3mm needles, 27 sts and 36 rows to 10cm (4in). Work a sample on 32 sts. Some of the patts will give a slightly tighter tension and more sts are allowed for these. The finished rectangles should all measure approximately 16cm × 18cm (6¼in × 7⅛in).

INSTRUCTIONS

RECTANGLES

The charts are worked 2, 3 or 4 times, using different colour combinations on various rectangles. The diagram shows the colours used and also the arrangement of rectangles. The arrow on each shows the direction of knitting. When they are joined some rectangles are placed sideways and some upside down to vary the effect.

Rectangle 1 With larger needles and **A** cast on 49 sts and working in st st work patt from Chart 1 using **D** and **A**.
1st row K 6 **A**, * 1 **D**, 11 **A**; * rep from * to * ending 1 **D**, 6 **A**. Cont in patt as now arranged until work measures 18cm (7⅛in) from beg. Cast off.
Rectangle 2 With larger needles and **C** cast on 45 sts and working in st st work 2 rows **C**, [2 rows **A**, 8 rows **C**] 6 times, 2 rows **A**, 2 rows **C**. Cast off.
Rectangle 3 With larger

needles and **B** cast on 49 sts and working in st st work patt from Chart 2 using **B** and **A**.

▦ *1st row* K [1 **A**, 1 **B**] twice, 1 **A**, ⁑ 3 **B**, [1 **A**, 1 **B**] 4 times, 1 **A**; ⁑ rep from ⁑ to ⁑ twice more, 3 **B**, [1 **A**, 1 **B**] twice, 1 **A**. Cont in patt as now set until work measures 18cm (7⅛in) from beg. Cast off.

▦ **Rectangle 4** With larger needles and **A** cast on 49 sts and working in st st work patt from Chart 3 using **A** and **C**.

▦ *1st row* K 2 **A**, ⁑ 9 **C**, 3 **A**; ⁑ rep from ⁑ to ⁑ twice more, 9 **C**, 2 **A**. Cont in patt as now set until work measures 18cm (7⅛in) from beg. Cast off.

▦ **Rectangle 5** This is worked from side to side. With larger needles and **A** cast on 49 sts and working in st st work 2 rows **A** then [7 rows **D**, 5 rows **A**] 4 times, 7 rows **D**, 2 rows **A**. Cast off.

▦ **Rectangle 6** With larger

needles and **A** cast on 49 sts and working in st st work patt from Chart 4 using **A** and **B**.

▦ *1st row* ⁑ K 2 **B**, 2 **A**; rep from ⁑ to last st, 1 **B**.

▦ *2nd row* P 1 **B**, ⁑ 2 **A**, 2 **B**; rep from ⁑ to end.

▦ *3rd row* K 1 **A**, ⁑ 2 **B**, 2 **A**; rep from ⁑ to end. Cont in patt as now set until work measures 18cm (7⅛in) from beg. Cast off.

▦ **Rectangle 7** With larger needles and **D** cast on 49 sts and work as given for rectangle 3 but using **D** in place of **B**.

▦ **Rectangle 8** With larger needles and **A** cast on 49 sts and work as given for rectangle 1 but using **C** in place of **D**.

▦ **Rectangle 9** With larger needles and **B** cast on 45 sts and working in st st work 2 rows **B**, then [2 row **A**, 8 rows **B**] 6 times, 2 rows **A**, 2 rows **B**. Cast off.

▦ **Rectangle 10** With larger

needles and **A** cast on 50 sts and work in small check patt using **A** and **C** as foll:

▦ *1st row* K 1 **A**, ⁑ 6 **C**, 6 **A**; ⁑ rep from ⁑ to ⁑ 3 times more, 1 **C**.

▦ *2nd row* P 1 **A**, ⁑ 6 **A**, 6 **C**; ⁑ rep from ⁑ to ⁑ 3 times more, 1 **C**.

▦ *3rd to 10th rows* Rep 1st and 2nd rows 4 times more.

▦ *11th row* K 1 **C**, ⁑ 6 **A**, 6 **C**; ⁑ rep from ⁑ to ⁑ 3 times more, 1 **A**.

▦ *12th row* P 1 **C**, ⁑ 6 **C**, 6 **A**; ⁑ rep from ⁑ to ⁑ 3 times more, 1 **A**.

▦ *13th to 20th rows* Rep 11th and 12th rows 4 times more. Rep these 20 rows twice more or until work measures 18cm (7⅛in) from beg. Cast off.

▦ **Rectangle 11** This is worked in window-pane checks using **A** and **C**; only the horizontal stripes are knitted; the vertical stripes are worked on afterwards by the Swiss darning method as explained below. With larger

needles and **A** cast on 46 sts and working in st st work 2 rows **A**, then [14 rows **C**, 2 rows **A**] 4 times. Cast off. Thread a tapestry needle with a length of **A** and beg on 3rd row miss the first 10 sts from right-hand edge and on next 2 sts work a vertical stripe by the Swiss darning method as described on page 6. Work 2 more stripes in **A** missing 10 sts between them and leaving 10 sts at end.

▦ **Rectangle 12** This is worked from side to side. With larger needles and **A** cast on 49 sts and working in st st work 2 rows **A** then [7 rows **B**, 5 rows **A**] 4 times, 7 rows **B**, 2 rows **A**. Cast off.

▦ **Rectangle 13** Work as for rectangle 4 but using **D** in place of **C**.

▦ **Rectangle 14** With larger needles and **C** cast on 49 sts and working in st st work patt from

Chart 2 using **C** for the background with **A** for the triangles. Cont in patt until work measures 18cm (7⅛in) from beg. Cast off.

▦ **Rectangle 15** Work as for rectangle 6 but using **D** in place of **B**.

▦ **Rectangle 16** Work as for rectangle 10 but using **D** in place of **C**.

▦ **Rectangle 17** Work as for rectangle 4, using same colours.

▦ **Rectangle 18** Work as for rectangle 10 but using **B** instead of **C**.

▦ **Rectangle 19** With larger needles and **D** cast on 45 sts and working in st st work 2 rows **D**, then [2 rows **A**, 8 rows **D**] 6 times, 2 rows **A**, 2 rows **D**. Cast off.

▦ **Rectangle 20** Work as for rectangle 11 but using **B** in place of **C**.

▦ **Rectangle 21** Work as for rectangle 4 but using **B** in place of **C**.

▦ **Rectangle 22** Work as for rectangle 11 but using **D** in place of **C**.

▦ **Rectangle 23** This is worked from side to side. With larger needles and **A** cast on 49 sts and working in st st work 2 rows **A**, then [7 rows **C**, 5 rows **A**] 4 times, 7 rows **C**, 2 rows **A**. Cast off.

▦ **Rectangle 24** Work as for rectangle 1 but using **B** in place of **D**.

▦ **Rectangle 25** Work as for rectangle 6 but using **C** in place of **B**.

▦ **Strips** With larger needles and **A** cast on 6 sts and k 1 row.

▦ *2nd row* Slip 1 pw, p 5.

▦ *3rd row* Slip 1 kw, k 5. Rep last 2 rows until strip measures 80cm (31½in) long. Cast off. Work 3 more strips in same way. Now work 4 similar strips each 90cm (35½in) long.

▦ **Borders** With smaller needles and **A** cast on 13 sts for one side border.

▦ *1st row* K 2, [p 1, k 1] 5 times, k 1.

▦ *2nd row* [K 1, p 1] 6 times, k 1. Rep these 2 rows until border measures 96cm (37¾in) from beg. Cast off in rib. Work another

1 ↑ Chart 1 □ = White ✕ = Yellow	2 ↑	3 ↑ Chart 2 □ = Beige ✕ = White	4 ↑ Chart 3 □ = White ✕ = Green	5 ←
6 ↑ Chart 4 □ = White ✕ = Beige	7 ↑ Chart 2 □ = Yellow ✕ = White	8 ↑ Chart 1 □ = White ✕ = Green	9 ↑	10 ↑
11	12 ←	13 ↑ Chart 3 □ = White ✕ = Yellow	14 ↓ Chart 2 □ = Green ✕ = White	15 ↑ Chart 4 □ = White ✕ = Yellow
16	17 ↑ Chart 3 □ = White ✕ = Green	18	19 ↑	20 ↑
21 ↓ Chart 3 □ = White ✕ = Beige	22 ↑	23 ←	24 ↑ Chart 1 □ = White ✕ = Beige	25 ↑ Chart 4 □ = White ✕ = Green

border in same way. Work 2 borders for upper and lower edges each 80cm (31½in) long.

▦ **Finishing** Assemble the 25 rectangles as shown on diagram, oversewing the seams closely. Press work on wrong side with warm iron and damp cloth. Now pin the narrow strips in place; with p side of strip to k side of main part pin the longer strips so that they cover the seams with the seam at centre of strip. There are almost bound to be minor differences in size between the

finished patches. These can be evened out when you join them with the long strips if you first divide each strip equally into five, marking the divisions with pins. Pin the strips in position at these points and then carefully ease out any fulness when sewing. Slip-st the strips in place then pin and sew the shorter strips in place in same way. Sew shorter ribbed borders along upper and lower edges making backstitch joins then sew longer borders to side edges including ends of shorter borders.

Where one of the charts is used for working a rectangle the key to colours is shown above. Patterns used on the other rectangles are explained in the instructions. Arrows show the direction of knitting; take note of correct direction when sewing the rectangles together.

Chart 1 12-row patt

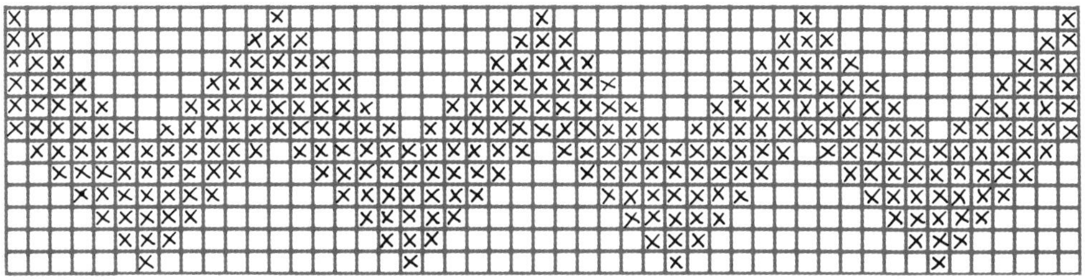

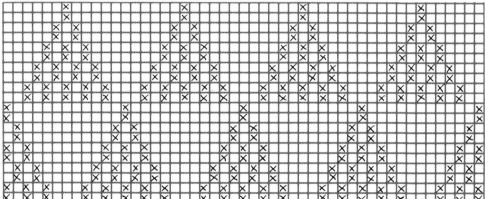

1st row

Chart 1

Use this chart for rectangles 1, 8 and 24. See diagram for colours. Chart shows full width; rep the 12-row patt until work is correct length.

Chart 2 20-row patt

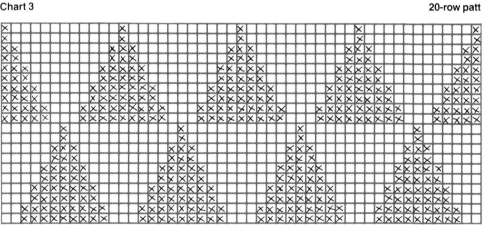

1st row

Chart 2

Use this chart for rectangles 3, 7 and 14. See diagram for colours. Chart shows full width; rep the 20-row patt until work is correct length.

Chart 3 20-row patt

1st row

Chart 3

Use this chart for rectangles 4, 13, 17 and 21. See diagram for colours. Chart shows full width; rep the 20-row patt until work is correct length.

Chart 4 8-row patt

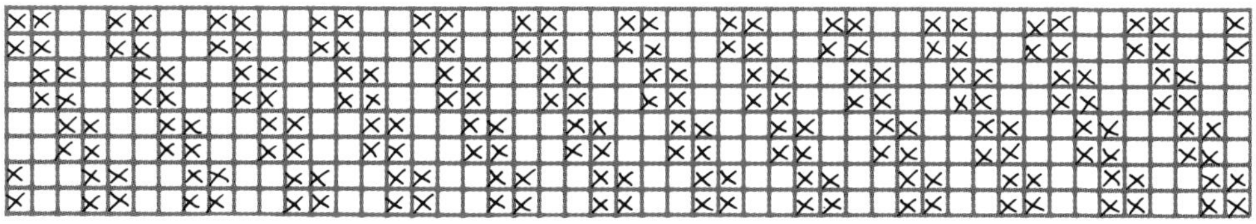

1st row

Chart 4

Use this chart for rectangles 6, 14 and 25. See diagram for colours. Chart shows full width; rep the 8-row patt until work is correct length.

FIRST BEST OUTFIT

This irresistably stylish outfit features the smart, multi-layered look – just the thing for your baby to wear when meeting an admiring host of grand-parents, aunts, uncles, friends and well-wishers. Knitted in a fine, soft yarn, it will keep baby warm without restricting his or her movements. Romper suit, buttoning down the back, bootees, socks and a pixie hat are all in garter stitch and rib. The finishing touch is a loose-fitting jacket in traditional Fair Isle patterns, adapted to make them easy to knit.

CHECKLIST

Materials
For the complete set, Chat Botté Shetland: 6 (7-7) balls mouette, pale grey (A); 2 balls azalée, rose pink (B); and one ball each of rocaille, green (C) and marron glacé, beige (D). Pair each of needles size 3mm and 3¼mm; 9 small buttons for rompers.

Sizes
Rompers and jacket are in three sizes to fit ages 3 (6-9) months. Hat, socks and bootees are in two sizes to fit ages 3 to 6 (6 to 9) months. Actual measurements of rompers and jacket shown on diagrams.

Stitches used
Single rib; g st; st st; patt *on the jacket is worked from charts as explained below. Some sections of the Fair Isle patt are embroidered on afterwards by the Swiss darning method and the small spot motifs on the rompers are also embroidered.*

Tensions
Over g st using 3¼mm needles, 27 sts and 48 rows to 10cm (4in); work a sample on 32 sts. Over Fair Isle patt using 3¼mm needles, 31 sts and 32 rows to 10cm (4in); work a sample on 38 sts working from Chart 1 below.

INSTRUCTIONS

ROMPERS

▦ **Main Part** Beg at lower edge of right leg, cast on 60 (64-70) sts using smaller needles and **B**. Work in single rib working 2 rows **B** then change to **A** and cont in rib until work measures 7cm (2¾in) from beg. Change to larger needles and using **A** only work in g st counting 1st row as right side of work. Cont until work measures 15 (17-19)cm, 5⅞(6¾-7½)in, from beg, ending with a wrong-side row. ** Cut yarn and leave sts on a spare needle. Work left leg in same way as far as ** then join legs adding sts for gussets.
▦ *1st row* Cast on 10, k these sts

and the sts of left leg, turn, cast on 20 sts; turn then, with right side facing, k the sts of right leg, turn and cast on 10 sts.
▦ *2nd row* K across 160 (168-180) sts.
▦ *3rd row* K 8, k 2 tog, k 60 (64-70), SKPO, k 16, k 2 tog, k 60 (64-70), SKPO, k 8.
▦ *4th row* K.
▦ *5th row* K 7, k 2 tog, k 60 (64-70), SKPO, k 14, k 2 tog, k 60 (64-70), SKPO, k 7. Cont working decs in these positions working 2 sts fewer at centre and 1 st at each end on 7th row then on every foll 4th row 4 times more.
▦ *24th row* K. Cast off 2 sts at beg of next 2 rows to make space for back borders to be worked afterwards. Cont on rem 128 (136-148) sts without shaping

until work measures 37(41-45)cm, 14½(16⅛-17¾)in, from beg, ending with a wrong-side row. Now divide for armholes.
▦ *Next row* K 31 (33-36), turn and cont on these sts for left back leaving rem sts on a spare needle. Cont in g st for 9(10-11)cm, 3½(4-4¼)in, ending at back opening edge.
▦ **Neck Shaping** Cast off 7 (8-9) sts at beg of next row and 4 sts at same edge on next 2 alt rows. Cast off rem 16 (17-19) sts for shoulder edge.

▦ **Front** With right side facing rejoin yarn to sts left unworked, k 66 (70-76) sts, turn and cont on these sts for front. Work 5(6-7)cm, 2(2⅜-2¾)in, without shaping, ending with a wrong-side row.
▦ **Neck Shaping** *1st row* K 27 (28-30) and leave these sts of left front on a spare needle, cast off next 12 (14-16) sts, k to end. Cont on 27 (28-30) sts now rem on needle for right front and k 1 row. *** Cast off 3 sts at beg of next row, 2 sts at same edge on next 2 alt rows and 1 st on next 4 alt rows. Cont on rem 16 (17-19) sts until work matches left back to shoulder. Cast off. Rejoin yarn to neck edge of left front sts and complete as for right front from *** to end.
▦ **Right Back** With right side facing rejoin yarn to rem 31 (33-36) sts left unworked at armhole opening, k to end. Complete as for left back reversing neck shaping.

▦ **Sleeves** With smaller needles and **B** cast on 36 (38-40) sts and work in single rib; work 2 rows in **B** then using **A** cont in rib until work measures 4cm (1½in) from beg.
▦ *Inc row* (wrong side) Rib 3 (1-4), [inc in next st, rib 5 (4-3)] 5 (7-8) times, inc in next st, rib 2 (1-3). 42 (46-49) sts. Change to 3¼mm needles and work in g st but inc 1 st at both ends of every foll 10th row 3 (4-4) times, then every foll 8th row 3 (3-4) times. Cont on 54 (60-65) sts until work measures 17(19-21)cm, 6¾(7½-8¼)in, from beg.

Cast off all sts.

▦ **Tie strip** With 3mm needles and **C** cast on 25 sts.
▦ *1st row* (right side) K 2, [p 1, k 1] 11 times, k 1.
▦ *2nd row* [K 1, p 1] 12 times, k 1. Rep these 2 rows 3 times more. Cast off in rib.

▦ **Back Borders** Beg above the 2 sts cast-off at end of gusset shaping, with right side of work facing and using smaller needles and **A**, pick up and k 82 (92-102) sts along left back edge. Work in single rib for 5 rows then cast off in rib. Work similar border on right back edge but after working 2 rows make buttonholes.
▦ *3rd row* Beg at lower edge, wrong side facing, rib 5 (7-9), cast off 2, [rib until there are 8 (9-10) sts on right needle after previous buttonhole, cast off 2] 7 times, rib to end. On foll row cast on 2 sts over each buttonhole. Rib 1 more row then cast off in rib.

▦ **Finishing and Neck Border** Join shoulder seams. With right side of work facing and using smaller needles and **A** pick up and k 22 (23-24) sts along left back neck edge including upper edge of back border, then 50 (52-54) sts around front neck edge and 22 (23-24) sts along right back edge including back border. 94 (98-102) sts. Work 2 rows in single rib.
▦ *3rd row* Beg at right back edge rib 2, cast off 2, rib to end. Change to **B** and cont in rib casting on 2 sts over buttonhole on next row then work 2 more rows. Cast off in rib.
▦ Before sewing rem seams work the motifs all over g st sections; thread a tapestry needle with 2 strands of **B** and sew twice over 2 sts and 2 rows, cut ends and tie close to work. Space knots approximately 9 sts and 18 rows apart in alternating positions as shown. Join sleeve seams and sew cast-off edge into armholes. Join inner leg seams and sew across cast-on edges of gussets. At back join outer edges of gussets below back borders. Sew centre of tie

strip to front just below neck border stitching tightly across centre to simulate a bow. Sew on buttons to correspond with buttonholes and slip-st lower edges of borders in place lapping right border over left.

JACKET

▦ **Main Part** This is worked in one piece up to armhole openings. With smaller needles and **B** cast on 141 (153-165) sts and work in rib.

▦ *1st row* (right side) P 1, * k 1, p 1; rep from * to end.

▦ *2nd row* K 1, * p 1, k 1; rep from * to end. K 1 row in **B**.

▦ *4th row* K 12 (14-16), [inc in next st, k 28 (30-32)] 4 times, inc in next st, k 12 (14-16). 146 (158-170) sts. Change to larger needles and working in st st work patt from Chart 1.

▦ *1st row* K 2 **B**, * 2 **A**, 2 **B**; rep from * to end. Cont working from chart for a further 5 (9-13) rows. Now work from Chart 2; note that the sts shown in **C** are embroidered on afterwards and they should be worked in **A** on the 10 rows of chart as foll:

▦ *1st row* K 2 **A**, * 2 **B**, 2 **A**; rep from * to end. Work 8 more rows with colours as set.

▦ *10th row* * P 3 **A**, 1 **B**; rep from * to last 2 sts, 2 **A**. Change to smaller needles and work in g st working 2 rows **C**, 2 rows **A**, 2 rows **B** but on last of these rows, for 1st size inc 1 st at centre (for 3rd size dec 1 st at centre). Change back to larger needles and cont on 147 (158-169) sts, working patt from Chart 3; note that the sts shown in **D** and the single st in **C** at centre of each motif are all embroidered on afterwards so these should be worked in **B**. When working more than 5 sts in **A** or **B** twist the other colour around the yarn in use once at centre of the group of sts; do not weave in as this distorts the tension.

▦ *1st row* K 4 **B**, * 7 **A**, 4 **B**; rep from * to end.

▦ *2nd row* P 5 **B**, * 5 **A**, 6 **B**; rep from * to last 10 sts, 5 **A**, 5 **B**. Cont as now set until chart is completed. Cut yarn and slip all

sts onto a smaller needle so that right side will be facing for next row. Using **B** k 1 row but for 1st size dec 1 st at centre (for 3rd size inc 1 st at centre). 146 (158-170) sts. Cont in g st and work 1 more row in **B** then 2 rows **A** and 2 rows **C**. Change back to larger needles and working in st st work patt from Chart 1, *at same time* dividing for armhole openings.

◫ *1st row* K [2 **B**, 2 **A**] 9 (10-11) times, 2 (1-0) **B**, turn and cont on these sts for right front, leaving rem sts on a spare needle. Cont on these 38 (41-44) sts keeping patt correct until work measures 6(7-8)cm, 2⅜(2¾-3⅛)in, from beg of this patt section, ending at front edge after a p row.

◫ **Neck Shaping** Cast off 10 (11-12) sts at beg of next row, 4 sts at same edge on next alt row, 2 sts on next 2 alt rows and 1 st on next 3 alt rows. Cont on rem 17 (19-21) sts until work measures 11(12-13)cm, 4¼(4¾-5⅛)in, from beg of this patt section. Cast off all sts.

◫ **Back** With right side facing and using larger needles, rejoin yarn to sts unworked and cont in patt; k 0 (1-2) **B**, [2 **A**, 2 **B**] 17 (18-19) times, 2 **A**, 0 (1-2) **B**, turn and cont on these 70 (76-82) sts for back; keep patt correct and cont without shaping until work matches right front to shoulder edge.
Cast off all sts.

◫ **Left Front** With right side facing and using larger needles, rejoin yarn to rem 38 (41-44) sts, k 2 (1-0) **B**, [2 **A**, 2 **B**] 9 (10-11) times. Cont in patt and complete as for right front reversing neck shaping.

◫ **Sleeves** With smaller needles and **B** cast on 57 (61-65) sts and work 2 rows in rib as on main part. K 1 row in **B**.

◫ *4th row* K 7 (9-11), [inc in next st, k 13] 3 times, inc in next st, k 7 (9-11). 61 (65-69) sts. Change to larger needles and working in st st work patt from Chart 4.

◫ *1st row* K 1 **A**, * 3 **B**, 1 **A**; rep from * to end.

◫ *2nd row* P 2 **A**, * 1 **B**, 3 **A**; rep from * ending 1 **B**, 2 **A**. Cont in

patt as now set but inc 1 st at both ends of every foll 8th row twice then every foll 6th row 2 (3-4) times working extra sts into patt. Cont on 69 (75-81) sts until work measures 13(15-17)cm, 5⅛(5⅞-6¾)in, from beg, ending with a p row. Change to smaller needles and working in g st work 2 rows **B**, 2 rows **A**, 2 rows **C**. Cast off all sts.

◫ **Finishing and Borders** First complete the panels of patt worked from Charts 2 and 3 by covering the sts shown by these symbols in the correct colour using the Swiss darning method described on page 6. To neaten front edges, with right side facing and using smaller needles and **B**, pick up and k 51 (57-63) sts along front edge of right front. P 1 row then cast off. Work similar edging on left front. Fold edgings inside and slip-st in place on wrong side.

◫ Sew shoulder edges of fronts to a corresponding width on top edge of back leaving centre 36 (38-40) sts of back free for neckline. With right side of work facing and using smaller needles and **B**, pick up and k 27 (28-29) sts along right front neck edge, 35 (37-39) sts across back neck and 27 (28-29) sts along left front neck. 89 (93-97) sts. K 1 row on wrong side then rep 1st and 2nd rows of rib border twice. Cast off in rib. Join sleeve seams. Sew cast-off edge of sleeves to sides of armhole openings.

SOCKS (both alike)

◫ Beg at upper edge cast on 52 (60) sts using smaller needles and **C**. Work in single rib for 11(12)cm, 4¼(4¾)in. Change to **B** and still using smaller needles work in g st counting 1st row as right side row. Work 10 rows in **B** then change to **D** and begin shaping.

◫ *11th row* K 2 tog, * k 23 (27), k 2 tog; rep from * once. Work 3 rows on rem 49 (57) sts.

◫ *15th row* K 2 tog, k 21 (25), k 2 tog, k 22 (26), k 2 tog. Work 1 (3) rows in **D** then change to **C** and work 2 (0) rows.

◫ *19th row* K 2 tog, * k 20 (24), k 2 tog; rep from * once. Cont to dec at each end of row and at centre, on every foll 4th row 5 (6) times more, and at same time cont stripes: work 7 (9) more rows in **C**, then 2 rows in **B**, 6 rows in **A** and 6 (8) rows in **D**. Decs have been completed, 28 (33) sts rem. Cont with **D** and work in st st; work 7(8)cm, 2¾(3⅛)in, ending with a p row, then shape toe.

◫ *1st row* [K 2 tog] 14 (16) times, k 0 (1). P 1 row.

◫ *3rd row* [K 2 tog] 7 (8) times, k 0 (1). Cut yarn, pass it through rem sts, draw up tightly and sew securely then join seam along foot and back of leg, matching stripes.

BOOTEES (both alike)

◫ Beg at upper edge cast on 40 (48) sts using smaller needles and **B**; work in g st for 23 rows then make holes for cord.

◫ *24th row* K 1, [k 2 tog, yfd, k 2] 9 (11) times, k 2 tog, yfd, k 1. Work 6 (8) more rows in g st then shape heel.

◫ *1st row* K 8 (10), turn and cont on these sts for one side of heel leaving rem sts on a spare needle. Cont in g st and dec 1 st at outer edge on next row and next 3 (4) alt rows. Cast off rem 4 (5) sts. Return to sts left unworked, slip next 24 (28) sts of instep onto a holder, rejoin yarn to rem 8 (10) sts, k to end. Complete as for first side of heel reversing shapings.

◫ With right side facing pick up and k 8 (10) sts along straight side edge of first heel section, k sts of instep then pick up and k 8 (10) sts along straight side of second heel section. Work 3 (7) rows on these 40 (48) sts then shape foot.

◫ *1st row* K 5 (7), SKPO, k 2,

KEY

☐	pale grey
▨	rose pink
▩	green
▨	beige

Charts 1, 2 and 3 are used for the main part of the jacket (in order 1, 2, 3 and then 1 again), and chart 4 is used for the sleeves only.

k 2 tog, k 18 (22), SKPO, k 2, k 2 tog, k 5 (7). Work 5 rows straight.

◫ *7th row* K 4 (6), SKPO, k 2, k 2 tog, k 16 (20), SKPO, k 2, k 2 tog, k 4 (6). Cont to work 4 decs in these positions, working 2 sts fewer at centre and 1 st at sides, on every foll 6th row 3 (4) times more. K 1 row on rem 20 (24) sts.

◫ *Next row* [K 2 tog] 10 (12) times. K 1 row.

◫ *Next row* [K 2 tog] 5 (6) times. Cut yarn, thread end through rem sts, draw up tightly and sew securely then join seam along foot and back of leg. Make a length of twisted cord and thread through holes at ankle to tie at front.

HAT

◫ With smaller needles and **B** cast on 90 (98) sts and work in single rib; work 2 rows in **B** then change to **A** and cont in rib until work measures 13(14)cm, 5⅛(5½)in, from beg. Still using smaller needles work in g st counting 1st row as right side. Work 4 rows then begin shaping.

◫ *5th row* K 2 tog, * k 42 (46), k 2 tog; rep from * once. Work 3 rows on rem 87 (95) sts.

◫ *9th row* K 2 tog, k 40 (44), k 2 tog, k 41 (45), k 2 tog. Work 3 rows on rem 84 (92) sts.

◫ *13th row* K 2 tog, * k 39 (43), k 2 tog; rep from * once. Cont to dec at each end and at centre of row on every foll 4th row 21 (22) times more. K 1 row on rem 18 (23) sts.

◫ *Next row* [K 2 tog] 9 (11) times, k 0 (1). Cut yarn, pass it through rem sts, draw up tightly and sew securely then sew back seam of hat reversing it on brim. Make a large pom-pon using **B**, **C** and **D**; sew it to point.

Chart no 1

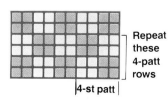

Repeat these 4-patt rows

4-st patt

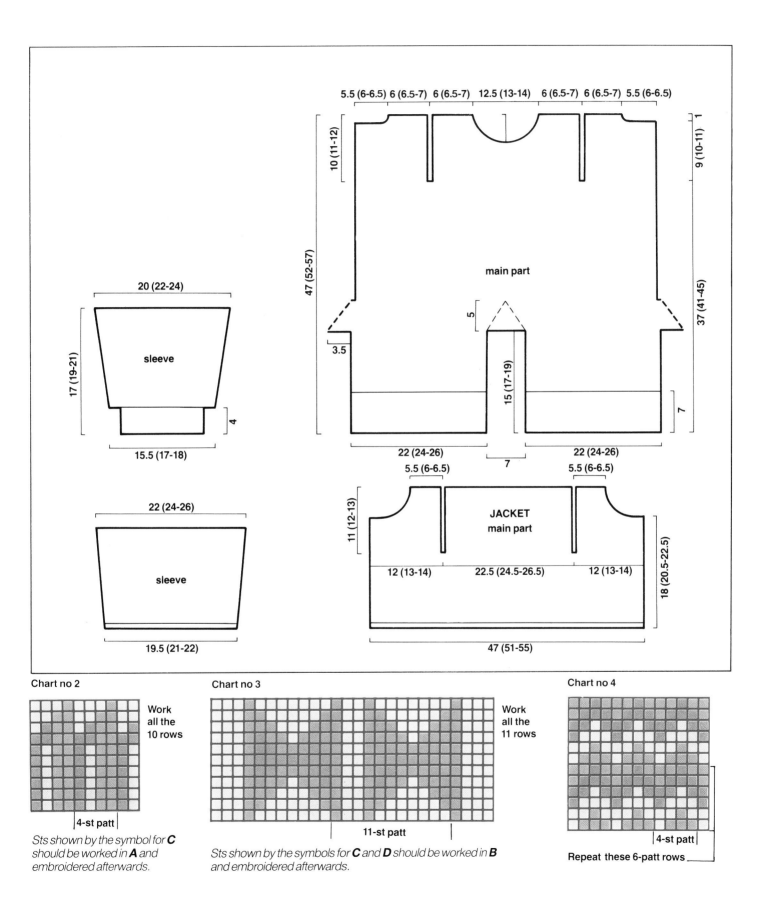

5.5 (6-6.5) 6 (6.5-7) 6 (6.5-7) 12.5 (13-14) 6 (6.5-7) 6 (6.5-7) 5.5 (6-6.5)

10 (11-12)

9 (10-11) 1

47 (52-57)

main part

37 (41-45)

5

3.5

15 (17-19)

7

22 (24-26)

7

22 (24-26)

20 (22-24)

17 (19-21)

sleeve

4

15.5 (17-18)

5.5 (6-6.5) 5.5 (6-6.5)

11 (12-13)

JACKET
main part

12 (13-14) 22.5 (24.5-26.5) 12 (13-14)

18 (20.5-22.5)

22 (24-26)

sleeve

19.5 (21-22)

47 (51-55)

Chart no 2

**Work
all the
10 rows**

|4-st patt|

*Sts shown by the symbol for **C**
should be worked in **A** and
embroidered afterwards.*

Chart no 3

**Work
all the
11 rows**

11-st patt

*Sts shown by the symbols for **C** and **D** should be worked in **B**
and embroidered afterwards.*

Chart no 4

|4-st patt|

Repeat these 6-patt rows

MIX AND MATCH SET

This wonderfully practical set, consisting of a sweater, rompers and matching bootees, is so quick and easy to knit that the temptation is to carry on knitting until you have several versions in different colourways, as here, for a versatile mix-and-match wardrobe. The sweater has a buttoned opening, worn either at the front or back, and is knitted in single yarn. For the rompers and bootees the yarn is used double stranded, to give extra firmness and warmth, and the only stitches used are stocking stitch, rib and garter stitch.

CHECKLIST

Materials

Phildar Prognostic 220 *or* Super Baby: *2 balls white and 2 balls pink or other contrast colour for sweater; 12 balls pink or other colour for rompers, and one ball for bootees. Pair each of needles size 2¼mm, 2¾mm and 4½mm; 3 buttons for sweater, 2 large buttons for rompers, 2 small buttons for bootees.*

Size

Two sizes, to fit ages 3 to 6 (9 to 12) months. Actual measurements of sweater and rompers are shown on diagram.

Stitches used

Single rib; st st; g st; k loop = pick up loop lying between needles and k it through the back.

Tension

Over st st and using 2¾mm needles and single yarn, 29 sts and 37 rows to 10cm (4in); work a sample on 35 sts. Over g st using 4½mm needles and double-stranded yarn, 17 sts and 34 rows to 10cm (4in); work a sample on 22 sts.

INSTRUCTIONS

SWEATER

▦ **Back** With 2¼mm needles and white, cast on 64 (70) sts and work in single rib for 8 rows. Change to 2¾mm needles and work in st st beg with a k row working stripes of 4 rows white, 4 rows pink (or other contrast colour) throughout. Cont until work measures 14(16)cm, 5½(6¼)in, from beg, ending with a p row.
▦ **Armhole Shaping** Cast off 5 sts at beg of next 2 rows. Work 2 (6) rows on rem 54 (60) sts.
▦ **Back Opening** *Next row* K 26 (29) and leave these sts of right back on a spare needle, cast off 2, k to end. Cont on 26 (29) sts

now rem on needle for left back, without shaping until work measures 24(27)cm, 9½(10⅝)in, from beg, ending at the opening edge.
▦ **Neck and Shoulder Shaping** Cast off for neck 10 (11) sts at beg of next row and 6 (7) sts at side edge of foll row. Cast off 3 sts at neck edge on next row then cast off rem 7 (8) sts to complete shoulder slope. Rejoin correct colour to sts of right back and complete as for left back reversing shapings.

▦ **Front** Work as for back until armhole shaping has been worked then cont on rem 54 (60) sts until work measures 20(23)cm, 7⅞(9)in, from beg, ending with a p row.

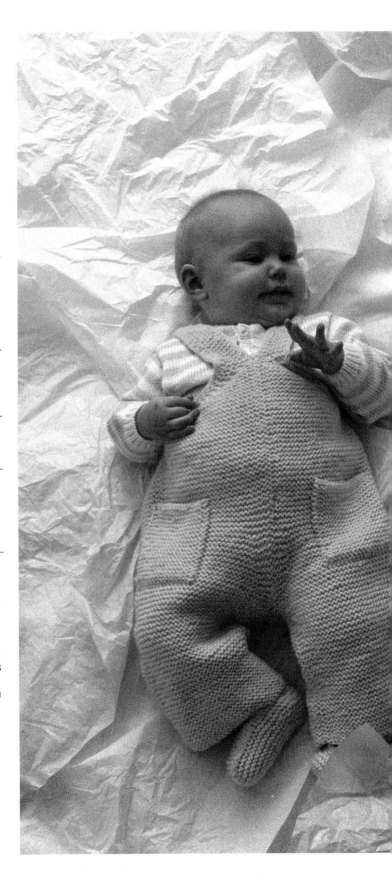

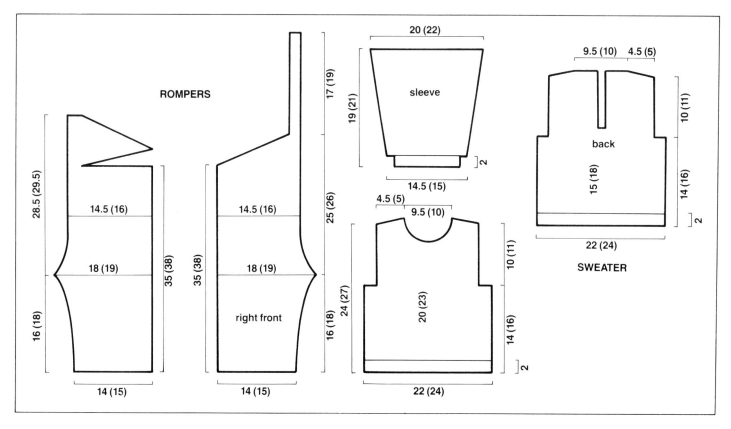

ROMPERS

28.5 (29.5)

14.5 (16)

18 (19)

16 (18)

35 (38)

14 (15)

right front

14.5 (16)

18 (19)

16 (18)

35 (38)

14 (15)

17 (19)

25 (26)

24 (27)

16 (18)

sleeve

20 (22)

14.5 (15)

19 (21)

2

4.5 (5)

9.5 (10)

20 (23)

14 (16)

22 (24)

10 (11)

2

back

9.5 (10)   4.5 (5)

15 (18)

22 (24)

10 (11)

14 (16)

2

SWEATER

Neck and Shoulder Shaping
1st row K 23 (25) and leave these sts of left front on a spare needle, cast off next 8 (10) sts, k to end. Cont on 23 (25) sts now rem on needle for right front and work 1 row. ** Cast off 4 sts at beg of next row, 2 sts at same edge on next 2 alt rows and 1 st on next 2 alt rows. Cont on rem 13 (15) sts until work matches back to beg of shoulder, ending at side edge. Cast off 6 (7) sts at beg of next row, work 1 row then cast off rem 7 (8) sts.

Rejoin correct colour to neck edge of left front sts; complete as for right front from ** to end.

Sleeves
With 2¼mm needles and white cast on 38 (40) sts and work 7 rows in single rib.

Inc row Rib 5 (6), [inc in next st, rib 8] 3 times, inc in next st, rib 5 (6). 42 (44) sts. Change to 2¾mm needles and work in striped st st as for back but inc 1 st at both ends of every foll 6th row 8 times (then at both ends of every foll 4th row twice for 2nd size). Cont on

58 (64) sts until work measures 19(21)cm, 7½(8¼)in, from beg. Cast off.

Neck Border
First join shoulder seams. With right side of work facing and using 2¾mm needles and white, pick up and k 14 (15) sts across left back neck edge, 40 (42) sts around front neck and 14 (15) sts across right back neck. Work 4 rows in single rib then cast off loosely in rib.

Back Borders
With right side of work facing and using 2¾mm needles and white, pick up and k 32 sts along left back edge of opening.

1st row K 1, p 1; rep from * to end. Now make buttonholes.

2nd row Beg at base of opening rib 4, [yrn, p 2 tog, rib 10] twice, yrn, p 2 tog, rib 2. Work 1 more row then cast off in rib. Work similar border on right back edge of opening omitting buttonholes.

Finishing
Sew cast-off edge of sleeves to sides of armholes

and sew armhole casting-off to a corresponding depth on sides of sleeves. Join side and sleeve seams matching stripes. Sew on buttons to correspond with buttonholes.

ROMPERS

Use double-stranded yarn throughout

Right Front
With 4½mm needles cast on 24 (26) sts and work in g st counting 1st row as right side. Cont until work measures 4(6)cm, 1½(2⅜)in, from beg, ending with a wrong-side row. Shape inner edge of leg.

1st row K 3, k loop, k to end. Cont to inc in this position on every foll 6th row 4 times then on every foll 4th row twice. Cont on 31 (33) sts until work measures 16(18)cm, 6¼(7⅛)in, from beg, ending at shaped edge.

Crotch Shaping
1st row K 3, k 2 tog, k to end. K 1 row then dec in same position on next row, then on every foll 4th row 4 times more. Cont on rem 25 (27) sts

until work measures 35(38)cm, 13¾(15)in, from beg, ending at shaped edge. **

Armhole Shaping
1st row K to last 6 sts, SKTPO, k 3. Work the double dec in this position on every alt row 9 times more then cont on rem 5 (7) sts for shoulder strap; work 17(19)cm, 6¾(7½)in, then cast off.

Left Front
Work leg section as for right front but working incs 3 sts in from the opposite edge. Cont on 31 (33) sts until work measures 16(18)cm, 6¼(7⅛)in, from beg, ending at straight side edge.

Crotch Shaping
1st row K to last 5 sts, SKPO, k 3. Dec 1 st in same position on next alt row then on every foll 4th row 4 times more. Cont on rem 25 (27) sts until work measures 35(38)cm, 13¾(15)in, from beg, ending at straight side edge. ***

Armhole Shaping
1st row K 3, k 3 tog, k to end. Cont to work the double dec in this position on every alt row 9 times more then cont on rem 5 (7) sts and work

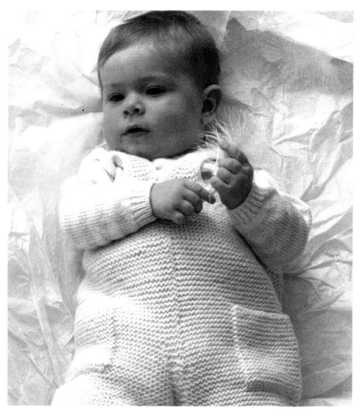

strap as for the right front.

Right Back Work as for left front to *** but ending at shaped edge then work shortened rows as foll:

- *1st row* K 21 (23), turn.
- *2nd and alt rows* K to end.
- *3rd row* K 18 (20), turn.
- *5th row* K 15 (17), turn. Cont to work 3 sts fewer before turning on next 3 alt rows; turn as usual and k to end. Work 1 row across all sts thus ending at side edge. Work armhole shaping as for left front and when shapings are completed cast off rem 5 (7) sts.

Left Back Work as for right front to ** thus ending at shaped edge. Work shortened rows as for right back until 2 rows have been worked on 6 (8) sts thus ending at shaped edge. Work armhole shaping as for right front and when shapings are completed cast off rem 5 (7) sts.

Pockets There are 2 pockets for front and 2 for back. With 4½mm needles cast on 16 (18)

sts for front pocket and work in g st for 8(9)cm, 3⅛(3½)in. Cast off.

- Make another in same way.
- For back pocket cast on 7 sts using 4½mm needles; work in g st but inc 1 st at both ends of every alt row 4 (5) times then cont on these 15 (17) sts until work measures 7(8)cm, 2¾(3⅛)in, from beg. Cast off.
- Make another pocket in same way.

Finishing and Borders Join side seams. With right side of work facing and using 2¼mm needles and yarn *single*, beg at centre back edge of left back pick up and k 124 (130) sts along entire left armhole edge and side of shoulder strap. Work 5 rows in g st then cast off rather tightly. Work similar border on right armhole beg at top of strap and ending at centre back. Join front seam. With right side facing and using 2¼mm needles and yarn *single*, pick up and k 108 (120) sts along inner edges of the 2

shoulder straps and work same border. Join centre back seam. Join inner leg seams.

- Sew front pockets to fronts as shown. Sew back pockets approximately at centre of each back placing them 21(23)cm, 8¼(9)in, above cast-on edge of legs. Make a buttonhole loop at end of each shoulder strap and sew buttons to back to correspond.

BOOTEES

Use yarn double-stranded throughout.

- With 4½mm needles cast on 26 (32) sts and work in g st, shaping both edges and centre.
- *1st and alt rows* K.
- *2nd row* K 1, k loop, k 11 (14), k loop, k 2, k loop, k 11 (14), k loop, k 1.
- *4th row* K 1, k loop, k 13 (16), k loop, k 2, k loop, k 13 (16), k loop, k 1. Cont working incs in these positions working 2 extra sts between them on next 3 alt rows then cont on 46 (52) sts and work

6 rows without shaping.

- **Instep Shaping** *1st row* K 27 (30), turn leaving 19 (22) sts unworked.
- *2nd row* K 8, turn, leaving 19 (22) sts at this edge also.
- *3rd row* K 7, k 2 tog, turn. Rep 3rd row 17 (19) times more thus taking in 1 st extra from those at sides on every row. Turn after last row and k to end. Cont on rem 28 (32) sts and work 4 rows across all sts. Cast off.
- For ankle strap cast on 12 sts.
- *1st row* K.
- *2nd row* K 9, yfd, k 2 tog, k 1. K 1 row then cast off. Fold cast-on edge of bootee in half and sew with a flat seam. Sew back seam of bootee.
- Sew ankle strap around front of leg section and sew on a button to correspond with buttonhole. When making 2nd bootee sew on strap the other way so that buttonhole of each bootee is at outside.

STYLISH STRIPES

The softest of baby yarns and a brilliant colour scheme are used for this simple but stylish sweater, which is knitted all in one piece and has a square neckline and a shoulder opening. The baby's snuggler is in a fine, soft mohair, in slightly different shades, and provides delightful warmth without weight.

CHECKLIST

Materials

FOR THE SWEATER
Berger du Nord Layette, *one ball in each of the foll colours: pacific (turquoise) No 8940* (**A**), *peppermint (pale green) No 8939* (**B**), *citron (yellow) No 8936* (**C**), *mandarine (orange) No 8937* (**D**), *pervenche (delphinium blue) No 8296* (**E**), *and framboise (raspberry red) No 8938* (**F**). *Pair of needles size 4mm; 2 buttons.*

FOR THE SNUGGLER
Berger du Nord Kid Mohair, *2 balls in each of the foll colours: turquoise No 8978* (**A**), *buvard (bright pink) No 7285* (**B**), *pervenche (delphinium blue) No 7991* (**C**), *and aigue-marine (blue-green) No 8458* (**D**). Kid Mohair No 5, *2 balls in each of the foll colours: melon (orange) No 8743* (**E**) *and paille (straw yellow) No 8146* (**F**). *A long pair of needles size 6mm.*

Size *Sweater, three sizes, to fit ages 3 (6-9) months. Actual measurements shown on diagram. Snuggler measures 81cm × 87cm (32in × 36in).*

Stitches used
Each item is knitted entirely in g st.
Note *When making the snuggler, Kid Mohair is used double-stranded and Kid Mohair No 5, which is thicker, is used single.*

Tension
Over g st using 4mm needles and Layette *double, 19 sts and 38 rows to 10cm (4in). Work a sample on 24 sts. Over g st and using 6mm needles and Kid Mohair double 13 sts and 26 rows to 10cm (4in). Work a sample on 20 sts.*

INSTRUCTIONS

SWEATER

▦ Each colour is used double. Wind a ball into 2 equal balls and rewind these tog to form a double-stranded ball which will be easier to use. Cut off each colour on completion of stripe.

▦ **Stripe sequence for sweater** Work 2 rows **C**, 2 rows **A**, 2 rows **D**, 2 rows **E**, 2 rows **F**, 2 rows **B**; rep these 12 rows 6 (7-8) times more, then 2 rows **C**, 2 rows **A**, 2 rows **D**, 2 rows **E**. Now work 2 rows **F** at the shoulder line then cont for back working

colours in reverse thus: 2 rows **E**, 2 rows **D**, 2 rows **A**, 2 rows **C**, then [2 rows **B**, 2 rows **F**, 2 rows **E**, 2 rows **D**, 2 rows **A**, 2 rows **C**] 7 (8-9) times.

▦ **To Make** Beg at lower edge of front cast on 42 (46-50) sts using 4mm needles and **C**. Count 1st row as right side and work in stripe sequence as given above. Cont until 52 (60-68) rows have been worked.

▦ **Sleeve Shaping** Cast on 7 (8-9) sts at beg of next 8 rows. Cont on 98 (110-122) sts and work 24 (28-32) rows; 84 (96-108) rows have been worked in all.

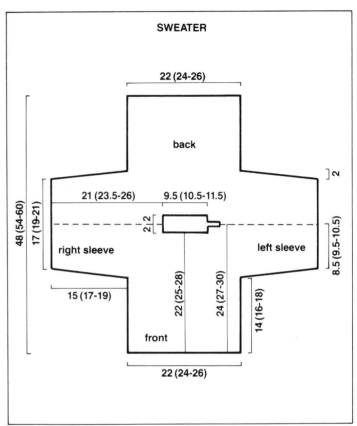

▦ **Neck Shaping** *Next row* Using **C**, k 40 (45-50) and leave these sts of left front on a spare needle, cast off next 18 (20-22) sts, k to end. Cont on 40 (45-50) sts now rem on needle for right front and work 7 more rows thus completing stripe in **E**. Work 2 rows in **F** which form shoulder line then cont for right back and work next 8 rows thus ending at neck edge. Cut yarn and leave sts on a spare needle. With wrong side facing rejoin **C** to neck edge of left front sts and work 7 rows. Change to **F** for the shoulder line rows.

▦ *Next row* K 30 (35-40), cast off rem 10 sts at neck edge and fasten off. Onto free needle using **F** cast on 10 sts, take this needle in right hand and k across the 30 (35-40) sts. Now cont for left back and work 8 rows thus completing a stripe in **C**.

▦ *Next row* With **B**, k the 40 (45-50) sts of left back, turn, cast on 18 (20-22) sts, turn then onto same needle k the 40 (45-50) sts of right back. Cont on these 98 (110-122) sts and work 23 (27-

31) rows.

▦ **Sleeve Shaping** Cast off 7 (8-9) sts at beg of next 8 rows. Cont on rem 42 (46-50) sts and work 52 (60-68) rows thus completing all stripes. Cast off.

▦ **Finishing** Join side and sleeve seams, matching stripes. Make 2 buttonhole loops on front edge of left shoulder opening and sew buttons to left back shoulder to correspond.

SNUGGLER

▦ Take a ball each of shades **A**, **B**, **C** and **D** and form double-thickness balls of each colour as explained for sweater; shades **E** and **F** are used single.

▦ With 6mm needles and **A** cast on 106 sts and working in g st work 2 rows **A**, 2 rows **E**, 2 rows **C**, 2 rows **B**, 2 rows **D**, 2 rows **F**. Cont to rep these 12 rows until 226 have been worked. Cast off.

so easy a child could knit them

2
CLOTHES CONSCIOUS KIDS

CALORIFIC COMFORT

Not the most suave and sophisticated of outfits, this cold weather combat suit is highly original and shows a strong sense of fun, as well as being comparatively easy to knit. It is also extremely practical: wide bands knitted in double-stranded yarn are alternated with narrow bands of single thickness, a design which guarantees thermal protection and comfort yet will keep its shape when washed.

CHECKLIST

Materials

Filatures de Paris Villageois *in 100g skeins:* 7 (8) *skeins in ecru. Pair each of needles size 3mm, 3¾mm and 6mm; strip of elastic 2cm (¾in) wide for waist of trousers.*

Sizes

Two sizes, to fit ages 9 to 12 (15 to 18) months. Actual measurements shown on diagram.

Stitches used

Single rib; g st; st st; k loop = *pick up loop lying between needles and k it tbl; patt, worked as foll:*

   1st to 12th rows *Work 12 rows in g st using yarn* double stranded *and 6mm needles.*

   13th to 16th rows *Beg with a k row work 4 rows st st using yarn single-stranded and 3mm needles. These 16 rows form one patt.*

Tension

Over patt 14 sts and 28 rows to 10cm (4in). Work a sample on 20 sts working 2 complete patts; when measuring the width tension, this must be done at centre of the g st band.

INSTRUCTIONS

SWEATER

▦ **Back** With 3¾mm needles and single yarn cast on 45 (49) sts and work in rib.
▦ *1st row* (right side) P 1, * k 1, p 1; rep from * to end.
▦ *2nd row* K 1, * p 1, k 1; rep from * to end. Rep these 2 rows until work measures 4cm (1½in) ending with a 1st row.
▦ *Dec row* Rib 5 (13), [p 2 tog, rib 6 (10)] 5 (3) times. 40 (46) sts. Now work in patt as given above and cont until 44 (52) rows have been worked in patt thus ending with 12th (4th) patt row.
▦ **Raglan Shaping** *1st size only* Work the 4 st st rows without shaping then dec 1 st at both ends of next 6 alt rows; rep last 16 rows once. Cast off rem 16 sts for back neck.
▦ **2nd size only** Dec 1 st at both ends of next 4 alt rows thus completing the g st section. Work the 4 st st rows without shaping then dec 1 st at both ends of next 6 alt rows; work the 4 st st rows without shaping then dec 1 st at both ends of next 4 alt rows. Cast off rem 18 sts for back neck.

▦ **Front** Work as for back until 24 (28) rows of raglan shaping.

have been worked. 24 (26) sts.
▦ **Neck Shaping** Rem rows are worked in g st with double-stranded yarn.
▦ *Next row* K 9 and leave these sts of left front on a spare needle, cast off 6 (8), k to end. Cont on 9 sts now rem on needle for right front. ** Dec 1 st at neck edge on alt rows 3 times but *at same time* dec 1 st at raglan edge on next row and next 3 alt rows. Cast off rem 2 sts.
▦ Rejoin yarn to neck edge of left front sts and complete as for right front from ** to end, reversing shapings.

▦ **Sleeves** With 3¾mm needles and single yarn cast on 33 (37) sts and work in rib as on welt for 3 (4)cm, 1⅛(1½)in, ending with a 1st rib row then work 1 more row working 1 dec at centre. 32 (36) sts.
▦ Now work in patt but inc 1 st at both ends of every foll 8th (10th) row 6 times then cont on 44 (48) sts until 60 (68) rows have been worked in patt thus ending with 12th (4th) patt row.
▦ **Raglan Shaping** Work as for correct size of back raglan but *at same time*, after 20 (24) rows of raglan have been worked, dec 1 st at centre of row on next row and next 5 alt rows, in addition to raglan shapings. When last raglan dec row has been worked cast off rem 14 sts.

▦ **Finishing and Neck Border** Join front raglan seams and right back seam making neat backstitch seams and taking care to match patts. With right side of work facing and using 3¾mm needles and single yarn, pick up and k 11 sts across top of left sleeve, 21 (23) sts around front neck edge, 11 sts across top of right sleeve and 16 (18) sts across back neck. 59 (63) sts. Beg with 2nd row work in rib for 7 rows then cast off loosely in rib. Join left back raglan seam and ends of neck border. Join side and sleeve seams.

TROUSERS

▦ **Back** This begins at waist

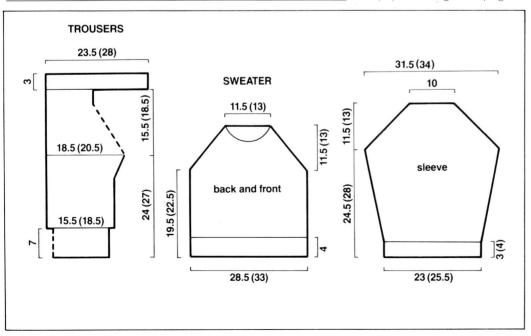

TROUSERS

23.5 (28)

3

15.5 (18.5)

18.5 (20.5)

15.5 (18.5)

24 (27)

7

SWEATER

11.5 (13)

19.5 (22.5)

back and front

28.5 (33)

31.5 (34)

10

11.5 (13)

11.5 (13)

24.5 (28)

sleeve

4

3 (4)

23 (25.5)

edge and is worked in one piece as far as crotch. With 3¾mm needles and single yarn cast on 43 (47) sts and work in rib as on sweater for 3cm (1⅛in) ending with a 1st rib row.

▦ *Dec row* Rib 3 (5), [p 2 tog, rib 2 (3)] 10 (8) times, rib 0 (2). 33 (39) sts. Now work in patt and cont until 12th row has been worked then begin centre shaping.

▦ *13th row* K 16 (19), k loop, k 1, k loop, k 16 (19). Cont to inc at each side of centre st on every foll 4th row 5 (9) times, then on every alt row 4 (0) times. Work 3 rows on these 53 (59) sts thus ending with 12th (4th) patt row. Divide legs as foll:

▦ *Next row* K 26 (29) and leave these sts on a spare needle, cast off 1, k to end. Cont on 26 (29) sts now rem on needle for one leg. Dec 1 st at inner leg next to opening on every foll 4th row 4 times then cont on rem 22 (25) sts until 92 (108) rows have been worked in patt from beg thus ending with a 12th patt row for both sizes. Cut yarn and leave sts on a piece of contrast yarn. With wrong side facing rejoin yarn to sts of other leg and complete in same way reversing shapings.

▯ **Front** Work as for back.

▦ **Finishing and Ankle Borders** Join side seams to within 2 rows of lower edges making neat backstitch seams and matching patt. With right side of work facing and using 3¾mm needles and single yarn work across the 2 groups of sts for right leg as foll: on back of leg k 7 (6), [k 2 tog, k 5 (4)] 2 (3) times, then k rem st tog with 1st st of front of leg, then [k 5(4), k 2 tog] 2 (3) times, k 7 (6). Cont on these 39 (43) sts and beg with 2nd rib row work in rib for 7cm (2½in) then cast off loosely in rib. Work left ankle border in same way, beg at front. Join remainder of side seams at centre of ankle border. Join inner leg seams. Cut elastic to fit baby's waist overlap ends forming a ring and sew securely. Attach elastic to inside of waistband with herringbone stitch.

THE YOUNGEST CABIN BOY

Walking already, even if he does sometimes look as though he is having trouble finding his legs on dry land, this young sailor is well equipped with a warm, double-breasted jacket, appropriately enough in an easy-to-work version of the popular favourite, fisherman rib. The jacket has a smart collar and revers, and the trousers have shoulder straps for a comfortable fit and are worked on smaller needles to give extra firmness.

CHECKLIST

Materials
Schaffhousen Salvatore: *6 (7-8) balls marine (dark blue) No 580 for jacket and 6 (7-8) balls rouge (red) No 71 for trousers. Pair each needles size 3¼mm, 3¾mm and 4mm; 4 buttons for jacket and 2 for trousers.*

Sizes
Three sizes to fit ages 12 months (18 months–2 years). Actual measurements shown on diagram.

Stitches used
Single rib; single-sided fisherman rib, *worked on an odd number of sts as foll:*

    1st row *(right side) K 1, * k next st but in row below, inserting needle through work and allowing st above to drop off needle, p 1; rep from * to last 2 sts, k 1 below as before, k 1.*

    2nd row *K 1, * p 1, k 1; rep from * to end. These 2 rows form patt. When casting off over this patt it should be done loosely in normal single rib as sts appear.*

Tension
Over patt using 4mm needles, 21 sts and 44 rows to 10cm (4in); work a sample on 25 sts. Over patt using 3¾mm needles, 22 sts and 48 rows to 10cm (4in); work a sample on 27 sts. When counting rows, each k rib showing on right side counts as 2 rows.

INSTRUCTIONS

JACKET

▦ **Back** With 3¾mm needles, cast on 63 (67-71) sts and work in single rib.

▦ *1st row* (right side) P 1, * k 1, p 1; rep from * to end.

▦ *2nd row* K 1, * p 1, k 1; rep from * to end. Rep these 2 rows once. Change to 4mm needles and work in patt as given above. Cont until work measures 16(18-20)cm, 6¼(7⅛-7⅞)in, from beg, ending with a wrong-side row.

▦ **Armhole Shaping** Cast off 3 sts at beg of next 2 rows, 2 sts at beg of next 2 rows and 1 st at beg of next 2 rows.

▦ Cont on rem 51 (55-59) sts until work measures 28(31-34)cm, 11(12¼-13⅜)in, from beg, ending with a wrong-side row.

▦ **Shoulder Shaping** Cast off 5 (5-6) sts at beg of next 4 rows and 6 (7-6) sts at beg of next 2 rows. Cast off rem 19 (21-23) sts for back neck.

▦ **Right Front** With 3¾mm needles cast on 41 (43-45) sts and work 4 rows in single rib as on back then change to 4mm needles and work in patt. Cont until work matches back to armhole but ending with a right-side row.

Armhole and Front Shaping
Cast off 3 sts at beg of next row, 2 sts at same edge on next alt row and 1 st on next alt row; work 4 rows on rem 35 (37-39) sts thus ending at front edge. Dec 1 st at beg of next row and next 18 (19-20) alt rows then cont on rem 16 (17-18) sts until work matches back to beg of shoulder, ending at side edge.

Shoulder Shaping Cast off 5 (5-6) sts at beg of next row and next alt row, work 1 row then cast off rem 6 (7-6) sts.

Left Front Work as for right front until work measures 5(6-7)cm, 2(2⅜-2¾)in, from beg, ending with a right-side row, then make buttonholes.
Next row Rib 4 sts, cast off 2, rib until there are 8 sts on right needle after previous buttonhole, cast off 2, rib to end. On foll row cast on 2 sts over each buttonhole. Cont until work measures 13(15-17)cm, 5⅛(5⅞-6¾)in, from beg, ending with a right-side row, then make 2 more buttonholes in same positions as before. Complete as for right front reversing all shapings.

Sleeves With 3¾mm needles cast on 31 (35-39) sts and work 4 rows in rib as on back then change to 4mm needles and work in patt. Inc 1 st at both ends of every foll 8th row 1 (5-9) times, then every foll 6th row 9 (5-1) times. Work extra sts into patt but do not k below on border st at sides. Cont on 51 (55-59) sts until work measures 18(20-22)cm, 7⅛(7⅞-8⅝)in, from beg.

Top Shaping Cast off 3 sts at beg of next 2 rows, 2 sts at beg of next 2 rows, 1 st at beg of next 10 (8-6) rows, 2 sts at beg of next 6 (8-10) rows and 4 sts at beg of next 2 rows. Cast off rem 11 (13-15) sts.

Revers For right front revers cast on 3 sts using 3¾mm needles and work in single rib shaping inner edge.
1st row P 1, k 1, p 1.
2nd row K 1, p 1, inc in last st. Cont to inc at this edge on every alt row 12 (13-14) times more. Cast off these 16 (17-18) sts loosely in rib. Work left front revers in same way but reversing shapings.

Collar With 3¾mm needles cast on 49 (53-57) sts and work in single rib as given at lower edge of back for 14 (16-18) rows then cast off loosely in rib.

Finishing Join shoulder seams matching patt ribs. Sew in sleeves then join side and sleeve seams. With right side of revers to wrong side of fronts, join shaped edges of revers to front shapings, making a flat join. With right side of collar to wrong side of jacket sew cast-on edge to back neck edges and front edges above the end of revers. Sew on buttons to correspond with buttonholes. Turn back collar and revers onto right side.

TROUSERS

Front With 3¼mm needles cast on 27 (29-31) sts for one leg. Work 2 rows in single rib as given for jacket then change to 3¾mm needles and work in patt; inc 1 st at both ends of every foll 20th row 4 times then cont on 35 (37-39) sts until work measures 22(24-27)cm, 8⅝(9½-10⅝)in, from beg, ending with a 2nd patt row. ✲✲
Cut yarn and leave sts on a spare needle. Work second leg in same way to ✲✲.
Next row Patt 34 (36-38), p rem st tog with 1st st of first leg, patt 34 (36-38) sts of first leg. Cont in patt on these 69 (73-77) sts until work measures 38(42-47)cm, 15(16½-18½)in from beg, ending with a 2nd patt row. Change to 3¼mm needles and work in single rib; work 2 rows then make buttonholes.
3rd row Rib 20 (22-22), cast off 2, rib until there are 25 (25-29) sts on right needle after previous buttonhole, cast off 2, rib to end. On foll row cast on 2 sts over each buttonhole. Rib 2 more rows then cast off loosely in rib.

Back Work as for front omitting buttonholes in waistband; after working the 6 rows in rib make shoulder straps:
Next row Cast off 18 (20-20) sts in rib, rib until there are 7 sts on right needle, leave these on a safety pin for right shoulder strap, cast off next 19 (19-23) sts in rib, rib until there are 7 sts on right needle, leave these on needle for left shoulder strap, cast off rem 18 (20-20) sts in rib and fasten off. Rejoin yarn with wrong side facing to sts of left shoulder strap.
Next row [K 1, p 1] 3 times, k 1.
Next row K 2, [p 1, k 1] twice, k 1. Rep these 2 rows until strap measures 31(35-39)cm, 12¼(13¾-15⅜)in, from beg. Cast off in rib. Work right shoulder strap in same way.

Finishing Join side and inner leg seams. Sew buttons to shoulder straps to match buttonholes.

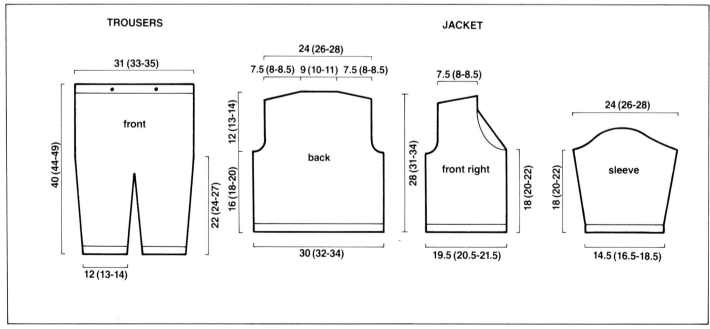

STYLISH AND PRACTICAL

Playing it cool and remaining seated when his girl friend comes to visit him – perhaps this young man's fashion sense is in advance of his manners? This smart yet practical outfit has great style and could prove particularly useful for a chubby youngster who tends to find cloth trousers just too tight across his middle. The cardigan is knitted in stocking stitch and the amusing patches in bright colours are added afterwards. The trousers are knitted in double stranded yarn to give extra strength and firmness.

CHECKLIST

Materials
Berger du Nord Alpaga: 3 (4-4) balls in grey for cardigan and 4 (5-6) balls for trousers. For the contrast patches on the cardigan, Layette: *1 ball or part-ball in yellow, red and jade green. Pair each of needles size 2¾mm, 3mm, 3¾mm and 4mm; a cable needle; 5 buttons in different colours for the cardigan; 2 buttons for the trousers.*

Sizes
Three sizes to fit ages 12 months (18 months–2 years). Actual measurements shown on diagram.

Stitches used
Single rib; st st; double rib; rib and cable patt, *worked on trousers, is explained in the instructions. Cable 4 front = slip next 2 sts on cable needle, leave at front, k 2, then k 2 from cable needle.*

Tension
Over st st using 3mm needles and yarn single, *28 sts and 36 rows to 10cm (4in); work a sample on 34 sts. Over rib and cable patt using 4mm needles and yarn* double, *24 sts and 27 rows to 10cm (4in); work a sample on 32 sts arranging patt on 1st row thus, [p 2, k 2] 4 times, p 2, k 4 for a cable, [p 2, k 2] 4 times, p 2. Flatten sample out when measuring.*

INSTRUCTIONS

CARDIGAN

▦ **Back** With 2¾mm needles cast on 81 (87-93) sts and work in rib.
▦ *1st row* (right side) P 1, * k 1, p 1; rep from * to end.
▦ *2nd row* K 1, * p 1, k 1; rep from * to end. Rep these 2 rows until work measures 3.5cm (1⅜in) from beg, ending with a 2nd rib row. Change to 3mm needles and beg with a k row work in st st. Cont until work measures 15(17-19)cm, 5⅞(6¾-7½)in, from beg, ending with a p row.
▦ **Armhole Shaping** Cast off 3 sts at beg of next 2 rows, 2 sts at beg of next 2 rows and 1 st at beg

of next 10 rows. Cont on rem 61 (67-73) sts until work measures 26(29-32)cm, 10¼(11⅜-12⅝)in, from beg, ending with a p row.
▦ **Shoulder and Neck Shaping** Cast off 6 (6-7) sts at beg of next 2 rows.
▦ *3rd row* Cast off 6 (6-7), k until there are 11 (13-13) sts on right needle, leave these for right back, cast off next 15 (17-19) sts, k to end.
▦ Cont on 17 (19-20) sts now rem at end of needle for left back. Cast off 6 (6-7) sts at beg of next row and 5 sts at neck edge on foll row. Cast off rem 6 (8-8) sts to complete shoulder slope. Rejoin yarn to neck edge of right back sts, cast off 5, p to end. Cast off rem 6 (8-8) sts.

▦ **Left Front** With 2¾mm needles cast on 39 (43-45) sts and work in rib as on back welt for same number of rows but for 1st and 3rd sizes inc 1 st in centre of last row. 40 (43-46) sts. Change to 3mm needles and work in st st; cont until work measures 15(17-19)cm, 5⅞(6¾-7½)in, from beg, ending with a p row.
▦ **Armhole and Front Shaping**
1st row Cast off 3 to begin armhole, k to last 2 sts, k 2 tog to begin front shaping. Cast off at armhole edge on alt rows 2 sts once and 1 st 5 times; *at same time,* dec 1 st at front edge on every row 11 (12-13) times more. When all shapings are completed cont on rem 18 (20-22) sts until work matches back to beg of shoulder, ending at armhole edge.
▦ **Shoulder Shaping** Cast off 6 (6-7) sts at beg of next row and next alt row, work 1 row then cast off rem 6 (8-8) sts.

▦ **Right Front** Work as for left front reversing all shapings.

▦ **Sleeves** With 2¾mm needles cast on 43 (45-49) sts and work in rib as on back welt for 3cm (1⅛in) ending with a 2nd rib row. Change to 3mm needles and work in st st but inc 1 st at both ends of every foll 6th row 8 (8-9) times, then every foll 4th row 0 (2-2) times. Cont on 59 (65-71) sts until work measures 18(20-22)cm, 7⅛(7⅞-8⅝)in, from beg.
▦ **Top Shaping** Cast off 3 sts at beg of next 2 rows, 2 sts at beg of next 2 rows, 1 st at beg of next 18 (16-14) rows, 2 sts at beg of next 4 (6-8) rows and 3 (4-5) sts at beg of next 2 rows. Cast off rem 17 (19-21) sts.

▦ **Front border** With 3mm needles cast on 6 sts.
▦ *1st row* (right side) K.
▦ *2nd row* K 1, p 4, k 1.
▦ *3rd row* K 1, cable 4 front, k 1.
▦ *4th row* As 2nd. These 4 rows form one patt. Cont in patt for 3 (3-1) rows then begin making buttonholes.
▦ *Next row* (wrong side) K 1, p 2, tog, yrn, p 2, k 1. ** Work 9 (11-13) rows in patt then make

another buttonhole on next row; rep from ** 3 times more. Cont in patt until border when slightly stretched fits along both front edges and across back neck. Leave sts on a safety pin without cutting yarn so that length can be adjusted.

▦ **Patches** Before sewing garment work the patches using the Swiss darning method described on page 8. Work the triangles, squares and circles in the positions indicated on diagrams using the colours shown.

▦ **Finishing** Join shoulder seams, sew in sleeves then join side and sleeve seams. Pin front border in place with buttonholes to left front for a boy or right front for a girl, stretching border slightly around neck edges so that it sits well. Replace sts on needle, adjust length if necessary so that it reaches to lower edge of right or left front then cast off. Sew border in place as pinned. Sew on buttons to correspond with buttonholes.

TROUSERS

▦ These are worked entirely in double-stranded yarn; take one ball and wind it into 2 equal balls then rewind these tog to form a double stranded ball which is easier to use.

▦ **Front** Beg at waist edge cast on 83 (87-91) sts using 3¾mm needles. Work in rib as given for cardigan and then after working 4 rows make buttonholes as foll:
▦ *5th row* Rib 21 (22-23), cast off 2, rib until there are 37 (39-41) sts on right needle after previous buttonhole, cast off 2, rib to end.
▦ *6th row* Rib 21 (22-23), turn, cast on 2, turn, rib 37 (39-41), turn, cast on 2, turn, rib 21 (22-23). Work 4 more rows in rib and inc 1 st in centre of last row. 84 (88-92) sts. Change to 4mm needles and work in rib and cable patt.
▦ *1st row* (right side) P 2 (0-2), [k 2, p 2] 4 (5-5) times, * k 4 for a cable, [p 2, k 2] 4 times, p 2; * rep

from * to * once, k 4 for a cable, [p 2, k 2] 4 (5-5) times, p 2 (0-2).

▦ *2nd row* K 2 (0-2), [p 2, k 2] 4 (5-5) times, * p 4, [k 2, p 2] 4 times, k 2; * rep from * to * once, p 4, [k 2, p 2] 4 (5-5) times, k 2 (0-2).

▦ *3rd row* Rib 18 (20-22) as on 1st row, * cable 4 front, rib 18; * rep from * to * once, cable 4 front, rib 18 (20-22).

▦ *4th row* As 2nd. These 4 rows form one patt. Cont in patt until work measures 19(20-21)cm, 7½(7⅞-8¼)in, from beg, ending with a wrong-side row. Now divide for legs.

▦ *Next row* Patt 40 (42-44), k

next 2 sts, turn and cont on these 42 (44-46) sts for one leg leaving rem sts on a spare needle. ✱✱ Work only one cable and keep rem sts in rib; dec 1 st at both ends of every foll 8th row 0 (3-6) times, then every foll 6th row 5 (3-0) times, then every foll 4th row 1 (0-0) times. Cont on rem 30 (32-34) sts until work measures 34(38-42)cm, 13⅜(15-16½)in, from beg, ending with a wrong-side row and working 1 dec at centre of last row. 29 (31-33) sts.

▦ Change to 3¾mm needles and work in single rib; work 4 rows straight, dec 1 st at both ends of next row then work 5

more rows in rib.

▦ Cast off loosely ribwise. Rejoin yarn with right side facing to sts left unworked, k 2, patt to end. Complete as for first leg from ✱✱ to end.

▦ **Back** Work as for left leg omitting buttonholes.

▦ **Shoulder Straps** Make 2 alike. With 3¾mm needles cast on 8 sts.

▦ *1st row* (right side) K 3, p 2, k 3.

▦ *2nd row* K 1, p 2, k 2, p 2, k 1. Rep these 2 rows until strap measures 46(50-54)cm, 18(19¾-21¼)in, from beg. Cast off.

▦ **Instep Straps** Make 2 alike. With 3¾mm needles cast on 4 sts.

▦ *1st row* K 2, p 1, k 1. Rep this row until strap measures 12(14-16)cm, 4¾(5½-6¼)in, from beg. Cast off.

▦ **Finishing** Join side seams and inner leg seams. Sew shoulder straps to back waistband and sew a button to other end of each strap. Sew instep straps to each side of the legs so that they will pass easily underneath the foot when worn, like ski pants.

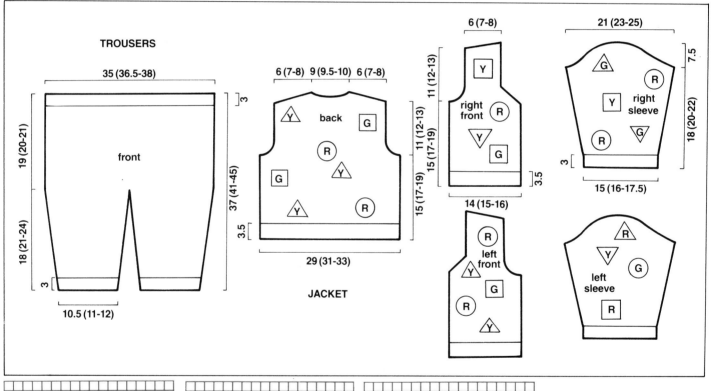

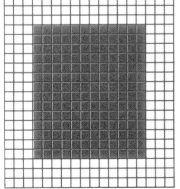 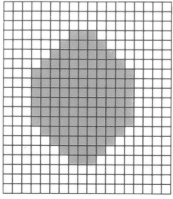 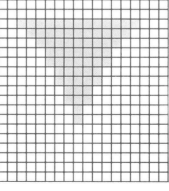

For the patches work shapes as shown on diagram placing them on back, fronts and sleeves as shown above; note that some of the triangles have the apex at the top and some at the bottom. Use the Swiss darning method on page 8. The exact placing of the motifs is not crucial, but you may find it easier to achieve a balanced arrangement if you first cut out paper circles, squares and triangles and pin them in place on the knitting.

APRIL TWOSOME

For days with just a hint of warmth, here is a pretty little outfit as fresh and welcome as fruit blossom. The button-up cardigan and skirt are knitted in a soft angora yarn and have a pattern of eyelet holes, with a line of zigzags across the yoke and below the skirt waistband. The cardigan has raglan armholes and the skirt finishes with a deep band of ribbing and an elasticated waist.

CHECKLIST

Materials
Berger du Nord Angora 70%: 8 (9-10) balls for the set. Pair each of needles size 2¾mm and 3mm; 6 buttons; narrow elastic for skirt.

Sizes
Three sizes, to fit ages 12 months (2-3 years). Actual measurements shown on diagram.

Stitches used
Single rib; eyelet patt, *worked on a multiple of 5 sts plus 1 as foll:*
    1st row *K.*
    2nd and alt rows *P.*
    3rd row *K 3, k 2 tog, yfd;* rep from * to * ending k 1.
    5th row *K.*
    7th row *K 1, * k 2 tog, yfd, k 3;* rep from * to *.
    8th row *P. These 8 rows form one patt.*
For the zig-zag lace patt *see instructions for each section.*

Tension
Over patt using 3mm needles, 26 sts and 38 rows to 10cm (4in). Work a sample on 31 sts.

INSTRUCTIONS

CARDIGAN

Back With smaller needles, cast on 71 (81-91) sts and work in rib.

1st row (right side) P 1, * k 1, 1; rep from * to end.

2nd row K 1, * p 1, k 1; rep from * to end. Rep these 2 rows 5 times more. Change to larger needles and work in eyelet patt as given above. Cont until work measures 19(21-23)cm, 7½(8¼-9)in, from beg, ending with a p row.

Raglan Shaping Cast off 2 sts at beg of next 2 rows, work 1 row then dec 1 st at both ends of foll row. Now begin zig-zag lace patt.

1st row K 5, * k 2 tog, yfd, k 1, yfd, SKPO, k 5; * rep from * to *.

2nd row P.

3rd row K 4, * k 2 tog, yfd, k 3, yfd, SKPO, k 3; * rep from * to * ending k 1.

4th row P 2 tog, p to last 2 sts, p 2 tog.

5th row K 2, * k 2 tog, yfd, k 5, yfd, SKPO, k 1; * rep from * to * ending k 1.

6th row P.

7th row K 1, k 2 tog, * yfd, k 7, yfd, SKTPO; * rep from * to * ending yfd, k 7, yfd, SKPO, k 1.

8th row As 4th. 61 (71-81) sts. This completes zig-zag patt. Cont in st st and dec 1 st at both ends of every foll 4th row 5 times, then at both ends of every alt row 4 times then at both ends of every row 10 (14-18) times. Cast off rem 23 (25-27) sts for back neck.

Right Front With smaller needles cast on 43 (49-53) sts and work in rib as on back welt for 6 rows then make buttonhole.

7th row Rib 3, cast off 3, rib to end. On foll row cast on 3 sts over buttonhole. Work 3 more rows in rib thus ending at side edge.

12th row For 1st size rib 17, inc in next st, rib 17 (for 2nd size rib 41 without inc; for 3rd size rib 22, inc in next st, rib 22), then for all sizes turn leaving 8 sts at front edge unworked and place these sts onto a safety pin for border to be worked later. Cont on rem 36 (41-46) sts; change to larger needles and work in eyelet patt until 1 more row has been worked than on back to beg of raglan shaping thus ending at side.

Raglan Shaping Cast off 2 sts at beg of next row, work 1 row then dec 1 st at beg of foll row. 33 (38-43) sts. Now work band of zig-zag lace patt.

1st row For 1st size: k 3, then rep from * to * in 1st row of this patt on back 3 times (for 2nd size k 1, yfd, SKPO, k 5, then rep from * to * in 1st row of this patt 3 times; for 3rd size k 3, then rep from * to * in 1st row of this patt 4 times).

2nd row P.

3rd row For 1st size k 2, then rep from * to * in 3rd row of this patt 3 times, k 1 (for 2nd size k 2, yfd, SKPO, k 3, then rep from * to * in 3rd row of this patt 3 times, k 1; for 3rd size k 2, then rep from * to * in 3rd row of this patt 4 times, k 1).

4th row P 2 tog, p to end.

5th row For 1st size k 1, then rep from * to * in 5th row of this patt 3 times, k 1 (for 2nd size k 3, yfd, SKPO, k 1, then rep from * to * in 5th row of this patt 3 times, k 1; for 3rd size k 1, then rep from * to * in 5th row of this patt 4 times, k 1).

6th row P.

7th row K 9 (4-9), yfd, SKTPO, rep from * to * in 7th row of this patt once (twice-twice), yfd, k 7, yfd, SKPO, k 1.

8th row As 4th. 31 (36-41) sts. Now work in st st and dec 1 st at raglan edge on every foll 4th row 5 times, then at same edge on every alt row 4 times, then dec 1 st at same edge on every row 0 (4-6) times; 22 (23-26) sts rem, ending at front edge.

Neck Shaping Cast off 4 (5-5) sts at beg of next row, 2 sts at same edge on next 2 alt rows and 1 st on next 2 (2-3) alt rows; *at same time,* cont to dec at raglan edge on next 10 (10-12) rows. Cast off rem 2 sts.

Left Front With smaller needles cast on 43 (49-53) sts and work in rib as on back for 11 rows.

12th row Rib 8 and slip these sts onto a safety pin for border, then for 1st size rib 17, inc in next st, rib 17 (for 2nd size rib 41 without inc; for 3rd size rib 22, inc in next st, rib 22). Change to larger needles and cont on these 36 (41-46) sts; work in eyelet patt until you have worked same number of rows as on back up to raglan thus ending at side edge.

Raglan Shaping Cast off 2 sts at beg of next row, work 2 rows straight then dec 1 st at same edge on foll row. Now work band of zig-zag lace patt.

1st row For 1st and 3rd sizes, k 5, then rep from * to * in 1st row of this patt ending last rep k 3 instead of k 5 (for 2nd size k 5, rep from * to * in 1st row of this patt 3 times, k 2 tog, yfd, k 1).

2nd row P.

3rd row For 1st and 3rd sizes, k 4, rep from * to * in 3rd row of this patt ending last rep k 2 instead of k 3 (for 2nd size k 4, rep from * to * in 3rd row of this patt 3 times, k 2 tog, yfd, k 2).

4th row P to last 2 sts, p 2 tog.

5th row For all sizes, k 2, rep from * to * in 5th row of this patt 3 (3-4) times (for 2nd size only, k 2 tog, yfd, k 3).

6th row P.

7th row K 1, k 2 tog, rep from * to * in 7th row of this patt 2 (3-3) times, yfd, k 9 (4-9).

8th row As 4th. 31 (36-41) sts. Cont in st st and complete as for right front reversing shapings.

Sleeves With smaller needles cast on 33 (37-39) sts and work in rib for 4cm (1½in) ending with a 1st rib row.

▦ *Inc row* Rib 2 (2-3), [inc in next st, rib 3 (3-2)] 7 (8-11) times, inc in next st, rib 2. 41 (46-51) sts. Change to larger needles and work in eyelet patt but inc 1 st at both ends of 4th row then every foll 6th row 9 (10-11) times working extra sts into patt. Cont on 61 (68-75) sts until work measures 21(23-25)cm, 8¼(9-9¾)in, from beg, ending with a p row.

▦ **Raglan Shaping** Cont in patt for remainder of sleeve; cast off 2 sts at beg of next 2 rows, dec 1 st at both ends of next alt row, then every foll 4th row 6 times, then dec at both ends of every alt row 6 (7-8) times after which dec 1 st at both ends of next 10 (12-14) rows.
Cast off rem 11 (12-13) sts.

▦ **Front Borders** Using smaller needles cast on 1 st, take needle with this st in right hand and beg at inner edge next to main part work in rib across sts of left front border. Cont in rib on these 9 sts until border when slightly stretched fits along front edge to neckline, ending with a 2nd rib row. Cut yarn and leave sts on a safety pin. Work right front border in same way but making 4 more buttonholes each 5.5(6-6.5)cm, 2⅛(2⅜-2½)in, above cast-off edge of previous one then cont until border is same length as left front border ending with a 2nd rib row. Leave sts on a safety pin but do not cut yarn.

▦ **Finishing and Neck Border** Join raglan seams, Sew on front borders stretching them slightly to fit. With right side facing and using smaller needles, rib sts of right front border, pick up and k 15 (16-18) sts around right front neck edge, 9 (10-11) sts across right sleeve top, 23 (25-27) sts across back neck, 9 (10-11) sts across left sleeve top and 15 (16-18) sts around left front neck edge then rib 9 sts of front border. 89 (95-103) sts. Beg with 2nd row cont in rib across all sts and after working 1 row make another buttonhole at right front edge on next 2 rows. Rib 3 more rows then cast off in rib. Join side

and sleeve seams. Sew on buttons to correspond with buttonholes.

SKIRT

⊞ **Back** With smaller needles cast on 125 (141-155) sts and work 2 rows in rib but inc 1 st at end of 2nd row on 1st and 3rd sizes. 126 (141-156) sts. Change to larger needles and work in eyelet patt; work 8 rows then shape to form curved edge as foll:

⊞ *1st row* K 111 (126-141), turn.

⊞ *2nd row* P 96 (111-126), turn. Keeping patt correct work 15 sts fewer before turning on each of next 6 rows. Turn after last row and k to end. Now work across all sts in patt until work measures 15(18-21)cm, 5⅞(7⅛-8¼)in, from beg, measured at centre, ending with a p row and working 1 dec at end of last row for 1st and 3rd sizes. 125 (141-155) sts. Now work band of zig-zag lace.

⊞ *1st row* K 5 (8-5), * k 2 tog, yfd, k 1, yfd, SKPO, k 5; * rep from * to * ending last rep k 5 (8-5).

⊞ *2nd and alt rows* P.

⊞ *3rd row* K 4 (7-4), * k 2 tog, yfd, k 3, yfd, SKPO, k 3; * rep from * to * ending last rep k 4 (7-4) instead of k 3.

⊞ *5th row* K 3 (6-3), * k 2 tog, yfd, k 5, yfd, SKPO, k 1; * rep from * to * 11 (12-14) times more, k 2 (5-2).

⊞ *7th row* K 2 (5-2), k 2 tog, * yfd, k 7, yfd, SKTPO; rep from * to * 10 (11-13) times more, yfd, k 7, yfd, SKPO, k 2 (5-2).

⊞ *8th row* For 1st size, p 4, [p 2 tog, p 3] 24 times, p 1 (for 2nd size p 5, [p 2 tog, p 2, p 2 tog, p 3] 15 times, p 1; for 3rd size p 6, [p 2 tog, p 2] 36 times, p 5).

⊞ *All sizes* Cont on rem 101 (111-119) sts; change to smaller needles and work in rib for 6cm (2½in) ending with a 1st rib row. K 1 row on wrong side to make a ridge for fold-line then beg with 1st rib row work a further 7 rows in rib for hem. Cast off loosely in rib.

⊞ **Front** Work exactly as for back.

⊞ **Finishing** Join side seams. Cut elastic to child's waist measurement, overlap ends to form a ring and sew securely. Fold hem section to inside along the foldline enclosing elastic and slip-st cast-off edge loosely in place.

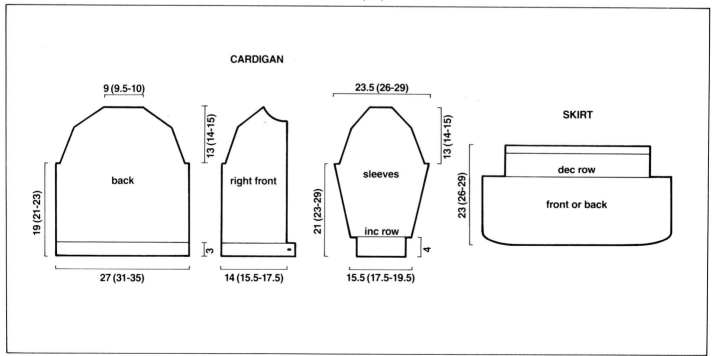

CARDIGAN

9 (9.5-10)

13 (14-15)

back

right front

19 (21-23)

3

27 (31-35)

14 (15.5-17.5)

23.5 (26-29)

13 (14-15)

sleeves

21 (23-29)

inc row

4

15.5 (17.5-19.5)

SKIRT

dec row

front or back

23 (26-29)

ANIMAL MAGIC

Children adore to dress up and have a natural love of animals, so they will instantly feel part of the animal kingdom when they wear these charming and imaginative sweaters, with their animal faces and matching hoods. The crafty fox and the gentle lamb, the mischievous mouse and the clever cat – for once they can all live together in harmony in a happy world of make-believe. All the designs are easy and quick to knit, using only simple stitches.

CHECKLIST

Materials

Fox *La Droguerie* Mohair: 180(190-200)g of rust (**A**), and 25(30-35)g of white (**B**). *Small amount of 4-ply yarn in black for nose. Pair each of needles size 3¾mm and 5mm; 2 buttons to fasten; 4 buttons for eyes.*

Lamb *La Droguerie* Igloo: 290(310-330)g of white (**A**), and 20g of peach (**B**). *Pair each of needles size 6mm and 8mm; 2 buttons to fasten; 4 buttons for eyes; yarn for embroidery.*

Mouse *La Droguerie* Mohair: 150(160-170)g of pink (**A**). *La Droguerie* Angora: 45(50-55)g of grey (**B**). *Pair each of needles size 3¾mm and 5mm; 2 buttons to fasten; 4 buttons for eyes; russia braid for whiskers; scrap of dress stiffening for teeth; yarn for embroidery.*

Cat *La Droguerie* Mohair: 90(100-110)g of grey (**A**), and 100(110-120)g of white (**B**). *Pair each of needles size 3¾mm and 5mm; 2 buttons to fasten; 4 buttons for eyes; russia braid for whiskers; pink yarn for embroidering nose.*

Sizes

Sweaters each have the same shape and are in three sizes, to fit ages 2 (4-6) years. Actual measurements shown on diagram.
Hoods are in one size, to fit a child of about 4 to 6 years. The hoods vary slightly in shape and are shown on separate diagrams.

Stitches used

Single rib; g st; st st.

Tensions

Over g st using 5mm needles and Mohair, 15 sts and 28 rows to 10cm (4in). Work a sample on 13 sts.
Over st st using 5mm needles and Mohair, 15 sts and 22 rows to 10cm (4in). Work a sample on 20 sts.
Over g st using 8mm needles and Igloo, 9 sts and 14 rows to 10cm (4in). Work a sample on 13 sts.

INSTRUCTIONS

FOX

▦ **Sweater Back** With smaller needles and **A** cast on 47 (49-53) sts and work in rib.
▦ ** *1st row* (right side) P 1, * k 1, p 1; rep from * to end.
▦ *2nd row* K 1, * p 1, k 1; rep from * to end. Rep these 2 rows until work measures 4cm (1½in) from beg, ending with a 2nd rib row (but for 2nd size inc 1 st in centre of last row). **.
▦ Change to larger needles and cont on 47 (50-53) sts working in g st. Cont until work measures 18(20-22)cm, 7⅛(7⅞-8⅝)in, from beg.

▦ **Armhole Shaping** Cast off 4 sts at beg of next 2 rows then cont on rem 39 (42-45) sts until work measures 33(36-39)cm, 13(14⅛-15⅜)in, from beg. Cast off all sts for shoulders and back neck.

▦ **Front** Work as for back until work measures 26(29-32)cm, 10¼(11⅜-12⅝)in, from beg, ending with a wrong-side row.
▦ **Neck Shaping** *1st row* K 17 (18-19) and leave these sts of left front on a spare needle, cast off next 5 (6-7) sts, k to end. Cont on 17 (18-19) sts now rem on needle for right front. *** Dec 1 st at neck edge on next 4 rows then at same edge on next 3 alt rows. Cont on rem 10 (11-12) sts until work matches back to shoulder edge. Cast off. Rejoin yarn to neck edge of left front sts and complete as for right front from *** to end reversing shapings.

▦ **Sleeves** With smaller needles and **A** cast on 31 (33-37) sts and work as for back welt from ** to **. 31 (34-37) sts. Change to larger needles and work in g st but inc 1 st at both ends of every foll 6th (6th-7th) row 8 times. Cont on 47 (50-53) sts until work measures 26(28-30)cm, 10¼(11-11¾)in, from beg. Cast off.

▦ **Finishing and Neck Border** On cast-off edge of back mark centre 19 (20-21) sts which will form neckline, leaving 10 (11-12) sts each side for shoulders. Join right shoulder seam. With right side of work facing and using smaller needles and **A**, pick up and k 41 (43-45) sts around front neck edge and 24 (24-26) sts across back neck. 65 (69-71) sts. Beg with 2nd row work 6 rows in rib as on welt then cast off in rib. Join right shoulder seam for the first 3 (4-5) sts from side edges. Along rem edge of front work 2 buttonhole loops, one near to neck edge and the other half-way along. Sew buttons to back shoulder to correspond. Sew cast-off edge of sleeves to sides of armholes and sew armhole casting-off to a corresponding depth on sides of sleeves. Join side and sleeve seams.

■ **Pocket** With larger needles and **A** cast on 3 sts for lower point; the nose is worked later. Work in st st but inc 1 st at both ends of 3rd row, work 4 rows straight, inc 1 st at both ends of next row and next 3 (4-5) alt rows. Cont on 13 (15-17) sts until work measures 10(11-11)cm, 4(4¼-4¼)in, from beg. Cast off.

■ For nose use the black 4-ply yarn double; cast on 3 sts using larger needles and work in st st. Inc 1 st at both ends of 2nd row then work 3 rows straight. Cast off. With p side of nose to k side of pocket slip-st nose to lower point.

■ With right side of work facing and using larger needles and **B**, pick up and k 15 (17-17) sts along one side edge of pocket. Rep 2nd rib row then keeping rib correct

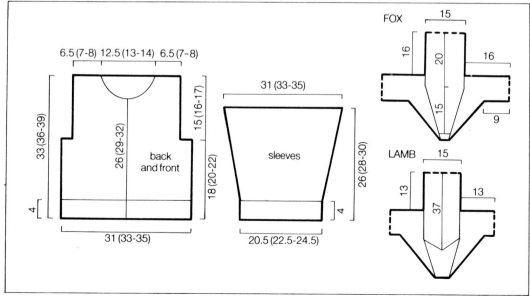

back and front diagram:
- 6.5 (7-8)   12.5 (13-14)   6.5 (7-8)
- 33 (36-39)
- 26 (29-32) — back and front
- 15 (16-17)
- 18 (20-22)
- 4
- 31 (33-35)

sleeves diagram:
- 31 (33-35)
- 26 (28-30)
- 4
- 20.5 (22.5-24.5)

FOX diagram:
- 15
- 16   20   16
- 15
- 9

LAMB diagram:
- 15
- 13   37   13

dec 1 st at lower edge of next 3 rows. Cast off in rib. Work similar border along other side edge.

▦ **Ears** For outer section cast on 3 sts using larger needles and **A**. Work in rib but inc 1 st at both ends of every alt row 4 times then work 4 rows straight. Cast off in rib.

▦ For inner section cast on 3 sts using larger needles and **B** work in rib, inc 1 st at both ends of every alt row 3 times then work 4 rows straight. Cast off in rib. Placing cast-off edges level sew outer and inner sections tog neatly. Sew ears to top of pocket and sew on eyes. Sew pocket to centre front just above welt.

▦ **Hood** For centre section cast on 3 sts using larger needles and **A**. Work in st st but inc 1 st at both ends of 2nd row, work 4 rows straight then inc 1 st at both ends of next row, then every foll 3rd row 8 times more. Cont on these 23 sts and work 20cm (7⅞in) without shaping, ending with a p row. Cut yarn and leave sts on a holder. Work nose as for pocket but after the inc row work 4 rows straight then cast off these 5 sts.

▦ Sew nose to lower point of hood in same way as for pocket. On left side edge of centre section mark off the first 19cm (7½in). With right side of work facing and using larger needles and **A**, pick up and k 39 sts on marked section. Rep 2nd rib row then keeping rib correct dec 1 st at lower edge on next 20 rows. Cont on rem 19 sts until work measures 16cm (6¼in) measured along straight side edge, ending with a wrong-side row. Cut yarn and leave sts on a holder.

▦ Work similar border along right side edge of centre section, reversing shapings; when work is same length as first side, ending with a wrong-side row, cont as foll. Work in rib across 19 sts of this side section, cont in rib across 23 sts of centre section then rib sts of first side section. 61 sts. Change to **A** and cont in rib across all sts for 9cm (3½in). Cast off in rib.

▦ **Ears** For outer section cast on

3 sts using larger needles and **A**. Work in rib but inc 1 st at both ends of every alt row 6 times. Work 2 rows on these 15 sts then cast off in rib.

▦ For inner section cast on 3 sts using larger needles and **B**. Work in rib but inc 1 st at both ends of every alt row 5 times. Work 1 row on these 13 sts then cast off in rib. Placing cast-off edges level sew inner section to outer section with neat sts.

▦ **Finishing** Join back seams of hood and make a neat backstitch seam at centre front. Sew ears to top of hood. Sew on buttons for eyes.

LAMB

▦ **Sweater Back** With smaller needles and **A** cast on 29 (31-33) sts and work in rib as for fox; cont until work measures 4cm (1½in) from beg, ending with a 2nd rib row. Change to larger needles and work in g st. Cont until work measures 18(20-22)cm, 7⅛(7⅞-8⅝)in, from beg.

▦ **Armhole Shaping** Cast off 3 sts at beg of next 2 rows then cont on rem 23 (25-27) sts until work measures 33(36-39)cm, 13(14⅛-15⅜)in, from beg. Cast off all sts for shoulder and back neck edges.

▦ **Front** Work as for back until you have worked 9 rows fewer than on back.

▦ **Neck Shaping** *1st row* K 10 (11-11) and leave these sts on a spare needle, cast off next 3 (3-5) sts, k to end. Cont on 10 (11-11) sts now rem on needle. Dec 1 st at neck edge on next 3 rows then at same edge on next alt row. Work 3 rows on rem 6 (7-7) sts then cast off these sts for shoulder edge. Rejoin yarn to neck edge of first group of sts and complete in same way, reversing neck shapings.

▦ **Sleeves** With smaller needles and **A** cast on 17 (19-21) sts and work in rib for 4cm (1½in) but inc 1 st in centre of last row. 18 (20-22) sts. Change to larger needles and work in g st but inc 1 st at both ends of every foll 4th (4th-5th) row 5 times. Cont on 28 (30-32) sts

until work measures 26(28-30)cm, 10¼(11-11¾)in, from beg. Cast off all sts.

▦ **Finishing and Neck Border** On cast-off edge of back mark centre 11 (11-13) sts for neckline leaving 6 (7-7) sts on each side for shoulders. Join right shoulder seam. With right side of work facing and using smaller needles and **A**, pick up and k 28 (28-30) sts around front neck edge and 15 (15-17) sts across back neck. 43 (43-47) sts. Beg with 2nd row work 4 rows in rib then cast off in rib. Work remainder of making up as for Fox.

▦ **Pocket** With smaller needles and **B** cast on 5 (5-7) sts and work in st st. Inc 1 st at both ends of 2nd row then cont on 7 (7-9) sts until work measures 6(6-7)cm, 2⅜(2⅜-2¾)in, from beg, ending with a p row. Now form point in **A** at centre.

▦ *1st row* K 3 (3-4) **B**, join on small ball of **A**, k 1 **A**, then 3 (3-4) **B**.

▦ *2nd row* P 2 (2-3) **B**, twist yarns, p 3 **A**, join on a small ball of **B**, p 2 (2-3) **B**. Always twisting yarns when changing colour work 2 extra sts in **A** at centre on next 2 (2-3) rows. Cast off all sts.

▦ **Ears** For outer section cast on 3 (3-5) sts using smaller needles and **A**. Work in rib but inc 1 st at

both ends of every alt row twice then work 4 rows on these 7 (7-9) sts. Cast off in rib. For inner section cast on 3 (3-5) sts using smaller needles and **B**. Work in rib but inc 1 st at both ends of every alt row twice. Work 2 rows on these 7 (7-9) sts then cast off in rib.

▦ Placing cast-off edges level sew inner and outer sections neatly tog. Sew ears to top of pocket and sew on eyes.

▦ Embroider the nose with a deeper peach colour. Sew the pocket to centre front just above welt.

▦ **Hood** Tension for this, working in st st on smaller needles is 11 sts and 14 rows to 10cm (4in).

▦ For centre section cast on 5 sts using smaller needles and **B**. Work in st st and inc 1 st at both ends of 3rd row, work 7 rows straight then inc 1 st at both ends of next row. 9 sts. Now begin forming point in **A** at centre.

▦ *12th row* P 4 **B**, join on a ball of **A**, p 1 **A**, then p 4 **B**.

▦ *13th row* K 3 **B**, twist yarns, k 3 **A**, join on a small ball of **B**, k 3 **B**.

▦ *14th row* P 2 **B**, twist yarns, p 5 **A**, 2 **B**. Inc 1 st at both ends of next row, then every foll 4th row 3 times more but *at same time* cont to work 2 extra sts in **A** at centre until all sts are in **A**. When incs are completed cont on these 17 sts and work 18cm (7⅛in) without shaping, ending with a p row. Cut yarn and leave sts on a holder.

▦ On each side edge mark a point 20cm (7⅞in) from beg. With right side of work facing and using smaller needles and **A**, pick up and k 29 sts along this marked section on left side. Rep 2nd rib row then keeping rib correct dec 1 st at lower edge on next 18 rows. Cont on rem 11 sts until work measures 13cm (5⅛in) along straight side edge, ending with a wrong-side row. Cut yarn and leave sts on a holder. Work similar border along right side edge of centre, reversing shapings, and when this section measures same length as first section ending with a wrong-side row cont as foll: work in rib across these 11 sts, cont in rib across 17 sts of centre section then cont in rib across 11 sts of first side section. 39 sts. Cont across all sts in rib for 10cm (4in). Cast off in rib.

▦ **Ears** For outer section cast on 5 sts using smaller needles and **A**; work in rib but inc 1 st at both ends of every alt row 3 times then cont on 11 sts until work measures 13cm (5⅛in) from beg. Cast off in rib.

▦ For inner section cast on 5 sts using smaller needles and **B**. Work in rib but inc 1 st at both ends of 3rd row then cont on these 7 sts until work measures 11cm (4¼in) from beg. Cast off in rib.

▦ **Finishing** Placing cast-off edges level sew inner and outer sections of ears neatly tog. Join back seams of hood and join ribbed section with a neat backstitch join at centre front. Sew ears to top of hood. Embroider nose with deeper peach shade. Sew on eyes.

MOUSE

▦ **Sweater** For back, front and sleeves work as for sweater of fox design but using col **A** (pink).

▦ **Finishing and Neck Border** As for Fox sweater.

▦ **Pocket** With larger needles and **B** cast on 4 (5-6) sts and work in st st but inc 1 st at both ends of

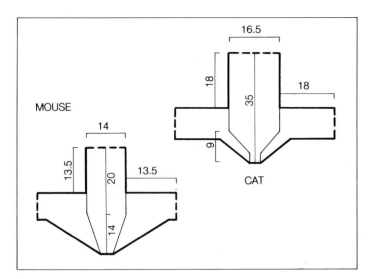

every alt row 6 times. Cont on 16 (17-18) sts until work measures 9(9-10)cm, 3½(3½-4)in, from beg. Cast off. With right side facing and using larger needles and **B**, pick up and k 15 (15-17) sts along one side edge of pocket. Rep 2nd rib row then keeping rib correct dec 1 st at lower edge on next 3 rows. Cast off in rib. Work similar border on other side.

▦ **Ears** With larger needles and **B** cast on 3 (3-5) sts for outer section and work in rib. Inc 1 st at both ends of every alt row 3 times then work 6 rows on these 9 (9-11) sts. cast off in rib. For inner section cast on 3 (3-5) sts using larger needles and **A**. Work in rib but inc 1 st at both ends of every alt row 3 times then work 3 rows on these 9 (9-11) sts. Cast off in rib.

▦ Placing cast-on and cast-off edges level sew inner and outer sections neatly tog. Sew ears to top of pocket. Sew pocket to centre front just above welt. Cut whiskers and pass through base of pocket. Cut out teeth from stiffened fabric and sew in place. Embroider nose in black yarn. Sew eyes in place.

▦ **Hood** With larger needles and **B** cast on 3 sts for centre section and work in st st; inc 1 st at both ends of every foll 3rd row 5 times then every foll 4th row 4 times. Cont on these 21 sts until work measures 34cm (13⅜in) from beg, ending with a p row. Cut yarn

and leave sts on a holder. On each side edge mark a point 20.5cm (8in) from beg. With right side of work facing and using larger needles and **B**, pick up and k 39 sts along this marked section on left side. Rep 2nd rib row then keeping rib correct dec 1 st at lower edge on next 20 rows. Cont on rem 19 sts until work measures 13.5cm (5¼in) from beg, ending with a wrong-side row. Cut yarn and leave sts on a holder.

▦ Work other side section along right edge of centre in same way, reversing shapings, and when this section measures same length ending with a wrong-side row cont as foll: work in rib across these 19 sts, cont in rib across 21 sts of centre section then cont in rib across 19 sts of left side section. 59 sts. Cont in rib across all sts for 9cm (3½in) then cast off in rib.

▦ **Ears** With larger needles and **B** cast on 5 sts for outer section and work in rib but inc 1 st at both ends of every alt row 5 times. Cont on these 15 sts and work 6 rows straight then cast off in rib. For inner section cast on 5 sts using larger needles and **A**. Work in rib but inc 1 st at both ends of every alt row 4 times. Cont on these 13 sts and work 5 rows straight. Cast off in rib. Placing cast-off edges level sew inner and outer sections tog neatly. Sew back seams of hood and make a neat backstitch seam at centre front. Sew ears to top of hood. Complete features as

for pocket of sweater.

CAT

▦ **Sweater** For back and front work as for sweater of Fox design using **A** for welts then change to larger needles and, working in st st, work in stripes of 4 rows **B**, 4 rows **A**; complete as for Fox design.

▦ **Sleeves** Work as for Fox sweater but after completing cuff change to larger needles and work in st st in stripes as for back and front; inc 1 st at both ends of every foll 6th row 2(3-4) times then every foll 4th row 6(5-4) times.

▦ Cont on these 47(50-53) sts until work measures 26(28-30)cm, 10¼(11-11¾)in, from beg, then cast off.

▦ **Pocket** With larger needles and **B** cast on 4 (5-6) sts and work in st st; work 2 rows straight then inc 1 st at both ends of next 10 rows. Cont on 24 (25-26) sts until work measures 8(8-9)cm, 3⅛(3⅛-3½)in, from beg. Cast off.

▦ With right side of work facing and using larger needles and **B**, pick up and k 19 (19-21) sts along right side edge of centre section. Rep 2nd rib row, then keeping rib correct shape both edges.

▦ *1st row* Cast off 3, rib to last 8 sts, turn.

▦ *2nd and alt rows* Rib to end.

▦ *3rd row* Cast off 2, rib to last 7 sts, turn.

▦ *5th row* Cast off 2, rib to last 6 sts, turn. Cont to cast off 2 sts at beg of every alt row and work 1 extra st before turning at end of same row 3 (3-4) times more. Work 1 row in rib on rem 6 sts then cast off in rib.

▦ Work similar border along other side reversing shapings.

▦ **Ears** With larger needles and **A** cast on 3 sts for outer section and work in rib but inc 1 st at both ends of every alt row 3 times then cont on 9 sts for 6 rows. Cast off in rib. For inner section cast on 3 sts using larger needles and **B**; work in rib but inc 1 st at both ends of every alt row twice then cont on 7 sts for 5 rows. Cast off in rib. Holding cast-off edges level sew

inner and outer sections tog neatly. Sew ears to top of pocket and sew pocket to centre front of sweater just above welt. Embroider nose in pink yarn. Cut whiskers and pass through base of pocket. Sew on eyes.

▦ **Hood** For centre section cast on 5 sts using larger needles and **B**. Beg with a k row work in st st for 9 rows then inc 1 st at both ends of next 5 rows. 15 sts. Now work in stripes of 4 rows **A**, 4 rows **B**; cont to inc 1 st at both ends of next 5 rows then cont on these 25 sts until work measures 35cm (13¾in) from beg, ending with a p row. Cut yarn and leave these sts on a holder.

▦ On each side edge of this section mark a point 6cm (2⅜in) from beg. With right side of work facing and using larger needles and **B**, pick up and k 13 sts along right side edge on marked section. Rep 2nd rib row then keeping rib correct shape both edges. Cast off 2 sts at beg of next row and next 5 alt rows – these shapings are at lower edge – *and at same time* inc 1 st at opposite edge on every alt row 5 times then cast on 15 sts at same edge on next alt row. 21 sts. Cont in rib without shaping for 18cm (7⅛in) ending with a wrong-side row. Cut yarn and leave sts on a holder. Work other side section in same way reversing shapings. With right side facing and using larger needles and **B**, rib sts of first side section, then cont in rib across sts of centre section then rib sts of second side section. Cont on these 67 sts and work in rib for 10cm (4in). Cast off in rib. Join side seams and make a neat back stitch seam at centre front.

▦ **Ears** For outer section cast on 3 sts using larger needles and **A**; work in rib but inc 1 st at both ends of every alt row 4 times then work 6 rows straight. Cast off in rib. For inner section cast on 3 sts using larger needles and **B**; work in rib but inc 1 st at both ends of every alt row 3 times. Work 5 rows straight then cast off in rib. Assemble ears as for pocket, sew to top of hood. Complete features as for pocket.

YOUNG SHRIMPERS

This lovely set of holiday sweaters is knitted in a soft cotton – ideal for those overcast days that are perfect for shrimping, and just right for evening wear in warmer climates. Back, front and sleeves are all divided in half at the start of the raglan armholes and are completed separately, which makes the colour changes much simpler and gives a well-shaped yoke. In an easy-to-knit mixture of rib and stocking stitch, the basic sweater covers an age range from three to fifteen (check the schema for actual sizes).

CHECKLIST

Materials
Coton *Sophie Desroches: 5 (6-7-8) balls in either blue, mustard, pale grey or beige = **A**, and 1 ball in each of four other colours. Using the picture as a guide, choose your own arrangement of colours and mark them as foll: **B** is used for the stripe on the right front yoke and for front of left sleeve; **C** is used for top of right front yoke and a stripe on each sleeve; **D** is used for stripe on left front yoke and for front half of right sleeve, and **E** is used for top of left front yoke and a stripe on each sleeve. Colours used for the original sweaters were: No 3214, sky blue; No 3070, mustard; No 3354, grey; No 3001, straw yellow; No 3212, clear blue; No 3020, salmon; No 3380, turquoise; No 3034, grey brown; No 3011, khaki; No 3242, dark green; No 3024, rust, and No 3341, mid green. Pair each of needles size 2¾mm and 3mm.*

Sizes
Four sizes, to fit ages 3 to 4 (6 to 7 – 9 to 11 – 13 to 15) years. Actual measurements shown on diagram.

Stitches used
Single rib; st st.

Tension
Over st st using larger needles, 29 sts and 40 rows to 10cm (4in). Work a sample on 35 sts.

INSTRUCTIONS

▦ **Front** With smaller needles and **A** cast on 91 (101-113-123) sts and work in rib.
▦ ** *1st row* (right side) P 1, * k 1, p 1; rep from * to end.
▦ *2nd row* K 1, * p 1, k 1; rep from * to end. Rep these 2 rows until work measures 5 (6-6-7)cm, 2(2⅜-2⅜-2¾)in, from beg, ending with 1st rib row. **
▦ *Inc row* Rib 9 (6-2-5), [inc in next st, rib 17 (10-8-6)] 4 (8-12-16) times, inc in next st, rib 9 (6-2-5). 96 (110-126-140) sts. Change to larger needles and work in st st; cont without shaping until work measures 22(27-31-35)cm, 8⅝(10⅝-12¼-13¾)in, from beg, ending with a p row.
▦ **Raglan Shaping** *1st row* Cast off 2 (3-5-6), k until there are 46 (52-58-64)sts on right needle, leave these on a holder, k rem 48 (55-63-70) sts. Cont on this group of sts and cast off 2 (3-5-6) sts at beg of foll row. Change to **B**.
▦ *3rd row* K without shaping.
▦ *4th row* K 1, p 2 tog, p to last 3 sts, p 2 tog tbl, k 1.
▦ *5th row* K without shaping.
▦ *6th row* K 1, p to last st k 1. Rep last 4 rows twice more. Change to **C**. Rep from 3rd to 6th rows inclusive 11 (13-15-17) times more. K 1 row then on foll row work dec at raglan edge only. 17 (19-21-23) sts. Change to smaller needles and work 6 (8-8-10) rows in rib as on welt.

▦ Cast off loosely in rib. With wrong side facing rejoin **A** to other group of 46 (52-58-64) sts, p to end.
▦ Change to **D** and cont as on first half of front for next 12 rows then change to **E** and complete as on first half.

▦ **Back** Work exactly as given for front; colours used for right front will thus be used on left back and vice versa.

[diagram: front and back]

15(17-19-21)

22 (27-31-35)

front and back

5 (6-6-7)

33 (38-43.5-48)

[diagram: sleeves]

31.5 (36-40-44)

15 (17-19-21)

sleeves

27 (32-37-42)

5 (6-6-7)

18 (20-22-24)

Sleeves With smaller needles and **A** cast on 47 (51-53-57) sts and work as for back welt from ✲✲ to ✲✲.

Inc row Rib 5 (4-1-4), [inc in next st, rib 8 (6-4-3)] 4 (6-10-12) times, inc in next st, rib 5 (4-1-4). 52 (58-64-70) sts.

Change to larger needles and work in st st but inc 1 st at both ends of every foll 6th row 1 (3-7-9) times then every foll 4th row 19 (20-19-20) times. Cont on 92 (104-116-128) sts until work measures 27(32-37-42)cm, 10⅝(12⅝-14½-16½)in, from beg, ending with a p row.

Raglan Shaping *1st row* Cast off 2 (3-5-6), k until there are 44 (49-53-58) sts on right needle, leave these on a holder, k rem 46 (52-58-64) sts. Cont on this group of sts and cast off 2 (3-5-6) sts at beg of foll row. Change to **C**. Rep from 3rd to 6th rows of raglan shaping on front 3 times. Change to **B** and cont as folls: Rep from 3rd to 6th rows 11 (12-11-13) times more. 16 (19-25-26) sts.

For 1st size work 1 row then on foll row dec at raglan edge only; *for 2nd size* work 5 rows straight then rep 4th row; *for 3rd size* work the decs at each end of every foll 6th row 3 times; *for 4th size* work the decs at each end of every foll 6th row twice, work 5 rows then dec at raglan edge only on foll row.

For all sizes change to smaller needles and cont on rem 15 (17-19-21) sts working in rib for 6 (8-8-10) rows then cast off loosely in rib.

With wrong side facing rejoin **A** to other group of 44 (49-53-58) sts, p to end. Complete as for first half of sleeve using **E** for next 12 rows and **D** for remainder.

Finishing Join seams along centre front and back and centre of each sleeve. Join raglan seams. Join side and sleeve seams.

GYM TONIC

From head to toe, these girls are ideally equipped to carry out all the movements and execute all the steps that their teacher asks of them. The set includes long and short sleeved sweaters, leg-warmers, shorts and a bandeau – all needed to keep the muscles warm and help to prevent chills and cramps when they stop exercising. Knitted in bright, zingy colours, all the items are simple and quick to make – in fact they are so easy that the girls could knit their own accessories – it might give them a taste for the craft!

CHECKLIST

Materials
La Droguerie Fluo: 450 (450-500)g for long-sleeved sweater; 300 (300-350)g for short-sleeved sweater; 150 (150-200)g for tank-top; 200g for leg-warmers, using either one colour or two or more colours; 150 g for shorts, and about 20g for bandeau. Pair each of needles sized 5mm and 6mm.

Sizes
Three sizes, to fit ages 10 (12-14) years. Actual measurements shown on diagrams.

Stitches used
Single rib; double rib; st st; g st.

Tension
For long and short-sleeved sweaters: over st st and using larger needles; 14 sts and 19 rows to 10cm (4in). Work a sample on 18 sts. For tank top: working in g st and using larger needles; 14 sts and 27 rows to 10cm (4in). Work a sample on 18 sts. For shorts and leg-warmers: working in double rib and using larger needles; 15sts and 19 rows to 10cm (4in), flattening work when measuring. Work a sample on 22 sts.

INSTRUCTIONS

LONG-SLEEVED SWEATER

▦ **Back** With larger needles, cast on 55 (58-61) sts and work in st st. Cont until work measures 53(56-59)cm, 20¾(22-23¼)in, from beg. Cast off loosely.

▦ **Front** Work exactly as for back.

▦ **Sleeves** With larger needles, cast on 33 (36-39) sts and work in st st but inc 1 st at both ends of every foll 10th row 2 (4-6) times then every foll 8th row 5 (3-1) times. Cont on 47 (50-53) sts until work measures 38(41-44)cm, 15(16⅛-17¼)in, from beg. Cast off all sts.

▦ **Finishing** Join shoulder seams for 9(10-11cm), 3½(4-4¼)in, from each side edge leaving centre section open for neckline. On each side edge place markers at a point 16.5(17.5-19)cm, 6½(7-7½)in, down from shoulder seams for armholes and then sew cast-off edge of sleeves between the markers. Join side and sleeve seams.

SHORT-SLEEVED SWEATER

▦ **Back** With larger needles, cast on 49(52-55) sts and work in st st. Cont until work measures 40(43-46)cm, 15¾(17-18)in, from beg, ending with a p row.
▦ **Neck Shaping** *1st row* K 18 (19-20) and leave these sts for

right back, cast off next 13 (14-15) sts, k to end. Cont on 18 (19-20) sts now rem on needle for left back and work 1 row. Cast off 3 sts at beg of next row and dec 1 st at neck edge on foll row. Cast off rem 14 (15-16) sts for shoulder edge. Rejoin yarn to neck edge of right back sts, cast off 3, p to end. Dec 1 st at neck edge on foll row, work 1 row on rem 14 (15-16) sts then cast off.

◻ **Front** Work as for back until work measures 37(40-43)cm, 14½(15¾-17)in, from beg, ending with a p row.

◻ **Neck Shaping** *1st row* K 19 (20-21) and leave these sts of left front on a spare needle, cast off next 11 (12-13) sts, k to end. Cont ·on 19 (20-21) sts now rem on needle for right front. ✷✷ Dec 1 st at neck edge on next 3 rows then dec 1 st at same edge on next 2 alt rows. Cont on rem 14 (15-16) sts until work matches back to shoulder edge. Cast off. Rejoin yarn to neck edge of left front sts and complete as for right front from ✷✷ to end, reversing shapings.

◻ **Sleeves** With larger needles,

cast on 53 (56-59) sts and work in st st for 15(16-17)cm, 5⅞(6¼-6¾)in. Cast off all sts.

◻ **Finishing** Join shoulder seams. On each side edge mark a point 19(20-21)cm, 7½(7⅞-8¼)in, down from shoulder seams for armholes and sew cast-off edge of sleeves between markers. Join side and sleeve seams.

TANK TOP

◻ **Back** With larger needles cast on 61 (64-67) sts and work in g st. Cont until work measures 14(15-

16)cm, 5½(5⅞-6¼)in, from beg, ending with a p row.

◻ **Armhole Shaping** Cast off 4 sts at beg of next 2 rows, 3 sts at beg of next 2 rows, 2 sts at beg of next 4 rows and 1 st at beg of next 4 (6-8) rows. 35 (36-37) sts.

◻ **Neck Shaping** *1st row* K 14 and leave these sts of right back on a spare needle, cast off next 7 (8-9) sts, k to end. Cont on 14 sts now rem on needle for left back and work 1 row. ✷✷ Cast off 2 sts at beg of next row and next 2 alt rows and 1 st at same edge on next 4 alt rows. Cont on rem 4 sts until work measures 27(29-31)cm,

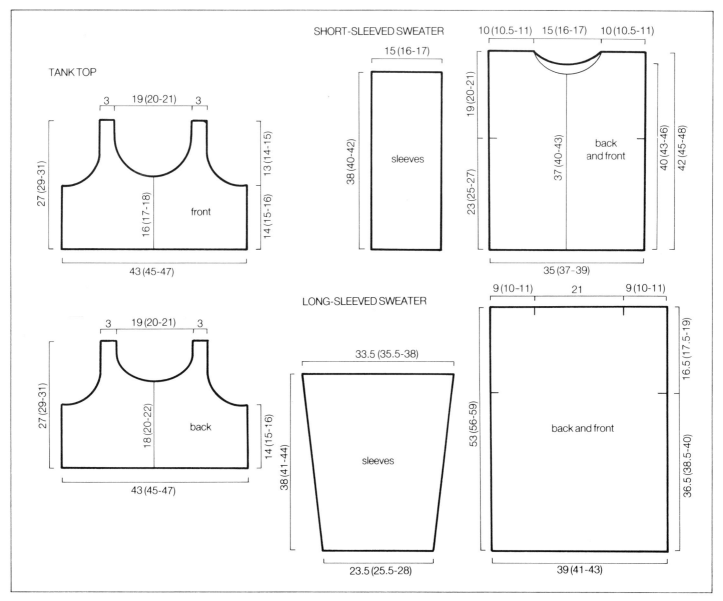

TANK TOP

SHORT-SLEEVED SWEATER

LONG-SLEEVED SWEATER

10⅝(11⅜-12¼)in, from beg. Cast off. Rejoin yarn to neck edge of right back sts and complete as for left back from ** to end reversing shapings.

▦ **Front** Work as for back until 6 rows of armhole shaping have been worked. 43 (46-49) sts.

▦ **Neck Shaping** *1st row* Cast off 2, k until there are 16 (17-18) sts on right needle, leave these for left front, cast off next 7 (8-9) sts, k to end. Cast off 2 sts at beg of foll row. *** Cont to dec 1 st at armhole edge on next 2 alt rows and *at same time* cast off at neck edge 2 sts on next row and next 2 alt rows and 1 st on next 4 alt rows. Cont on rem 4 sts until work matches back to shoulder edge. Cast off. Rejoin yarn to neck edge of left front sts and complete as for right front reversing shapings.

▦ **Finishing** Join shoulder and side seams.

SHORTS

▦ **Back** Beg at waist edge cast on 42 (46-50) sts using smaller needles and work in single rib for 6cm (2⅜in). Change to larger needles and work in double rib as foll:

▦ *1st row* (right side) K 2, * p 2, k 2; rep from * to end.

▦ *2nd row* P 2, * k 2, p 2; rep from * to end. Rep these 2 rows until work measures 23(25-27)cm, 9(9¾-10⅝)in, from beg.

▦ *Next row* Rib 20 (22-24), cast off 2, rib to end. Cont on 20 (22-24) sts now rem on needle keeping rib correct for 5cm (2in) then cast off

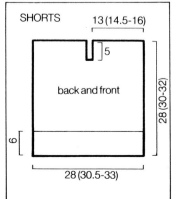

SHORTS
13 (14.5-16)
5
back and front
28 (30-32)
6
28 (30.5-33)

in rib. Complete other leg section in same way.

▦ **Front** Work as for back.

▦ **Finishing** Join side seams. Join inner leg and crotch seams.

LEG-WARMERS

▦ Beg at lower edge cast on 50 sts using smaller needles and work in double rib as given for shorts.

▦ If you are using one colour, cont until work measures 40cm (15¾in) from beg then cast off in rib.

▦ If you are using 2 or more colours, decide on main colour and cast on with this. Work in double rib ⁑ working 8cm(3⅛in) in main colour then 4cm (1½in) in

another colour; ⁑ rep from ⁑ to ⁑ twice more; then work 4cm (1½in) in main colour.

▦ Cast off in rib. Join back seam. Make second leg-warmer to match.

BANDEAU

▦ This is so simple – with only 5 sts to count – that it would make an ideal learning project for a complete beginner to knitting. With smaller needles cast on 5 sts and work in g st for 70cm (27½in). Cast off.

COUNTRY KIDS

Here is a bold, colourful trio of sweaters designed for lucky boys and girls between the ages of 6 and 14, and ideally suited to children who like the outdoor life and wide open spaces. There are three completely different styles, each with its own distinctive colour scheme, but all feature panels of colour outlined and separated by narrow stripes, added after the knitting is finished. Colours are suggested, but in practice most children will enjoy choosing their own designs: if they need a holiday project, they could even dye the yarns themselves, in earthy, natural colours.

STYLE 1 (yellow, tan and orange)

CHECKLIST

Materials
*Novita, Florica: 50 (50-100)g each of No 1524, gold (**A**); No 1521, tan (**B**); No 1512, red (**C**); No 1563, pale fawn (**D**); No 1514, pale yellow (**E**), and 50g (all sizes) No 1519, grey (**F**). Pair each of needles size 3mm and 4mm; crochet hook size 3.00mm for working the vertical stripes, or alternatively these can be embroidered in chain stitch, using a tapestry needle.*

Sizes
Three sizes, to fit ages 10 (12-14) years, fitting very loosely. Actual measurements shown on diagram.

Stitches used
Single rib; st st.

Tension
Over st st using larger needles, 25 sts and 32 rows to 10cm (4in). Work a sample on 30 sts.
The sweater consists of five separate sections, each worked vertically, beg at front and ending at back; welts and cuffs are worked on afterwards.

INSTRUCTIONS

▦ **Panel 1** This is for the centre front and back. With larger needles and **A**, cast on 43 (47-49) sts and work in st st; cont until work measures 12(13-14)cm, 4¾(5⅛-5½)in, from beg then change to **B** and work 13(14-15)cm, 5⅛(5½-5⅞)in, in **B** then change to **C**. Cont until work measures 31(34-37)cm, 12¼(13⅜-14½)in from beg, ending with a p row.
▦ **Neck Shaping** *1st row* K 12 (13-13) and leave these sets of left front on a spare needle. Cast off next 19 (21-23) sts, k to end. Cont on 12 (13-13) sts now rem on needle for right front. ✴✴ Dec 1 st at

neck edge on next 5 rows then at same edge on next 2 alt rows; work 3 rows on rem 5 (6-6) sts. You are now at the shoulder level; cont for right back and work 3 rows straight then inc 1 st at neck edge on next row and next alt row, work 1 row then inc 1 st at same edge on next 5 rows. ✴✴ Work 1 row on these 12 (13-13) sts thus ending at neck edge. Cut yarn and leave sts on a spare needle. Rejoin **C** at neck edge to sts of left front and cont as for right front and back from ✴✴ to ✴✴ reversing shapings. Work 1 row on these 12 (13-13) sts thus ending at side edge.
▦ *Next row* K 12 (13-13), turn, cast on 19 (21-23) sts, turn, then onto same needle, k the 12 (13-13)

sts of right back. Cont on these 43 (47-49) sts without further shaping until work measures 20(22-24)cm, 7⅞(8⅝-9½)in, from beg of the section in **C**. Work 13(14-15)cm, 5⅛(5½-5⅞)in, in **B** then 12(13-14)cm, 4¾(5⅛-5½)in, in **A**. Cast off.

▦ **Panel 2** This is for the right front and back, and part of right sleeve. With larger needles and **B** cast on 30 (32-34) sts and work in st st; cont until work measures 8(9-10)cm, 3⅛(3½-4)in, from beg then change to **E**. Cont until work measures 17(19-21)cm, 6¾(7½-8¼)in, from beg, ending with a k row.
▦ **Sleeve Shaping** Cast on 5 sts at beg of next row and next 4 alt rows. Cont on 55 (57-59) sts until you have worked 14(15-16)cm, 5½(5⅞-6¼)in, in **E** then change to **D** and work 26(28-30)cm, 10¼(11-11¾)in, without shaping. Change to **E** and work 2(3-4)cm, ¾(1⅛-1½)in, ending at shaped side edge. Cast off 5 sts at beg of next row and next 4 alt rows then cont on rem 30 (32-34) sts until you have worked 14(15-16)cm, 5½(5⅞-6¼)in, in **E** then change to **B** and work 8(9-10)cm, 3⅛(3½-4)in. Cast off.

▦ **Panel 3** This is for the left front and back, and part of left sleeve. With larger needles and **C** cast on 30 (32-34) sts and work in st st; cont until work measures 8(9-10)cm, 3⅛(3½-4)in, from beg then change to **D** and work a further 9(10-11)cm, 3½(4-4¼)in, ending with a p row.
▦ **Sleeve Shaping** Change to **E** and cast on 5 sts at beg of next row and next 4 alt rows then cont on these 55 (57-59) sts and work 30(32-34)cm, 11¾(12⅝-13⅜)in, ending at shaped edge. Cast off 5 sts at beg of next row and next 4 alt rows. Change to **D** and cont on rem 30 (32-34) sts; work 9(10-11)cm, 3¾(4-4¼)in, in **D** then change to **C** and work 8(9-10)cm, 3⅛(3½-4)in. Cast off.

▦ **Panel 4** End of right sleeve With larger needles and **C** cast on 5 (6-7) sts and k 1 row; cont in st st and cast off 5 (6-6) sts at beg of

next row and next 2 alt rows and 6 (6-7) sts at same edge on next 3 alt rows; 12 rows have been worked and there are 38 (42-46) sts. Cont without shaping for 22.5(24.5-26.5)cm, 8⅞(9⅝-10½)in, ending with a k row. Cast off 6 (6-7) sts at beg of next row and next 2 alt rows and 5 (6-6) sts at same edge on next 3 alt rows. Cast off rem sts.

▦ **Panel 5** End of left sleeve With larger needles and **A** cast on 5 (6-7) sts and p 1 row; work as for Panel 4 reversing shapings by working cast-on and cast-off sts at beg of k rows.

▦ **Neck border** With smaller needles and **C** cast on 96 (100-104) sts and work in single rib for 3cm (1⅛in). Cast off loosely in rib.

▦ **Finishing and stripes** Sew straight side edge of Panel 2 to left-hand edge of Panel 1 and sew corresponding edge of Panel 3 to other side edge of Panel 1, making flat seams. Sew longer side edge of Panel 4 to outer edge of Panel 2, and sew longer side edge of Panel 5 to outer edge of Panel 3. Along seams joining the panels, work 2 lines of chain-st using **F**; either work with the crochet hook or embroider the lines, placing them close tog to hide seams. Ensure that all lines run in same direction from cast-on edges to cast-off edges.

▦ **Welts and cuffs** With right side of work facing and using smaller needles and **C**, pick up and k 100 (108-116) sts across lower edge of back and work in single rib for 5cm (2in). Cast off loosely in rib. Work front welt in same way.
▦ With right side of work facing and using smaller needles and **C**, pick up and k 54 (58-62) sts across outer edge of right sleeve. Work in single rib for 7cm (2¾in) then cast off loosely in rib. Work left cuff in same way.

▦ **Finishing** Join entire side and sleeve seams. Join ends of neck border and sew cast-on edge all round neck edge placing seam at left side of neckline.

STYLE 2 (red, orange and brown)

CHECKLIST

Materials
Novita Florica: *100g each of No 1542, light brown (**A**); No 1513, rust (**B**), and No 1512, orange (**C**); 50(50-100)g each of No 1545, bright red (**D**), and No 1539, geranium (**E**), and 50g each of 1534, dark brown (**F**), and No 1548, dark red (**G**). Pair each of needles size 3mm and 4mm.*

Sizes
Three sizes, to fit ages 6 (8-10) years. Actual measurements shown on diagram.

Stitches used
Single rib; st st. *For the arrangement of colours on back and front see instructions; when changing colour during a row always twist yarns on wrong side, picking up the new colour from underneath the one previously used.*

Tension
Over st st using 4mm needles, 25 sts and 32 rows to 10cm (4in); work a sample on 30 sts.

INSTRUCTIONS

▦ **Back** With smaller needles and **A** cast on 90 (96-102) sts and work in single rib for 5cm (2in), working 5 incs evenly spaced along last row. 95 (101-107) sts. Change to larger needles and cut off **A**; work in st st with colours arranged as foll, joining on **C** at beg.
▦ *1st row* K 45 (48-51) **C**, join on a small ball of **F** and k 5 **F**, join on a ball of **B** and k 45 (48-51) **B**.
▦ *2nd row* P 45 (48-51) **B**, twist yarns, p 5 **F**, twist yarns, p 45 (48-51) **C**. Cont as now set until work measures 23(24-25)cm, 9(9½-9¾)in, from beg, ending with a p row. Cut off all colours and join on **F** at beg. Work 6 rows in **F**, cut **F** and join on **D** at beg. Cont as foll:
▦ 1st row K 45 (48-51) **D**, join on small ball of **F** and k 5 **F**, join on a ball of **E** and k 45 (48-51) **E**.
▦ *2nd row* P 45 (48-51) **E**, twist yarns, p 5 **F**, twist yarns, p 45 (48-51) **D**. Cont with colours as now set until work measures 43(46-49)cm, 17(18-19¼)in, from beg, ending with a p row.
▦ **Neck Shaping** *1st row* K 36 (38-40) and leave these sts of right back on a spare needle, cast off next 23 (25-27) sts using correct colours, k to end. Cont on 36 (38-40) sts now rem on needle for left

back, using **E**; dec 1 st at neck edge on next row, cast off 4 sts at beg of foll row then p 1 row without shaping. Cast off rem 31 (33-35) sts for shoulder edge. Rejoin **D** to neck edge of right back sts, cast off 4, p to end. Dec 1 st at neck edge on next row then work 1 row straight. Cast off rem 31 (33-35) sts.

▦ **Front** Work as for back until work measures 37(40-43)cm, 14½(15¾-17)in, from beg, ending with a p row.
▦ **Neck Shaping** *1st row* K 41 (43-45) and leave these sts of left front on a spare needle, cast off next 13 (15-17) sts, k to end. Cont on 41 (43-45) sts now rem on needle for right front, using **E**, and work 1 row. ** Cast off 3 sts at beg of next row, 2 sts at same edge on next 2 alt rows and 1 st on next 3 alt rows. Cont on rem 31 (33-35) sts until work matches back to shoulder edge. Cast off. Rejoin **D** to neck edge of left front sts and complete as for right front from ** to end.

▦ **Right Sleeve** With smaller needles and **A** cast on 48 (50-52) sts and work in single rib for 3cm (1⅛in) working 4 (5-6) incs evenly spaced along last row. 52 (55-58) sts. Change to larger needles and

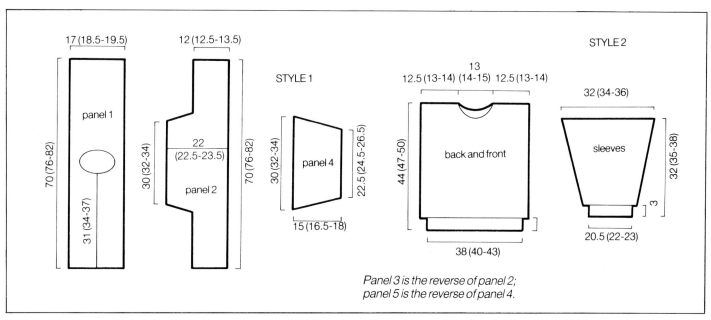

STYLE 1

17 (18.5-19.5)

12 (12.5-13.5)

panel 1

70 (76-82)

31 (34-37)

30 (32-34)

22
(22.5-23.5)

panel 2

70 (76-82)

30 (32-34)

panel 4

22.5 (24.5-26.5)

15 (16.5-18)

STYLE 2

13
12.5 (13-14) (14-15) 12.5 (13-14)

44 (47-50)

back and front

38 (40-43)

32 (34-36)

sleeves

32 (35-38)

3

20.5 (22-23)

*Panel 3 is the reverse of panel 2;
panel 5 is the reverse of panel 4.*

C. Work in st st and inc 1 st at both ends of every foll 6th row 12 (15-16) times then every foll 4th row twice for *1st size only; at same time,* when work measures 16(18-20)cm, 6¼(7⅛-7⅞)in, from beg cut off **C** and work 6 rows in **F** then change to **A** and cont until all incs are completed. Cont on these 80 (85-90) sts until work measures 30(33-36)cm, 11¾(13-14⅛)in, from beg. Work 6 rows in **F** then cast off all sts.

◫ **Left Sleeve** Work as for right sleeve but work the first wide section after cuff in **B** and after the band of **F** work the next section in **G** ending with 6 rows in **F** as on right sleeve. Cast off.

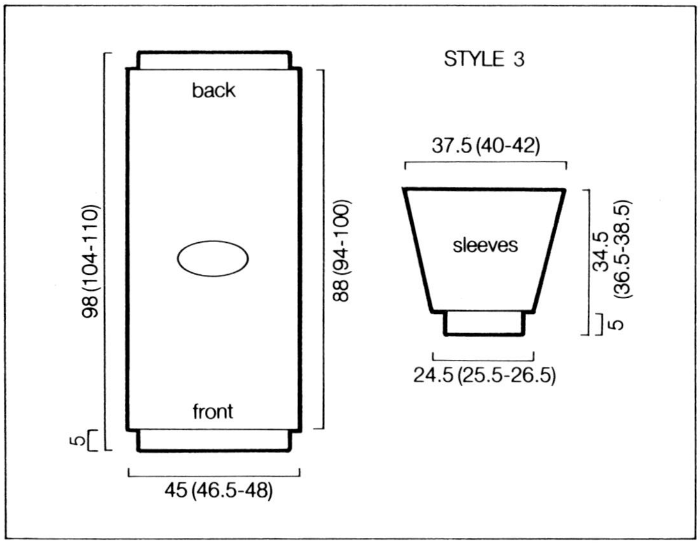

STYLE 3 (grey, blue, green)

CHECKLIST

Materials
*Novita Fauna: 150g each of No 2019, green (**A**), and No 2024, mid-blue (**B**), and 100g each of No 2006, grey (**C**), and No 2021, royal blue (**D**). Quality Florica: 50g of No 1531, navy (**E**). The latter yarn is used double throughout. Pair each of needles size 3¾mm and 4½mm; a crochet hook size 4.00mm for working the vertical stripes, or alternatively these can be embroidered in chain stitch, using a tapestry needle.*

Sizes
Three sizes, to fit ages 8 (10-12) years. Actual measurements shown on diagram.

Stitches used
Single rib; st st; *check patt as explained below. Only the horizontal stripes are worked in; all the vertical stripes are added afterwards.*

Tension
Over st st using 4½mm needles, 18 sts and 25 rows to 10cm (4in). Work a sample on 24 sts.
Note: *The colour* **E** *is used double throughout; wind the yarn into 2 equal balls then rewind these tog into a double thickness ball which will be easier to use. When working the check patt, take care always to twist yarns around each other when changing colour during a row, picking up the new colour from under the colour previously used.*

INSTRUCTIONS

◫ **Main part** Beg at lower edge of front cast on 76 (78-82) sts using smaller needles and **C**. Work in single rib for 5cm (2in) working 5 (6-5) incs evenly spaced along last row. 81 (84-87) sts. Change to larger needles and patt.
◫ *1st row* K 27 (28-29) **C**, join on **D** and k 27 (28-29) **D**, join on **A**

and k 27 (28-29) **A**.
◫ *2nd row* P 27 (28-29) **A**, twist yarns, p 27 (28-29) **D**, twist yarns, p 27 (28-29) **C**. Cont in patt as now set until you have worked 14(15-16)cm, 5½(5⅞-6¼)in, in patt, ending with a p row. Cut off all colours and work 2 rows st st in **E**. Cut **E** and join on **B** at beg; cont as folls:
◫ *1st row* K 27 (28-29) **B**, join on

◫ **Neck border** With smaller needles and **A** cast on 96 (100-104) sts and work in single rib for 7 rows. Cast off loosely in rib.

◫ **Finishing** Join shoulder seams. Pin cast-off edge of sleeves to sides of sweater placing centre of sleeve level with shoulder seam and ensuring that sides of sleeves reach to same position on patt at each side. Sew in place as pinned then join side and sleeve seams matching **F** stripes. Join ends of neck border and sew cast-on edge to neck edges, placing seam level with left shoulder seams.

STYLE 3

37.5 (40-42)

back

front

98 (104-110)

88 (94-100)

45 (46.5-48)

5

sleeves

34.5 (36.5-38.5)

5

24.5 (25.5-26.5)

A, k 27 (28-29) **A**, join on **C**, k 27 (28-29) **C**. Cont with colours as set until this panel is same length as previous panel, ending with a p row. Cut off all colours and work 2 rows st st in **E**; cut **E** and join on **C** at beg. Start new panels working 1st panel in **C**, 2nd panel in **B** and 3rd panel in **D**. Cont as now set for 7(8-9)cm, 2¾(3⅛-3½)in, ending with a p row.
◫ **Neck Shaping** *1st row* Keeping colours correct, k 33 (34-35) and leave these sts of left front on a spare needle, cast off next 15 (16-17) sts, k to end. Cont on 33 (34-35) sts now rem on needle for right front and work 1 row. Cast off 3 sts at beg of next row, 2 sts at same edge on next alt row and 1 st on next alt row. Cont on rem 27 (28-29) sts using **D** only until this panel is same length as previous panels, ending with a p row. Cut **D** and join on **E**; work 2 rows st st in **E** to mark shoulder line then cont for right back. Change to **C** and cont in st st casting on 3 sts at beg of next row and next alt row working these extra sts in **B**. P 1 row on these 33 (34-35) sts thus ending at neck edge. Cut **B** and leave these sts for the present.
◫ With wrong side facing rejoin **B** to neck edge of left front sts, cast off 3, p to end using correct colours. Cast off 2 sts at neck edge on next alt row and 1 st on next alt row then cont on rem 27 (28-29) sts using **C** only until this panel is same length as previous

panels, ending with a p row. Cut **C** and work 2 rows st st in **E** for shoulder line then cont for left back. Join on **A** and k 1 row then cast on 3 sts at beg of next row and next alt row working these extra sts in **B**.
◫ *Next row* K 27 (28-29) **A**, twist yarns, k 6 **B**, turn, cast on 15 (16-17), turn then working sts of right back k 6 **B**, twist yarns, k 27 (28-29) **C**. Cont across all sts until side panels are same length as previous panels ending with a p row then work 2 rows st st in **E**. Start new panels working 1st panel in **B**, 2nd panel in **D** and 3rd panel in **A** and when these are same length as before work 2 rows st st in **E**. For last line of panels work 1st panel in **A**, 2nd panel in **C** and 3rd panel in **B**. Cont until these are same length as before ending with a p row. Cut all colours and join on **C**. K 1 row working 5 (6-5) decs evenly spaced. 76 (78-82) sts. Change to smaller needles and work in single rib for 5cm (2in) then cast off in rib.

◫ **Right Sleeve** With smaller needles and **C** cast on 40 (42-44) sts and work in single rib for 5cm (2in) working 4 incs evenly spaced along last row. 44 (46-48) sts. Change to larger needles and patt joining on **A** at beg.
◫ *1st row* K 22 (23-24) **A**, join on **D**, k 22 (23-24) **D**. Cont with colours as set twisting yarns at centre and work 4 (6-8) more rows

then inc 1 st at both ends of next row, then every foll 4th row 4 times more so that there are 27 (28-29) sts in each colour. Cont until work measures 14(15-16)cm, 5½(5⅞-6¼)in, from beg of patt ending with a p row then cut colours and work 2 rows in **E**. Now start new panels joining on **C** at beg.
▦ *1st row* K 27 (28-29) **C**, join on **B** and k 27 (28-29) **B**. Cont with colours as set for 3 more rows. Now join on a small ball of **D** at each side and working all extra sts in **D** inc 1 st at both ends of next row then every foll 4th row 6 (7-8) times more. Cont on 68 (72-76) sts until panels are same length as before. Work 2 rows st st in **E**. Cast off all sts.

▦ **Left Sleeve** Work as for right sleeve but with colours as foll: after the cuff work 1st panel in **D** and 2nd panel in **B**. After the stripe in **E** work 1st panel in **C** and 2nd panel in **A** and work all the extra sts at sides in **D**. Complete as for right sleeve.

▦ **Neck border** With smaller needles and **C** cast on 84 (86-88) sts and work in single rib for 3cm (1⅛in). Cast off in rib.

▦ **Vertical stripes** These can either be worked with the crochet hook working in line of slip-sts or else embroidered using a tapestry needle and working a line of chain-st. Beg at bottom of patt on front and using **E** work 2 lines next to each other at the change of colour on each panel; cont lines until the centre panels are eliminated at the neck and begin again on back. Work similar lines along centre of each sleeve and at the change of colour where the small sections are worked in **D** at top of sleeves.

▦ **Finishing** Pin cast-off edge of sleeves to sides of sweater with sleeves at correct side edges and matching centre vertical stripe on sleeves to the stripe at shoulder line. Sew in place, then join side and sleeve seams matching stripes. Join ends of neck border. Sew cast-on edge to neck edges: seam at left side of neckline level with the shoulder stripe.

3
FAMILY FAVOURITES

HEADS IN THE CLOUDS

On course for the moon, this father and son (or it could equally well be mother and daughter) wear easy-to-knit sweaters featuring a subtle design showing the moon shrouded in clouds. The sweater has a straight, loose shape, with hems instead of the more usual bands of ribbing at the cuffs and lower edge, and with a slash neck. The back and sleeves are worked in varying shades of grey lightened with ecru. If grey skies don't appeal to you, you could use the same motif but switch to a mixture of reds and wines, or alternatively rose pinks, dusty blues and pale yellows, transforming the moonlit scene to a stormy sunset or a gentle sunrise.

CHECKLIST

Materials

Georges Picaud Shetland: 1 (2) balls of No 62, dark grey; 2 (3) balls of No 10, light grey; 2 (4) balls of No 8, medium grey, and 1 (4) balls of No 39, ecru. Orient Express: 1 (1) ball in No 4, gold. Pair of double-pointed needles size 4½mm; circular needle size 4½mm; medium-size crochet hook (child's version only).

Sizes

Two sizes, one adult's and one child's, to fit a child aged 4 years, or an adult size 97/102cm (38/40in) chest.

Stitches used

St st, patt, worked from charts.
Use separate balls or short lengths of yarn for each of the sections shown on chart, taking care to wind yarns around each other when changing colour. The back is worked in stripes to match those on the front. The stripes are made by alternating 1 row in each colour. Use the double-pointed needles or the circular needle to avoid cutting the yarn, then always work from the side where you find the colour you need. The yarn is used double throughout.

Tension

Over st st with yarn used double, 18 sts and 27 rows to 10cm (4in).

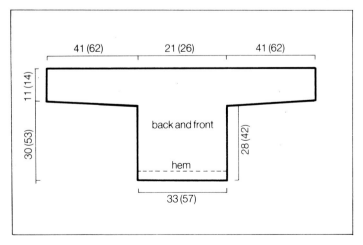

CHILD'S SWEATER front

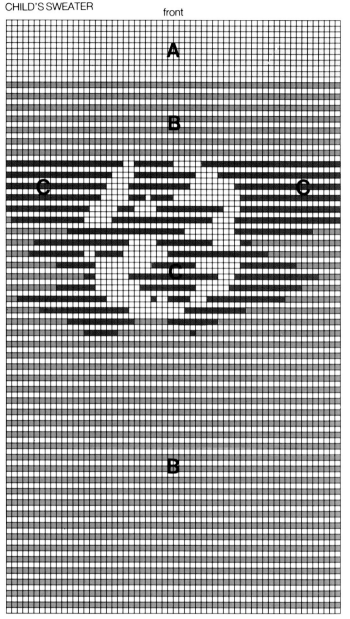

KEY

A = 1 row light gray, 1 row ecru
B = 1 row medium gray, 1 row ecru
C = 1 row dark gray, 1 row ecru
⊡ = gold

ADULT'S SWEATER

front

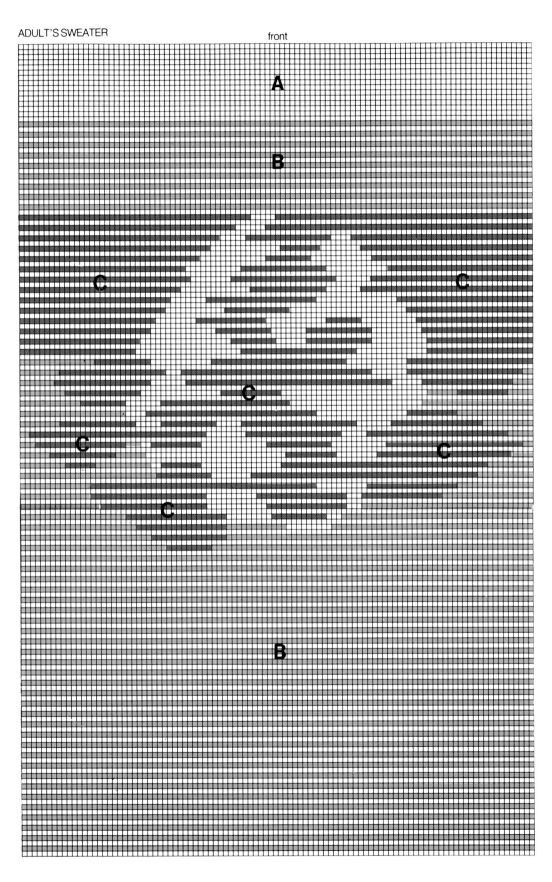

INSTRUCTIONS

▦ **Back** Use the yarn double.
With double-pointed needles and
medium grey, cast on 60 (102) sts
for lower edge and work 2 rows s
st for hem.

▦ Cont in st st, alternating 1 row
medium grey and 1 row ecru until
work measures 28(42)cm,
11(16½)in.

▦ Alternating 1 row ecru and 1
row dark grey, work 12 (32) rows
and *at the same time* at the 1st
(11th) row cast on extra sts for
sleeves, as foll, changing to
circular needle for the extra sts: *for
child's sweater* cast on 21 sts at
beg of next 6 rows; *for adult's
sweater* cast on 4 sts at beg of
next 12 rows and 12 sts at beg of
foll 10 rows. 186 (270) sts.

▦ Work 13 (18) rows, alternating
1 row ecru and 1 row medium
grey, then cont with ecru and light
grey until work measures
41(67)cm, 16⅛(26⅜)in, from beg.
Cast off the 186 (270) sts.

▦ **Front** Foll the instructions for
the back until work measures
20(29.5)cm, 7⅞(11½)in.

▦ Foll chart, commence moon
motif as foll:

▦ *1st row* K 41 (65) **B**, 2 (7) **C**, 17
(30) **B**.

▦ Cont in patt as now set to end
of motif, then finish with stripes to
match the back.

▦ **Finishing** Join shoulder and
upper sleeve seams of back and
front for 41(62)cm, 16⅛(24⅜)in,
leaving 21(26)cm, 8¼(10¼)in,
free at the centre for neck.

▦ Join side and sleeve seams.
Turn up the hem at base of back
and front.

▦ Make a 2cm (¾in) hem on
sleeves. Make a narrow hem
around neck edge of adult's
sweater. For the child's sweater,
work a row of d c around the neck
edge with ecru.

SNOW SET

Marvellous mohair is ideal for the snow – so light, yet so beautifully warm. To emphasize its wonderful cold-beating qualities, each item of this outdoor set is made in two thicknesses, using contrasting colours. After it is made up, each jacket is thus completely reversible, with cuffs turned back to show the contrast. Photographed on the ski slopes of Couchevel in the French alps, these colourful clothes are all easy to make.

JACKET WITH ROLL COLLAR

CHECKLIST

Materials
*Anny Blatt Soft' Anny, Kid Mohair: 17 balls of No 1602, mulberry (**A**), and 17 balls of No 1382, olive (**B**). Pair of needles size 5mm; large size crochet hook for making up.*

Size
One size only, to fit 82/97cm (32/38in) bust. Actual measurements shown on diagram.

Stitches used
St st; double rib; slip st *(in crochet).*

Tension
Over st st using needles given, 15 sts and 24 rows to 10cm (4in). Work a sample on 20 sts.

INSTRUCTIONS

FIRST SECTION

▦ **Back** Using **A**, cast on 94 sts and work in st st. Cont until work measures 58cm (22¾in) from beg, ending with a p row.
▦ **Armhole Shaping** Cast off 3 sts at beg of next 2 rows and 1 st at beg of next 4 rows. Cont on rem 84 sts until work measures 86cm (33⅞in) from beg, ending with a p row.
▦ **Shoulder Shaping** Cast off 7 sts at beg of next 6 rows and 9 sts at beg of next 2 rows. Cast off rem 24 sts for back neck.

▦ **Right Front** Using **A** cast on 60 sts and work in st st. Cont until work measures 32cm (12⅝in) from beg, ending with a p row.
▦ **Pocket Opening** *1st row* K 30, turn and cont on these sts for front section leaving rem 30 sts of side section on a spare needle. Work a further 19cm (7½in)

ending with a k row. Cut yarn and rejoin to 30 sts of side section, k to end. Work 19cm (7½in) on these sts ending with a k row.
▦ *Next row* P 30 sts of side section then p 30 sts of front section. Cont on 60 sts until work matches back to armhole, ending with a k row.
▦ **Armhole Shaping** Cast off 3 sts at beg of next row and dec 1 st at same edge on next 2 alt rows. Cont on rem 55 sts until work matches back to shoulder, ending at side edge.
▦ **Shoulder Shaping** Cast off 7 sts at beg of next row and next 2 alt rows and 9 sts at same edge on next alt row.
▦ Cont on rem 25 sts for collar. Inc 1 st at shaped edge on every foll 4th row 4 times then cont on 29 sts until work measures 9cm (3½in) from beg of collar ending at shaped edge. Cast off 6 sts at beg of next row and next 3 alt rows. Work 1 row and then cast off rem 5 sts.

Left Front Work as for right front reversing all shapings.

Sleeves Using **A** cast on 68 sts and work in st st. Cont until work measures 10cm (4in) from beg then inc 1 st at both ends of next row then every foll 14th row 7 times more. Cont on 84 sts until work measures 54cm (21¼in) from beg.

Top Shaping Cast off 3 sts at beg of next 2 rows, 4 sts at beg of next 4 rows and 6 sts at beg of next 2 rows. Cast off rem 50 sts.

Pocket Borders With right side of work facing and using **A**, pick up and k 38 sts along front edge of pocket opening on right front.

1st row (wrong side) P 2, * k 2, p 2; rep from * to end.

2nd row K 2, * p 2, k 2; rep from * to end. Rep these 2 rows until border measures 2.5cm (1in) then cast off in rib. Work similar border on left front pocket opening.

SECOND SECTION

Work all parts as for first section but using **B**.

Finishing For each section join shoulder seams, sew in sleeves then join side and sleeve seams. Join cast-off edges of collar and sew inner edge along back neck easing it to fit. Neatly sew ends of pocket border in place. Slip one section inside the other, having both wrong sides tog. Working on

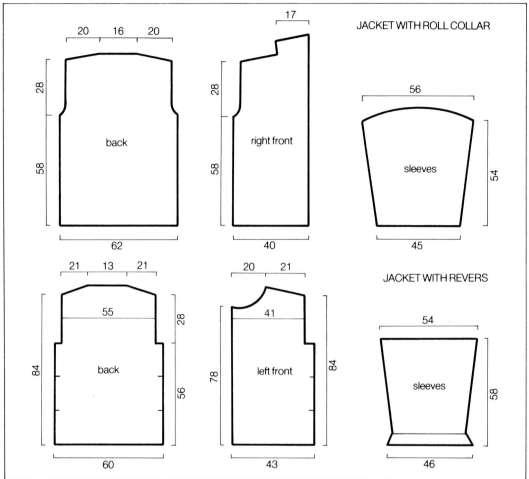

JACKET WITH ROLL COLLAR

JACKET WITH REVERS

wrong side and using the crochet hook, slip-st the sections tog at top and bottom of opening. Working on right side join the sections on all outer edges with a

row of slip sts, using the crochet hook. Hold the 2 thicknesses tog by sewing along both shoulder seams.

JACKET WITH REVERS

CHECKLIST

Materials
Bouton d'Or 100 per cent Mohair Gratté: 700g of mustard (A), and 700g of mint (B). Pair of needles size 7mm.

Size
One size only, to fit 82/97cm (32/38in) bust. Actual measurements shown on diagram.

Stitch used
St st.

Tension
Over st st using needles given, 12 sts and 16 rows to 10cm (4in). Work a sample on 16 sts.

INSTRUCTIONS

FIRST SECTION

Back Using **A**, cast on 72 sts and work in st st. Cont until work measures 56cm (22in) from beg, ending with a p row.

Armhole Shaping Cast off 3 sts at beg of next 2 rows then cont on rem 66 sts until work measures 84cm (33in) from beg, ending with a p row.

Shoulder and Neck Shaping Cast off 8 sts at beg of next 2 rows.

3rd row Cast off 8, k until there are 11 sts on right needle, leave these for right back, cast off next 12 sts, k to end. Cont on 19 sts now rem at end of needle for left back. Cast off 8 sts at beg of next row and 2 sts at neck edge on foll row. Cast off rem 9 sts to complete shoulder slope. Rejoin yarn to neck edge of right back sts, cast off 2, p to end. Cast off rem 9 sts.

▦ **Left Front** Using **A** cast on 52 sts and work in st st. Cont until work measures 56cm (22in) from beg, ending with a p row.

▦ **Armhole Shaping** Cast off 3 sts at beg of next row then cont on rem 49 sts until work measures 78cm (30¾in) from beg, ending at front edge after a k row.

▦ **Neck and Shoulder Shaping** Cast off 15 sts at beg of next row, 5 sts at same edge on next alt row, 2 sts on next alt row and 1 st on next 2 alt rows. Now keeping neck edge straight cast off for shoulder 8 sts at beg of next row and next alt row, work 1 row then cast off rem 9 sts.

▦ **Right Front** Work as for left front reversing all shapings.

▦ **Sleeves** Using **A** cast on 55 sts and work in st st but dec 1 st at both ends of every foll 4th row twice. Cont on 51 sts until work measures 12cm (4¾in) from beg; inc 1 st at both ends of next row then every foll 10th row 3 times, then every foll 8th row 3 times more. Cont on 65 sts until work measures 58cm (22¾in) from beg. Cast off all sts.

SECOND SECTION

▦ Work all parts as for first section but using **B**.

▦ **Finishing** For each section join shoulder seams; sew cast-off sleeve edges to armhole sides and armhole casting-off to last 4 rows of sleeves. Join sleeve seams. On each side edge put markers 20cm (7⅞in) from lower edge and 18cm (7⅛in) higher, to mark pocket openings. Join side seams above and below openings. Place one jacket inside the other having both right sides tog. Join along front and neck edges and along edges of pocket openings. Turn right sides out. Working from inside and using the crochet hook, slip-st sections tog at upper and lower levels of pocket openings for 20cm (7⅞in) from sides and slip-st vertically to form pockets. On outside neatly sew the sections tog along lower edges and edges of sleeves. Hold thicknesses tog by sewing along shoulder seams.

PARKA

CHECKLIST

Materials
Laine Plassard Florès: *14 balls of No 7, rust* (**A**)*, and 14 balls of No 21, pink* (**B**)*. Pair of needles size 5mm; large size crochet hook for making up. An open-ended 70cm (21in) zip for front opening and 2 ordinary 13cm (5in) zips for pockets.*

Size
One size only, to fit 82/97cm (32/38in) bust. Actual measurements shown on diagram.

Stitches used
St st; slip-st *(in crochet).*

Tension
Over st st, using needles given, 16 sts and 24 rows to 10cm (4in). Work a sample on 20 sts.

INSTRUCTIONS

FIRST SECTION

Back Using **A** cast on 100 sts and work in st st. Cont until work measures 50cm (19¾in) from beg, ending with a p row.

Armhole Shaping Cast off 3 sts at beg of next 2 rows and 2 sts at beg of next 2 rows. Cont on rem 90 sts until work measures 78cm (30¾in) from beg, ending with a p row.

Shoulder Shaping Cast off 8 sts at beg of next 8 rows. Cast off rem 26 sts for back neck.

Right Front Using **A** cast on 52 sts and work in st st; cont until work measures 16cm (6¼in) from beg, ending with a p row.

Pocket Opening *1st row* K 32, turn and cont on these sts for front section leaving rem 20 sts of side section on a spare needle. Dec 1 st at beg of next row and at same edge on next 17 rows; you have ended at the opening after a k row

Cut yarn and leave rem 14 sts on a spare needle. With right side facing rejoin yarn to 20 sts of side section, k to end. Inc 1 st at end of next row and at same edge on next 17 rows; you have ended at side edge after a k row and there are 38 sts on needle.

20th row P 38 then p 14 sts of front section. Cont on 52 sts until work measures 50cm (19¾in) from beg, ending with a k row.

Armhole Shaping Cast off 3 sts at beg of next row and 2 sts at same edge on next alt row. Cont on rem 47 sts until work measures 72cm (28¼in) from beg, ending at front edge.

Neck and Shoulder Shaping Cast off 3 sts at beg of next row, 2 sts at same edge on next 5 alt rows and 1 st on next 2 alt rows. Now keeping neck edge straight cast off for shoulder 8 sts at beg of next row and next 2 alt rows, work 1 row then cast off rem 8 sts.

Left Front Work as for right front reversing pocket opening and all shapings.

Sleeves Using **A** cast on 72 sts and work in st st; inc 1 st at both ends of every foll 12th row 9 times then cont on 90 sts until work measures 54cm (21¼in) from beg.

Top Shaping Cast off 3 sts at beg of next 2 rows, 5 sts at beg of next 4 rows and 6 sts at beg of next 2 rows. Cast off rem 52 sts.

Hood Using **A** cast on 60 sts and work in st st for 50cm (19¾in).

Cast off.

SECOND SECTION

Work all parts as for first section but using **B**.

Finishing For each section join shoulder seams, sew in sleeves then join side and sleeve seams. Fold hood in half and join one side of row ends forming upper seam. Sew hood to neck edges. Place one section inside the other having the p sides tog. Join sections around lower edges of main part and sleeves with a row of slip st, using crochet hook. Join front edges of hood in same way. Sew open-ended zip between the 2 thicknesses along front edges leaving last 2cm (¾in) open at neck edge and at waistline. Leave an opening for the depth of 4 rows to allow cord to be passed through. Slip-st front edges above top of zip.

Sew short zips to pocket openings between the 2 sections. Slip-st the sections tog on inside of openings to form pockets. To make cord work a length of crochet chain 90cm (35½in) long, using **A**, then cont for same length in **B**; work back along the chain in slip st, matching colours.

At waistline backstitch through both thicknesses 4 rows apart for casing and thread cord through.

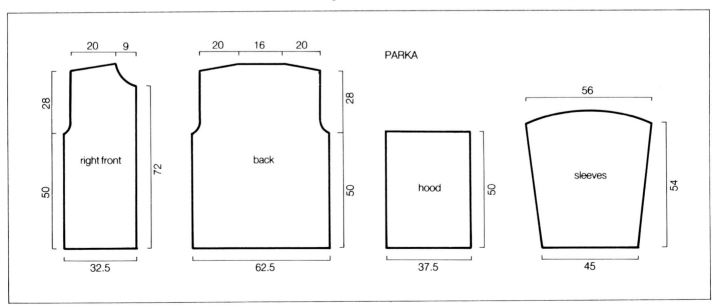

CHILD'S JACKET

CHECKLIST

Materials
*Berger du Nord Kid Mohair: 8 (8-9) balls of No 7991, bright blue (**A**); 6 (6-7) balls of No 8245, dark green (**B**), and 2 (2-3) balls of No 8250, green (**C**). Pair of 4mm needles; 8 buttons.*

Sizes
Three sizes, to fit ages 6 (8-10) years. Actual measurements shown on diagram.

Stitches used
Single rib; st st.

Tension
Over st st and using needles given, 16 sts and 23 rows to 10cm (4in). Work a sample on 24 sts.

Note *Section 1 is worked entirely in **A** and has patch pockets. Section 2 is worked in **B** with zigzag panels worked in **C** from chart; the small diamonds in **A** and **C** are embroidered afterwards by the Swiss darning method described on page 6.*

See instructions for arrangement of patt on each section. Arrow shows centre st for back sleeves and hood.

INSTRUCTIONS

FIRST SECTION

▦ **Back** Using **A** cast on 67 (73-79) sts and work in st st. Cont until work measures 54(58-62)cm, 21¼(22¾-24½)in, from beg.
▦ **Shoulder Shaping** Cast off 7 (8-9) sts at beg of next 4 rows and 8 sts at beg of next 2 rows. Cast off rem 23 (25-27) sts for back neck.

▦ **Left Front** Using **A** cast on 35 (38-41) sts and work in st st. Cont until work measures 50(53-57)cm, 19¾(20¾-22⅜)in, from beg ending with a k row.
▦ **Neck and Shoulder Shaping** Cast off 5 (6-7) sts at beg of next

| centre stitch
Work the zigzag patt during the course of the work and emboider the diamonds afterwards in Swiss darning.

row, 2 sts at same edge on next 2 alt rows and 1 st on next 4 alt rows. Now cast off for shoulder 7 (8-9) sts at beg of next row and next alt row, work 1 row then cast off rem 8 sts.

▦ **Right Front** Work as for left front reversing all shapings.

▦ **Sleeves** Using **A** cast on 45 (49-53) sts and work in st st but inc 1 st at both ends of every foll 10th row 2 (5-8) times then every foll 8th row 6 (3-0) times. Cont on 61 (65-69) sts until work measures 34 (37-40)cm, 13⅜(14½-15¾)in, from beg. Cast off all sts.

▦ **Hood** Beg at top edge cast on

61 (65-69) sts and work in st st; cont until work measures 23(24-25)cm, 9(9½-9¾)in, from beg. Cast off.

◻ **Pockets** Make 2 alike. Using **A** cast on 19 (19-21) sts and work in st st for 10(10-12)cm, 4(4-4¾)in, ending with a p row then work in rib.
◻ *1st row* P 1, * k 1, p 1; rep from * to end.
◻ *2nd row* K 1, * p 1, k 1; rep from * to end. Rep 1st and 2nd rows once then 1st row again. Cast off loosely in rib.

◻ **Buttonhole Loops** Make 8 alike. Cast on 3 sts using **A** and work in st st for 5cm (2in). Cast off.

◻ **Finishing** Join shoulder seams. On each side edge mark a point 19(20-21.5)cm, 7½(7⅞-8½)in, down from shoulder seam for armholes; sew cast-off edge of sleeves between markers. Join side and sleeve seams. Slip st pockets to fronts. Fold cast-on edge of hood in half and sew forming upper seam. Sew lower edges to neck edges easing in fullness. The buttonhole loops are sewn on later.

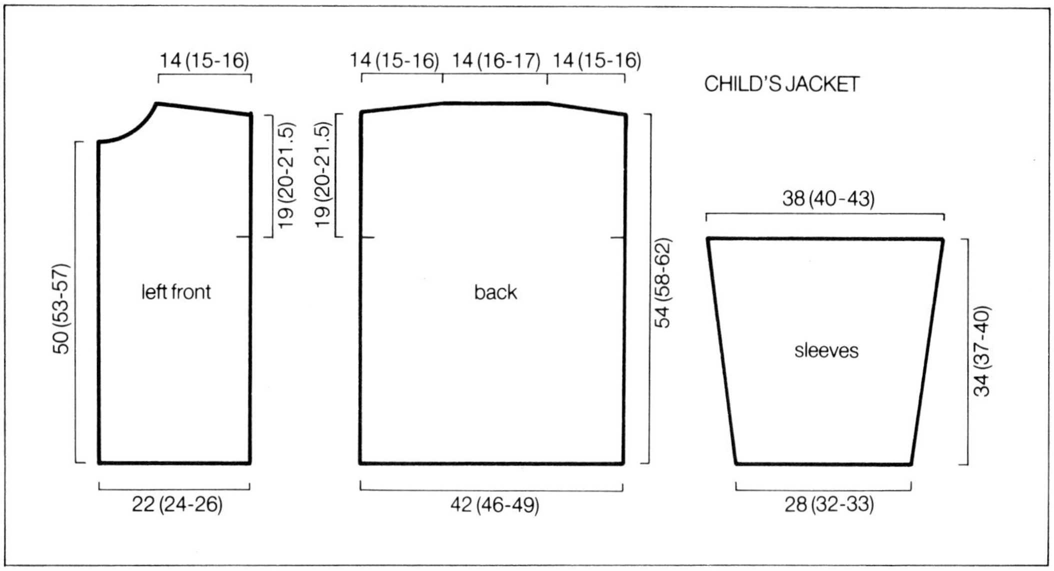

SECOND SECTION

◻ **Back** using **B** cast on 67 (73-79) sts and work 4 rows in st st then work patt from chart, joining on **C**.
◻ *1st row* K 5 (0-3) **B**, * 1 **C**, 7 **B**; * rep from * to * ending 1 **C**, 5 (0-3) **B**. Mark on chart the position where row begins and ends according to size. Cont working from chart until the zigzag is completed on 8th row, taking great care not to pull the yarn tightly on wrong side.
◻ Work next 5 rows in **B**; the spots will be embroidered afterwards. Work rem 8 rows of chart then cont in **B** only until work measures 44(48-52)cm, 17¼(18⅞-20½)in, from beg, ending with a p row. Work the 21 rows of patt as before then cont in **B** until work measures 54(58-62)cm, 21¼(22¾-24½)in, from beg. Work shoulder shaping as for Section 1.

◻ **Left Front** Using **B** cast on 35 (38-41) sts and work 4 rows in st st then work patt from chart.
◻ *1st row* K 5 (0-3) **B**, * 1 **C**, 7 **B**; * rep from * to * 2 (2-3) times more, 1 **C**, 5 **B**. Cont in patt as now set until 21st row has been worked then cont in **B** only until work measures 44(48-52)cm, 17¼ (18⅞-20½)in, from beg, ending with a p row. Work patt as before and *at same time*, when work measures 50(53-57)cm, 19¾(20¾-22⅜)in, from beg, ending with a k row work neck and shoulder shaping as for Section 2, changing to **B** after patt is completed.

◻ **Right Front** Work as for left front reversing arrangement of patt and all shapings.

◻ **Sleeves** Using **B** cast on 45 (49-53) sts and work 4 rows in st st then work patt from chart.
◻ *1st row* K 2 (4-6) **B**, * 1 **C**, 7 **B**; * rep from * to * ending 1 **C**, 2 (4-6) **B**. Cont working from chart but shape sides of sleeve as for Section 1, working 1st inc at each side on 6th row of patt. When the 21 rows have been worked complete as for Section 2 using **B** only.

◻ **Hood** Using **B** cast on 61 (65-69) sts and work 4 rows in st st. Now begin working patt from chart arranging it as for sleeves; when

the 21st row has been worked, cont in **B** only and complete as for Section 1.

◻ **Buttonhole Loops** Make these as for Section 1 but using **B**.

◻ **Finishing** Join as Section 1 apart from pockets. Swiss darn spots in **C** and **A** on back and fronts, leaving 4 or more rows at top before start of zigzag. Embroider spots on sleeves and

hood. Slip one section inside the other with p sides tog. Neatly slip-st sections tog all along front and lower edges, around front edge of hood and lower edges of sleeves. Fold buttonhole loops in half and sew to fronts of each section placing top one just below neck and rem 3 on each front spaced about 9.5(10-10.5)cm, 3¾(4-4⅛)in, apart. Sew 4 buttons to the loops on right front of each section if for a boy or left front for a girl.

SCARF, ROLL COLLAR HOOD WITH VISOR, LEGWARMERS AND CHILD'S MITTENS

CHECKLIST

Materials
Scarf *Laine Plassard* Florès: 4 balls of No 9, yellow. Pair of needles size 5mm.

Roll Collar *Bouton d'Or* 100 per cent Mohair Gratté: *2 balls of Prunelle, pink. pair each of needles size 5mm and 6mm.*

Hood with Visor *Ann Blatt Soft'Anny Kid Mohair: 2 balls of No 1349, blue. Pair each of needles size 4½mm and 5mm.*

Leg-warmers *Bouton d'Or 11 per cent Mohair Gratté: 2 balls of Prunelle, pink (**A**), and 1 ball of Anemone (**B**). Pair of 5mm needles.*

Child's Mittens *Berger du Nord Kid Mohair: 1 ball of No 8246, coral. Pair each of needles size 3mm and 4mm.*

Sizes
Scarf, roll collar hood with visor and leg-warmers are adult sized, and can easily be adjusted to be larger or smaller. Mittens are in two sizes, to fit ages 6 (8) years.

CHILD'S JACKET

left front — 14 (15-16) / 19 (20-21.5) / 50 (53-57) / 22 (24-26)

back — 14 (15-16) 14 (16-17) 14 (15-16) / 19 (20-21.5) / 54 (58-62) / 42 (46-49)

sleeves — 38 (40-43) / 34 (37-40) / 28 (32-33)

INSTRUCTIONS

■ **Scarf** Cast on 35 sts and work in rib.

■ *1st row* (right side) K 2, * p 1, k 1; rep from * to last st, k 1.

■ *2nd row* K 1, * p 1, k 1; rep from * to end. Rep these 2 rows until work measures 210cm (82½in) from beg. Cast off in rib.

■ **Roll Collar** Using smaller needles, cast on 90 sts and work in double rib.

■ *1st row* (right side) K 2, * p 2, k 2; rep from * to end.

■ *2nd row* P 2, * k 2, p 2 *; rep from * to end. Rep these 2 rows until work measures 12cm (4¾in) from beg then change to larger needles and cont in same rib but inc 1 st at both ends of every foll alt row until work measures 30cm (11¾in) from beg. Cast off loosely in rib. Join side edges with a neat

backstitch seam.

■ **Hood with Visor** Beg at lower edge cast on 104 sts using smaller needles and work in single rib for 9cm (3½in).

■ *Dec row* Rib 5, [p 2 tog, rib 2] 24 times, rib 3. Cont on rem 80 sts; change to larger needles and beg with a k row work in st st. Cont until work measures 19cm (7½in) from beg, ending with a p row.

■ **Front Opening** *1st row* K 34 and leave these sts on a spare needle, cast off next 12 sts, k to end. Cont on 34 sts now rem on needle and p 1 row. ** Cast off 3 sts at beg of next row, 2 sts at same edge on next alt row and 1 st on next 3 alt rows then dec 1 st at same edge on foll 4th row. Cont on rem 25 sts until work measures 30cm (11¾in) from beg, ending at opening after a p row. ** Cut yarn and with wrong side facing rejoin

to first group of sts. Cont in same way from ** to ** but ending at side edge after a p row.

■ *Next row* K 25, turn, cast on 30 sts, turn, then k across other group of 25 sts. Cont on these 80 sts in st st until work measures 35cm (13¾in) from beg, ending with a p row then shape top.

■ *1st row* K 3, [k 2 tog, SKPO, k 6] 7 times, k 2 tog, SKPO, k 3. Work 5 rows on rem 64 sts.

■ *7th row* K 2, [k 2 tog, SKPO, k 4] 7 times, k 2 tog, SKPO, k 2. Work 5 rows on rem 48 sts.

■ *13th row* K 1, [k 2 tog, SKPO, k 2] 7 times, k 2 tog, SKPO, k 1. Work 3 rows on rem 32 sts.

■ *17th row* [K 2 tog] 16 times. Cut yarn, thread end through rem 16 sts, draw up tightly and sew securely then join back seam of hood.

■ **Visor** With right side of work

facing and using larger needles, pick up and k 32 sts along cast-on edge at top of front opening. Shape by working shortened rows as foll:

■ *1st row* (wrong side) P 22, turn.

■ *2nd row* K 12, turn; there are 10 sts left unworked at each side.

■ *3rd row* P 16, turn.

■ *4th row* K 20, turn.

■ *5th row* P 23, turn.

■ *6th row* K 26, turn.

■ *7th row* P 29, turn.

■ *8th row* K all the 32 sts. Now k 1 row on wrong side to form a ridge for foldline. Cont in st st beg with another k row and cast off 3 sts at beg of next 4 rows and 4 sts at beg of next 2 rows. Cast off rem 12 sts.

■ **Front Border** With right side of work facing and using smaller needles, pick up and k 54 sts around rem edges of opening, beg and ending next to visor. Work 2 rows in g st. Sew ends of this border at sides of visor; fold last part of visor to inside along fold-line and slip-st cast-off edges in place.

▦ **Leg-warmers** Beg at lower edge cast on 60 sts using **A** and work in single rib. Cont until work measures 20cm (7⅞in) from beg then work 4 rows in **B**, 6 rows in **A**, 4 rows in **B**, 4 rows in **A**. Cast off in rib. Make another leg-warmer in same way. Join back seams.

▦ **Child's Mitts** *Both mitts alike* With smaller needles cast on 26 (30) sts and work in single rib for 4cm (1½in). Change to larger needles and beg with a k row work in st st. Work 2 rows then shape for thumb.

▦ *3rd row* K 12 (14), pick up loop lying between needles and k it through the back = k loop, k 2, k loop, k 12 (14). Work 3 rows.

▦ *7th row* K 12 (14), k loop, k 4, k loop, k 12 (14). Cont to inc in these positions on every foll 4th row once (twice) more. P 1 row on 32 (38) sts.

▦ **Thumb** K 12 (14) and leave these sts on a holder, k next 8 (10) sts, turn leaving rem 12 (14) sts on another holder. Cast on 1 st at beg of next 2 rows then cont on 10 (12) sts until thumb measures 2.5(3)cm, 1(1⅛)in, from beg. On foll row work 2 sts tog all along row, cut yarn, pass end through rem sts, draw up tightly and sew securely. Join thumb seam. With right side facing and using larger needles, pick up and k 2 sts at base of thumb, k rem 12 (14) sts left on second holder.

▦ *Next row* P 14 (16), then p sts from first holder. Cont on 26 (30) sts until work measures 13(15)cm, 5⅛(5⅞)in, from beg, ending with a p row then shape top.

▦ *1st row* K 1, SKPO, k 7 (9), k 2 tog, k 2, SKPO, k 7 (9), k 2 tog, k 1. P 1 row.

▦ *3rd row* K 1, SKPO, k 5 (7), k 2 tog, k 2, SKPO, k 5 (7), k 2 tog, k 1. Cont to dec in same positions on next 2 (3) alt rows.

▦ Cut yarn, pass end through rem sts, draw up tightly and sew securely then join seam along side of hand.

LIGHTNING FLASH

Just the thing for a mutual admiration society of two (or more) members: small children love to be dressed like their parents, so this smart sweater in a two-tone pattern with an embroidered multicoloured zigzag comes in sizes for adults as well as children. Although a father and son are featured here, the adult version provides a comfortable loose fit for a woman, so you could make a sweater for each member of the family, perhaps changing the background colours to add interest and variety.

ADULT'S VERSION

CHECKLIST

Materials
*Laine Marigold 4 fils: 7(7-8) balls of No 8767, dark grey (**A**), and 6(6-7) balls of No 8673, light grey (**B**). For the lightning flash, small amounts of 4-ply yarn in several different bright colours. Pair each of needles size 3mm and 3¾mm.*

Sizes
Three sizes, to fit chest sizes 97 (102-107)cm, 38 (40-42)in, normal fit for a man, or 87 (92-97)cm, 34(36-38)in, loose fit for a woman. Actual measurements shown on diagram.

Stitches used
Single rib; st st; patt, worked from chart; the lightning flash is embroidered on afterwards by the Swiss darning method explained on page 6 and the placing of the motif is explained below.

Tension
Over patt using larger needles, 28 sts and 30 rows to 10cm (4in). Work a sample on 33 sts as given for 1st size on back.

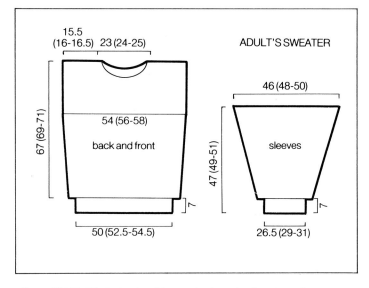

INSTRUCTIONS

■ **Back** With smaller needles and **A**, cast on 131 (137-143) sts and work in rib.
■ ** *1st row* (right side) P 1, * k 1, p 1; rep from * to end.
■ *2nd row* K 1, * p 1, k 1; rep from * to end. Rep these 2 rows until work measures 7cm (2¾in) from beg, ending with a 1st rib row. **
■ *Inc row* Rib 7 (10-13), [inc in next st, rib 12] 9 times, inc in next st, rib 6 (9-12). 141 (147-153) sts. Change to larger needles, join on B and working in st st work patt from chart.
■ *1st row For 1st and 3rd sizes:* k 1 **A**, 1 **B**, 2 **A**, 1 **B**, * 2 **A**, [1 **B**, 1 **A**] 3 times, 1 **B**, 2 **A**, 1 **B**; * rep from * to * ending 2 **A**, 1 **B**, 1 **A**. *For 2nd size:* k 1 **A**, 1 **B**, then rep from * to * as for 1st size ending 1 **A**.

■ *2nd row For 1st and 3rd sizes:* p 2 **A**, 1 **B**, 1 **A**, * 2 **A**, [1 **B**, 1 **A**] 5 times; * rep from * to * ending 2 **A**, 1 **B**, 2 **A**. *For 2nd size:* p 1 **A**, rep from * to * in 1st size row ending 2 **A**. Cont in patt as now set for a further 16 (18-20) rows then inc 1 st at both ends of next row then every foll 20th row 4 times more working extra sts into patt. Cont on 151 (157-163) sts until work measures 65(67-69)cm, 25⅝(26⅜-27⅞)in, from beg, ending with a p row.
■ **Neck Shaping** *1st row* Patt 55 (57-59) and leave these sts of right back on a spare needle, cast off next 41 (43-45) sts, patt to end. Cont on 55 (57-59) sts now rem on needle for left back and work 1 row. Cast off 5 sts at beg of next row and next alt row then dec 1 st at same edge on next 2 rows. Cast

off rem 43 (45-47) sts for shoulder edge. Rejoin yarns to neck edge of right back sts, cast off 5, patt to end. Cast off 5 sts at neck edge on next alt row, dec 1 st at same edge on next 2 rows, work 1 row then cast off rem 43 (45-47) sts.

■ **Front** Work as for back until work measures 61(63-65)cm, 24(24¾-25⅝)in, from beg, ending with a p row.
■ **Neck Shaping** *1st row* Patt 59 (61-63) and leave these sts of left front on a spare needle, cast off next 33 (35-37) sts, patt to end. Cont on 59 (61-63) sts now rem on needle for right front and work 1 row. *** Cast off 4 sts at beg of next row and next alt row, 2 sts at same edge on next 3 alt rows and 1 st on next 2 alt rows. Cont on rem 43 (45-47) sts until work matches back to shoulder edge. Cast off. Rejoin yarns to neck edge of left front sts and complete as for right from *** to end.

■ **Sleeves** With smaller needles and **A** cast on 65 (69-73) sts and work as for back welt from ** to **.
■ *Inc row* Rib 5 (1-4), [inc in next st, rib 5 (5-4)] 9 (11-13) times, inc in next st, rib 5 (1-3). 75 (81-87) sts. Change to larger needles and patt.
■ *For 1st and 3rd sizes:* work as for *2nd size* on back; for *2nd size* work as for *1st and 3rd sizes* on back. Cont thus in patt until 4 rows have been worked then inc 1 st at

both ends of next row then every foll 6th row 2 (5-8) times then every foll 4th row 24 (21-18) times working extra sts into patt. Cont on 129 (135-141) sts until work measures 47(49-51)cm, 18½(19¼-20)in, from beg. Cast off all sts.

■ **Lightning** Use oddments of 4-ply yarn in as many bright colours as possible arranging them to suit your taste. Miss the first 22 (24-26) sts at left-hand edge on 1st row of patt on back and using one of the colours embroider over the next 2 sts; on next 2 sts use another colour and on foll 2 sts a 3rd colour. Move the whole group of 6 sts 1 st over to the right on every row, joining on new colours to give a random effect. Cont moving the group of 6 sts over to the right until a point 31(32-33)cm, 12¼(12⅝-13)in, from cast-on edge of back then change direction and move the group back towards the left on every row until the point 49(51-53)cm, 19¼(20-20¾)in, above cast-on edge is reached. Now change direction again and cont to top edge. Work similar line on front; this line will end at the neck. On sleeve work a short line beg 16 (18-20) sts from left-hand edge of sleeve and moving to the right 1 st at a time for the first 28 rows then back again for 27 rows to end in same position.

■ **Neck border** Join right

shoulder seam. With right side of work facing and using smaller needles and **A**, pick up and k 83 (85-87) sts around front neck edge and 68 (70-72) sts across back neck. 151 (155-159) sts. Beg with 2nd row work in rib for 5cm (2in). Cast off loosely in rib.

■ **Finishing** Join left shoulder

seam and ends of neck border. Fold border in half to wrong side; slip-st cast-off edge to back of picked-up sts. Mark sides 23(24-25)cm, 9(9½-9¾)in down from shoulder seam. Join in sleeves between markers. Join side and sleeve seams.

CHILD'S VERSION

CHECKLIST

Materials
*Laine Marigold 4 fils: 3 (3-3) balls of No 8673, light grey (**A**), and 3 (3-3) balls of No 8767, dark grey (**B**). Small amounts of 4-ply yarn for the lightning flash. Pair each of needles size 3mm and 3¾mm.*

Sizes
Three sizes, to fit ages 4 (6-8) years. Actual measurements shown on diagram.

Stitches used and tension are the same as for the adult version.

INSTRUCTIONS

■ **Back** With smaller needles and **B** cast on 87 (93-99) sts and work in rib as on adult's sweater for 5cm (2in), ending with a 1st rib row.
■ *Inc row* Rib 8 (11-14), [inc in next st, rib 13] 5 times, inc in next st, rib 8 (11-14). 93 (99-105) sts. Change to larger needles and working in st st work patt from chart. All sizes fit in same way as for adult's sweater but note the change of colour; light grey is used

for the background and dark grey for the patt. Cont in patt until 14 (16-18) rows have been worked then inc 1 st at both ends of next row then every foll 14th row 3 times more, working extra sts into patt. Cont on 101 (107-113) sts until work measures 40(43-46)cm, 15¾(17-18)in, from beg, ending with a p row.
■ **Neck Shaping** *1st row* Patt 39 (41-43) and leave these sts of right back on a spare needle, cast off next 23 (25-27) sts, patt to end. Cont on 39 (41-43) sts now rem on needle for left back and work 1 row. Cast off 4 sts at beg of next row and next alt row then dec 1 st at same edge on next 2 rows. Cast off rem 29 (31-33) sts for shoulder edge. Rejoin yarn to neck edge of right back sts, cast off 4, patt to end. Cast off 4 sts at same edge on next alt row, dec 1 st at same edge on next 2 rows, work 1 row then cast off rem 29 (31-33) sts.

■ **Front** Work as for back until work measures 37(40-43)cm, 14½(15¾-17)in, from beg, ending with a p row.
■ **Neck Shaping** *1st row* Patt 40 (42-44) and leave these sts of left front on a spare needle, cast off next 21 (23-25) sts, patt to end. Cont on 40 (42-44) sts now rem on needle for right front and work 1 row. *** Cast off 4 sts at beg of next row, 2 sts at same edge on next 3 alt rows and 1 st on next alt row. Cont on rem 29 (31-33) sts until work matches back to shoulder edge. Cast off all sts. Rejoin yarns to neck edge of left front sts and complete as for right front from *** to end.

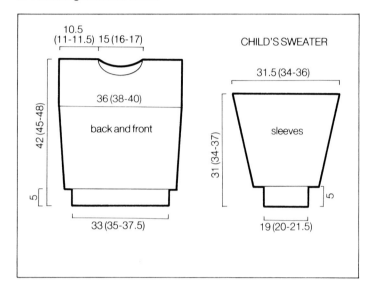

CHILD'S SWEATER

10.5 (11-11.5) 15 (16-17)

36 (38-40)

back and front

42 (45-48)

5

33 (35-37.5)

CHILD'S SWEATER

31.5 (34-36)

sleeves

31 (34-37)

5

19 (20-21.5)

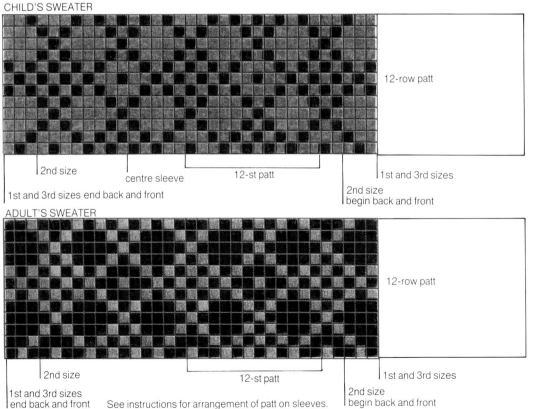

CHILD'S SWEATER

2nd size

centre sleeve   12-st patt

1st and 3rd sizes end back and front

12-row patt

1st and 3rd sizes

2nd size begin back and front

ADULT'S SWEATER

2nd size

12-st patt

1st and 3rd sizes end back and front   See instructions for arrangement of patt on sleeves.

12-row patt

1st and 3rd sizes

2nd size begin back and front

▦ **Sleeves** With smaller needles and **B** cast on 47 (49-53) sts and work in rib as for adult's sweater for 5cm (2in), ending with a 1st rib row.

▦ *Inc row* Rib 6 (3-5), [inc in next st, rib 6 (5-5)] 5 (7-7) times, inc in next st, rib 5 (3-5). 53 (57-61) sts. Change to larger needles and work in patt.

▦ *1st row 1st size* K [1 **A**, 1 **B**] 3 times, * 2 **A**, 1 **B**, 2 **A**, [1 **B**, 1 **A**] 3 times, 1 **B**; * rep from * to * twice more, 2 **A**, 1 **B**, 2 **A**, [1 **B**, 1 **A**] 3 times.

▦ *2nd size* K [1 **A**, 1 **B**] 4 times, rep from * to * in 1st size row 4 times, 1 **A**.

▦ *3rd size* K 1 **B**, 2 **A**, [1 **B**, 1 **A**] 3 times, 1 **B** rep from * to * in 1st size row 4 times, 2 **A**, 1 **B**.

▦ *All sizes* Cont in patt as now set for 4 more rows then inc 1 st at both ends of next row, then every foll 6th row 0 (2-4) times, then every foll 4th row 17(16-15) times working extra sts into patt. Cont on 89 (95-101) sts until work measures 31(34-37)cm, 12¼(13⅜-14½)in, from beg. Cast off all sts.

▦ **Lightning Flash** Work as for adult's sweater beg the line 22 (24-26) sts from left side edge on 1st patt row of back and front and moving it to the right 1 st on every row. Change direction 17(19-21)cm, 6¾(7½-8¼)in, above cast-on edge, moving to the left for the next 10(11-12)cm, 4(4¼-4¾)in, then move to the right for remainder of back or front. On sleeves begin the line 12 (14-16) sts from left side edge and move right for 24 rows then left for the next 23 rows.

▦ **Neck border** Join right shoulder seam. With right side of work facing and using smaller needles and **B**, pick up and k 59 (61-63) sts around front neck edge and 46 (48-50) sts across back neck. 105 (109-113) sts. Beg with 2nd row work in rib for 4cm (1½in), then cast off loosely in rib.

▦ **Finishing** As for adult's sweater placing markers for armholes 16(17-18)cm, 6¼(6¾-7⅛)in, down from shoulders.

SCANDINAVIAN SNOWFLAKES

Here's a tough family, all set to go cross-country skiing – Norwegian style – in their richly patterned sweaters; but note that there is plenty of room for additional warm clothing under these outsize knits. The girl wears the same size and shape sweater as the man, though the patterning is different and his version has a roll collar. The child's sweater is a smaller version of the mother's, with the snowflake motifs reversed out. Even the baby joins in with a matching sleeping bag. There are two cosy, double thickness scarfs; other accessories are purchased.

SLEEPING BAG

CHECKLIST

Materials
*Laine Marigold 4 fils: 4 balls of No 8098, pale rose (**A**), and 3 balls of No 8623, red (**B**). Pair each of needles size 4mm and 4½mm; 6 red buttons.*

Size
One size, to fit baby from birth to 3 months. Actual measurements shown on diagram.

Stitches used
Single rib; st st; patt, *worked from charts as explained below. Strand yarn not in use loosely across wrong side of work to keep fabric elastic and weave in only when working across 5 or more sts. Take great care to position patt correctly each time, by matching centre of work to centre of chart. Read k rows from right to left and p rows from left to right.*

Tension
For Sleeping bag and for Man's and Girl's sweaters: over patt using 4½mm needles, 23 sts and 24 rows to 10cm (4in). Work a sample on 34 sts.

INSTRUCTIONS

▨ **Back** With larger needles and **A** cast on 65 sts. Beg with a k row, work in st st. Work 4 rows, casting on 4 sts at beg of first 2 rows, then 3 sts at beg of next 2 rows. 79 sts.
▨ Now begin working from charts. * Work 19 rows of Chart 2, 1 row in **A**, 7 rows of Chart 9, 33 rows of Chart 6, 7 rows of Chart 1, * 2 rows in **A**; rep from * to * once more, 1 row in **A**, then 1 row in **B**, *at the same time* casting on 3 sts at beg of first 4 rows, 2 sts at beg of next 2 rows, then 1 st at beg of next 2 rows, work 8 rows straight, then dec 1 st at each end of next and every foll 8th row until 73 sts rem. 142 rows have been worked

from beg. Break off **B**.
▨ **Neck Shaping** *143rd row* K 25 and leave these sts of right back on a spare needle, cast off next 23 sts, then k to end. Cont on 25 sts now rem on needle for left back. Change to smaller needles and work in rib.
▨ *1st row* (wrong side) K 1, * p 1, k 1; rep from * to end.
▨ *2nd row* P 1, * k 1, p 1; rep from * to end. Rep these 2 rows once more, then the 1st row again. Cast off in rib. Rejoin **A** to neck edge of right back sts and rib to end. Cont to match first side.

▨ **Front** Work as given for back until 133 rows in all have been worked, keeping patt correct to

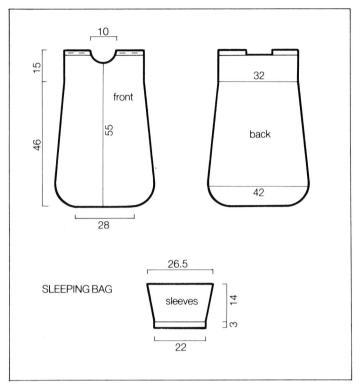

10

15

front

55

46

28

SLEEPING BAG

32

back

42

26.5

sleeves

14

3

22

match back.

▦ **Neck Shaping** *134th row* Patt 32 and leave these sts of right front on a spare needle, cast off next 9 sts, then patt to end. Cont on 32 sts now rem on needle for left front; work 1 row straight. Cast off at neck edge 3 sts at beg of next row, 2 sts at beg of foll alt row, then 1 st at beg of foll 2 alt rows. 25 sts. Break off **B**. Work 1 row straight, then work 1 row in rib as on back.
▦ *Next row* Rib 3, [cast off 2 sts, rib 9] twice.
▦ *Next row* Rib to end, casting on 2 sts over each 2 cast off. Work 2 more rows as set, then cast off in rib. Rejoin yarns to neck edge of right front sts, cast off 3 sts and patt to end. Cont to match first side, reversing shaping and position of buttonholes.

▦ **Sleeves** With smaller needles and **A** cast on 51 sts and beg with a 2nd row, work in rib as on shoulders for 3cm (1¼in), ending with a 1st rib row. Change to larger needles. Beg with a k row work in st st. Work 7 rows of Chart 1, 19 rows of Chart 2, 7 rows of Chart 1, then 1 row in **A**, *at the same time* inc 1 st at both ends of the 5th and

every foll 6th row until there are 61 sts. Cast off *loosely*.

▦ **Back Neck Border** With smaller needles, **A** and right side facing, pick up and k 41 sts evenly around back neck. Work 5 rows in rib as on shoulders. Cast off in rib.

▦ **Front Neck Border** With smaller needles, **A** and right side facing, pick up and k 49 sts evenly around front neck. Work 1 row in rib as on shoulders.
▦ *Next row* Rib 3, cast off 2 sts, rib 39, cast off 2 sts, rib 3.
▦ *Next row* Rib to end, casting on 2 sts over each 2 cast off. Work 2 more rows as set, then cast off in rib.

▦ **Finishing** At this stage darn in all loose ends. Lay front ribs on top of back ribs and catch down at armhole edge. On each side edge mark a point 13cm (5⅛in) down from shoulder line for armholes and sew cast-off edge of sleeves between marked points. Join side, sleeve and lower edge seams matching patt. Sew on buttons.

GIRL'S SCARF

CHECKLIST

Materials
*Laine Marigold 3 fils: 3 balls of No 8623, red (**A**), and 5 balls of No 8690, banana (**B**). Pair of needles size 4mm.*

Size
168cm (66in) long and 20cm (7¾in) wide.

Stitches used
As for Sleeping bag.

Tension
Over patt using needles given, 30 sts and 31 rows to 10cm (4in). Work a sample on 34 sts.

INSTRUCTIONS

▦ **First Section** With smaller needles and **A**, cast on 61 sts. Beg with a k row, work in st st. Work [8 rows of Chart 8, 25 rows of Chart 5, 7 rows of Chart 9, 33 rows of Chart 6, 1 row in **B**, 27 rows of Chart 3, 4 rows in **A**, 1 row in **B**, 2 rows in **A**, 19 rows of Chart 2, 1 row in **B**, 2 rows in **A**] twice. This is now the centre of work.
▦ Reverse patt for second half, that is read charts from top to

bottom thus making a mirror image of first half. Cast off using **A**.

▦ **Section Section** With smaller needles and **B** cast on 60 sts. Beg with a k row cont in st st until work measures the same as first piece, ending with a p row. Cast off.

▦ **Finishing** At this stage darn in all loose ends. With right side tog, join seams, leaving gap for turning. Turn right side out and close.

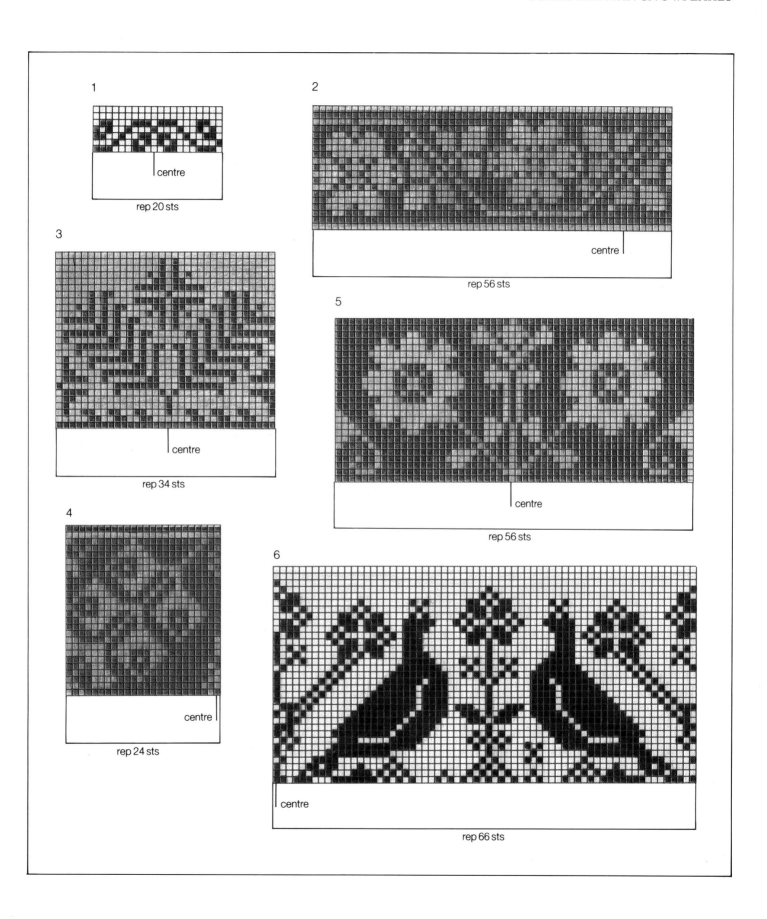

1

centre

rep 20 sts

2

centre

rep 56 sts

3

centre

rep 34 sts

5

centre

rep 56 sts

4

centre

rep 24 sts

6

centre

rep 66 sts

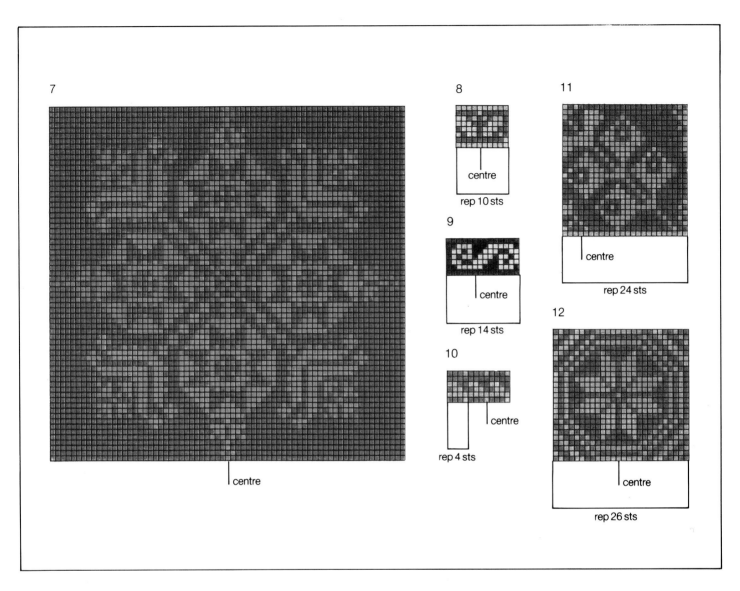

MAN'S SWEATER

CHECKLIST

Materials
Laine Marigold 4 fils: 9 balls of No 8690, yellow (A), and 6 balls of No 8740, blueberry (B). Pair each of needles size 3mm, 4mm and 4½mm.

Size
One size only, to fit 107/112cm (42/44in) chest.

Stitches used and tension
As for Sleeping bag.

INSTRUCTIONS

▦ **Back** With 4mm needles and **A** cast on 141 sts and work in rib.

▦ *1st row* (right side) P 1, * k 1, p 1; rep from * to end.

▦ *2nd row* K 1, * p 1, k 1; rep from * to end. Rep these 2 rows until work measures 6cm (2⅜in) from beg, ending with a 2nd rib row. Change to 4½mm needles and beg with a k row work in st st. **

▦ Work 19 rows of Chart 2, [1 row in **A**, 7 rows of Chart 9, 33 rows of Chart 6, 7 rows of Chart 1, 1 row in **A**, 19 rows of Chart 2, 2 rows in **A**] twice. 159 rows have been worked in st st. Working in patt from Chart 1:

▦ *** **Neck Shaping** *160th row* Patt 60 and leave these sts of left back on a spare needle, cast off next 21 sts, then patt to end. Cont on 60 sts now rem on needle for right back; work 1 row straight. Cast off at neck edge 9 sts at beg of next and foll alt row. 42 sts.

Work 2 rows straight, then cast off. Rejoin yarns to neck edge of left back sts, cast off 9 sts and patt to end. Cont to match first side, reversing shaping.

▦ **Front** Work as given for back until 145 rows have been worked in st st. Keep patt matching back.

▦ **Neck Shaping** *146th row* Patt 65 and leave these sts of right front on a spare needle, cast off next 11 sts, then patt to end. Cont on 65 sts now rem on needle for left front; work 1 row straight.

▦ Cast off at neck edge 5 sts at beg of next row, 4 sts at beg of foll alt row, 3 sts at beg of foll 3 alt rows, 2 sts at beg of foll 2 alt rows,

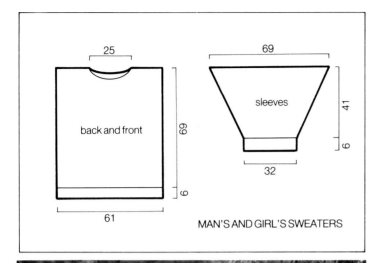

MAN'S AND GIRL'S SWEATERS

then 1 st at beg of foll alt row. 42 sts. Work 4 rows straight. Cast off. Rejoin yarns to neck edge of right front sts, cast off 5 sts and patt to end. Cont to match first side, reversing shaping.

▦ **Sleeves** With 4mm needles and **A** cast on 73 sts and work in rib as on back welt for 6cm (2⅜in), ending with a 2nd rib row. Change to 4½mm needles. Beg with a k row work in st st. ※※※ Work 1 row. Now begin working from charts. Work 19 rows of Chart 2, 7 rows of Chart 1, 19 rows of Chart 2, 3 rows in **A**, 7 rows of Chart 9, 33 rows of Chart 6, 7 rows of Chart 1, 3 rows in **A**, *at the same time* inc 1 st at both ends of the 5th and every foll 4th row until there are 81 sts, then every foll alt row until there are 159 sts. Cast off *loosely*.

▦ **Collar** With 3mm needles and **A** cast on 143 sts. Beg with a k row work 4 rows in st st.
▦ *5th row* P to end. Change to 4½mm needles and beg with a p row work in st st. Work 4 rows. Now begin working from charts. Beg with row 3, work 17 rows of Chart 2, 3 rows in **A**, 7 rows of Chart 1, 2 rows **A**. Cast off, knitting 2 sts tog across the row.
▦ **Finishing** At this stage darn in all loose ends. Join shoulder seams. On each side edge mark a point 34.5cm (13½in) down from shoulder seam for armholes and sew cast off edge of sleeves between marked points. Join side and sleeve seams. Join ends of collar to form a circle. Fold cast on edge in on p ridge and slip-st hem. With seam to centre back neck, sew cast off edge of collar to neck.

GIRL'S SWEATER

CHECKLIST

Materials
*Laine Marigold 4 fils: 10 balls of No 8685, Van Dyck red (**A**), and 5 balls of No 8626, periwinkle blue (**B**). Pair each of needles size 4mm and 4½mm; set of four double-pointed needles size 4mm.*

Size
One size, to fit 87/92cm (34/36in) bust very loosely.

Stitches used and tension
As for Sleeping bag.

INSTRUCTIONS

▦ **Back** Work as given for Man's sweater to ※※. Work 3 rows in **A**, 1 row in **B**, then 2 rows in **A**. Now begin working from charts. Work 19 rows of Chart 2, 3 rows in **A**, 27 rows of Chart 3, 3 rows in **A**, 26 rows of Chart 4, 25 rows of Chart 12, 26 rows of Chart 11, 2 rows in **A**, 6 rows of Chart 10, 16 rows of Chart 2. 159 rows have been worked in st st.
▦ Working 3 more rows of Chart 2, then 4 rows in **A**, read as given for Man's sweater from ※※※ on back neck shaping to ※※※ on sleeves. Work 2 rows in **A**.
▦ Now begin working from charts. Work 6 rows of Chart 10, 1 row in **B**, 3 rows in **A**, 26 rows of Chart 4, 25 rows of Chart 12, 26 rows of Chart 11, 2 rows in **A**, 6 rows of Chart 10, 1 row in **A**, *at the same time* inc 1 st at both ends of the 5th and every foll 4th row until there are 81 sts, then every foll alt row until there are 159 sts. Cast off *loosely*.

▦ **Neckband** Join shoulder seams. With set of four double-pointed needles and **A**, pick up and k 160 sts evenly round neck edge. Work 3cm (1¼in) in rounds of single rib. Cast off *loosely* in rib.

▦ **Finishing** Darn in loose ends. Put markers on side edges 34.5cm (13½in) down from shoulders. Sew cast-off edge of sleeves between markers. Join side and sleeve seams.

WOMAN AND CHILD'S SCARF

CHECKLIST

Materials
Woman's version *Malourène Elk: 1 skein each of No 24, turquoise* (**A**), *and No 601, red* (**B**). *Pair of needles size 3¾mm.*

Child's version *Chat Botté Nénuphar: 3 balls of No 4689, bright green* (**A**), *5 balls of No 4600, ruby* (**B**). *Pair of needles size 3¾mm.*

Size
One size only; 181.5cm (71½in) long and 27cm (10¾in) wide. Work a sample on 34 sts.

Stitches used
As for Sleeping bag.

Tension
For Woman and Child's scarf and sweaters: over patt using needles given, 25 sts and 32 rows to 10cm (4in). Work a sample on 34 sts.

INSTRUCTIONS

▦ With needles given and **A**, cast on 69 sts. Beg with a k row work in st st. Work 5 rows. Now begin working from charts. Work [67 rows of Chart 7, 5 rows in **A**] 8 times. Cast off using **A**.

▦ With given needles and **B** cast on 68 sts. Beg with a k row cont in st st until work measures the same as first piece, ending with a p row. Cast off.

▦ **Finishing** As for Girl's scarf.

WOMAN AND CHILD'S SWEATER

CHECKLIST

Materials
Malourène Elk: 3 (2½) skeins of No 24, turquoise (**A** *child,* **B** *mother), and 1 (5) skeins of No 60, red* (**B** *child,* **A** *mother). Pair each of needles size 3mm and 3¾mm.*

Sizes
Two sizes: small, to fit a child aged 6 to 8 years loosely; large, to fit 92/97cm (36/38in) bust. Actual measurements shown on diagram.

Stitches used
As for Sleeping bag.

Tension
As for Mother and Child's scarf.

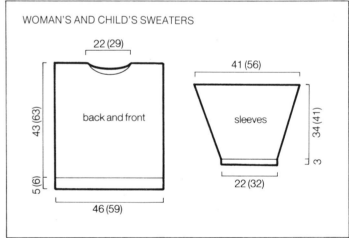

WOMAN'S AND CHILD'S SWEATERS

22 (29)

43 (63)

back and front

5 (6)

46 (59)

41 (56)

sleeves

34 (41)

3

22 (32)

INSTRUCTIONS

▦ **Back** With smaller needles and **A** cast on 115 (147) sts and work in rib as on back welt of Man's sweater for 5(6)cm, 2(2⅜)in, ending with a 2nd rib row.

▦ Change to larger needles and beg with a k row work in st st. Work 2 rows. Now begin working from charts. Work 0 (8) rows of Chart 8, 27 (25) rows of Chart 3 (5), 18 (40) rows in **A**, 67 rows of Chart 7, placing motif in centre with sts at each end in **A**, 14 (23) rows in **A**, 0 (27) rows of Chart 3, but reading chart from top to bottom thus reversing patt, 1 row in **A**, 2 rows of Chart 1. 131 (195) rows have been worked in st st. Work 5 more rows of Chart 1, then 2 rows in **A**.

▦ **Neck Shaping** *Next row* Patt 47 (58) and leave these sts of left back on a spare needle, cast off next 21 (31) sts, then patt to end. Cont on 47 (58) sts now rem on needle for right back; work 1 row straight.

▦ Cast off at neck edge 7 sts at beg of next row, then 5 (7) sts at beg of foll 2 alt rows. 30 (37) sts.

▦ Rejoin yarn to neck edge of left back sts, cast off 7 sts and patt to end. Cont to match first side, reversing shaping.

▦ **Front** Work as given for back until 117 (175) rows have been worked in st st. Keeping patt correct to match back:

▦ **Neck Shaping** *Next row* Patt 48 (59) and leave these sts of right front on a spare needle, cast off next 19 (29) sts, then patt to end. Cont on 48 (59) sts now rem on needle for left front; work 1 row straight. Cast off at neck edge 2 sts at beg of next and every foll alt row until 30 (37) sts rem. Work 2 (4) rows straight. Cast off. Rejoin yarns to neck edge of right front sts, cast off 2 sts and patt to end. Cont to match first side, reversing shaping.

▦ **Sleeves** With smaller needles and **A** cast on 55 (81) sts and work in rib as on back welt for 3cm (1¼in) ending with a 2nd rib row. Change to larger needles. Beg with a k row work in st st. Work 1 row. Now begin working from charts. Work 7 rows of Chart 1, 59 (14) rows in **A**, 0 (67) rows of Chart 7 placing motif in centre, 12 rows in **A**, 27 rows of Chart 3 with patt reversed, 2 rows in **A**, *at the same time*, inc 1 st at both ends of the 5th and every foll 6th row until there are 65 (91) sts, then every foll 4th row until there are 103 (141) sts. Cast off *loosely*.

▦ **Neckband** Join left shoulder seam. With smaller needles, **A** and right side facing, pick up and k 139 (179) sts evenly along neck edge. Beg with a 2nd row, work 2(3)cm, ¾(1⅛)in, in rib as on back welt. Cast off *loosely* in rib.

▦ **Finishing** At this stage darn in all loose ends. Join right shoulder and neckband seam. On each side edge mark a point 20.5(28)cm, 8(11)in, down from shoulder seams for armholes and sew cast-off edge of sleeves between marked points. Join sides and sleeve seams.

PAISLEY PAIR

This time it is a father and and daughter who are relaxing together, in sweaters decorated with traditional Paisley motifs, though the design could just as easily be for father and son. Knitted in a luxurious alpaca yarn, both sweaters are identical in their patterning and their drop-shoulder styling, but they are knitted in different colour schemes. Back, front and sleeves are each made in two panels which are then joined down the centre. Use the colours in separate balls to avoid having long strands across the back.

CHILD'S SWEATER

CHECKLIST

Materials
Anny Blatt Alpaga: 2 balls of No 2047, larch green (A), and 2 balls of No 1497, mulberry (B). Anny Blatt No 4: 2 balls of No 1563, emerald (C), and 1 ball of No 1564, petrol (D). Pair each of needles size 3mm and 3¼mm.

Sizes
Two sizes, to fit ages 6 to 7 (8 to 9) years. Actual measurements shown on diagram.

Stitches used
Single rib; st; patt worked from charts as explained below.
Square No 1 This consists of 4 (6) rows worked in A, 41 rows working from Chart No 1, then 3 (5) rows in A. When working the patt begin at position indicated according to size, work the sts of patt twice on back and front, once on sleeves, cont to end of row and mark the last st worked; next row will begin at this point.
Square No 2 This consists of 4 (6) rows worked in B, 4 rows working from Chart No 2, then 3 (5) rows in B. When working patt, begin at position indicated according to size, work the sts of patt 3 times on back and front, once on sleeves, cont to end of row and mark the last st worked; next row will begin at this point.

Tension
Over st st, using 3¼mm needles and Alpaga, 29 sts and 37 rows to 10cm (4in). Work a sample on 35 sts; patt will give the same tension.

INSTRUCTIONS

▥ **Back** With smaller needles and **A** cast on 117 (125) sts and work in rib.
▥ *1st row* (right side) P 1, * k 1, p 1; rep from * to end.
▥ *2nd row* K 1 * p 1, k 1; rep from * to end. Rep these two rows until work measures 4cm (1½in) from beg, ending with a 1st rib row.
▥ *Inc row* Rib 10 (6), [inc in next st, rib 15 (13)] 6 (8) times, inc in next st, rib 10 (6). 124 (134) sts. Change to larger needles and patt, dividing work at centre.

▥ *1st row* With **A**, k 61 (66), inc in next st, turn and cont on these 63 (68) sts, leaving rem 62 (67) sts on a spare needle. This row counts as 1st row of Square No 1.
▥ Cont on sts for right back and complete Square No 1 then begin a Square No 2; after working 30 (34) rows of this square cast off 3 sts at beg of next row for armhole shaping.
▥ Cont on rem 60 (65) sts until square is completed then work a Square No 1, placing motifs in same positions as on previous square worked in this patt. Cont

until 43rd (47th) row of this square has been worked thus ending at centre.
▥ **Neck Shaping** Cast off 15 sts at beg of next row and 5 (6) sts at same edge on next 2 alt rows. This completes the square. Cast off rem 35 (38) sts for shoulder.
▥ With right side facing and using **B**, rejoin yarn to group of sts left unworked after welt, inc in 1st st, k to end. Cont on these 63 (68) sts for left back, work rem rows of Square No 2, then work a square No 1 and then a Square No 2. Work armhole shaping 1 row below that of right back and begin neck shaping 1 row below right back; after last shaping row work 1 row then cast off rem 35 (38) sts.

▥ **Front** Work as for back working squares in same positions; right back will thus be

left front and vice versa. Work armhole shaping after 30 (34) rows of second square worked, then cont on rem 60 (65) sts until 33 (35) rows of third square have been worked thus ending at centre.
▥ **Neck Shaping** Cast off 10 sts at beg of next row, 4 sts at same edge on next 2 alt rows, 2 sts on next 2 (3) alt rows and 1 st on next 3 alt rows. This completes the square. Cast off rem 35 (38) sts for shoulder. Work right front as for left back with squares in same order. Work armhole shaping 1 row below that of left front and begin neck shaping 1 row below left front; after last shaping row work 1 row then cast off rem 35 (38) sts.

▥ **Sleeves** Both alike. With smaller needles and **A** cast on 61 (65) sts and work in rib as on back welt but cont until work measures

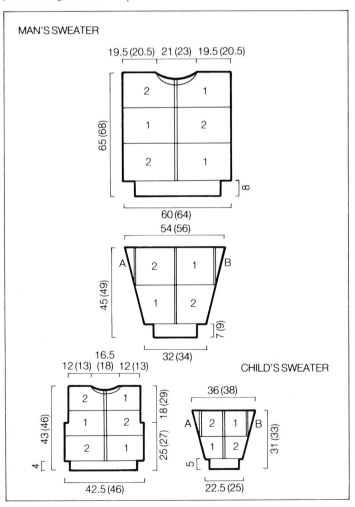

114

5cm (2in) from beg, ending with a 1st rib row.

⊞ *Inc row* Rib 6 (2), [inc in next st, rib 11 (9)] 4 (6) times, inc in next row rib 6 (2). 66 (72) sts. Change to larger needles and patt, dividing work at centre: change to **B**.

⊞ *1st row* K 32 (35), inc in next st, turn and cont on these 34 (37) sts leaving rem sts on a spare needle. Cont working a Square No 2 but inc 1 st at side edge on every foll 6th row 7 times then cont on these 41 (44) sts until this square is completed. Cont without shaping and work a Square No 1; when this is completed cast of all sts. Return to sts left unworked and with right side facing join on **A**, inc in 1st st, k 32 (35). Cont working a Square No 1 with incs at side edge in same way as on first half of sleeve then a Square No 2 without shaping. Cast off.

⊞ **Triangular Insertions** With larger needles and **B** cast on 3 sts and work in st st beg with a k row. Work 2 (4) rows then inc 1 st at beg of next row then at same edge on every foll 4th row 11 times more.

MAN'S SWEATER

CHECKLIST

Materials
Anny Blatt Alpaga: *5 balls of No 1770, caramel* (**A**), *and 5 balls of No 1759, pumpkin* (**B**). *Anny Blatt* No 4: *5 balls of No 1565, mustard* (**C**), *and 3 balls of No 1566, copper* (**D**). *Pair each of needles size 3mm and 3¼mm.*

Sizes
Two sizes, to fit 97/102 (107/112)cm, 38/40 (42/44)in, chest. Actual measurements shown on diagram.

Stitches used
Single rib; st st; patt, *worked from charts as explained below.*
Square No 1 *This consists of 4 (6) rows worked in* **A**, *60 rows of patt from Chart No 1, then 6 (8) rows in* **A**. *When working patt begin at position indicated according to size, work the sts of patt 3 times on back and front, once on sleeves, then cont to end of row and mark the last st worked; next row will begin at this point.*
Square No 2 *This consists of 2 (4) rows worked in* **B**, *then 65 rows in patt from Chart No 2, then 3 (5) rows in* **B**. *When working patt begin at position indicated according to size; work the sts of patt 4 times on back and front, twice on sleeves, then cont to end of row and mark last st worked; next row will begin at this point.*

Tension
As for Child's sweater.

Cont on 15 sts until 48 (52) rows have been worked. Work another triangle in same way but using **A** and reversing shapings. Two triangles are needed for each sleeve.

⊞ **Neck Border** With smaller needles and **A** cast on 123 (129) sts and work in rib as on welt for 10 rows. Cast off loosely in rib.

⊞ **Finishing** Join seam at centre back, centre front and along centre of each sleeve making neat backstitch seams. Sew straight side edge of each triangle to sides of the second square worked on each sleeve so that the triangle in **B** is joined to side of Square No 1 and the triangle in **A** is joined to side of Square No 2. Sew cast-off edge of sleeves to sides of armholes and sew armhole shapings to a corresponding depth on sides of sleeves. Join side and sleeve seams. Join ends of neck border; placing seam level with left shoulder seam sew cast-on edge of neck border to neck edges.

INSTRUCTIONS

⊞ **Back** With smaller needles and **A** cast on 163 (173) sts and work in rib as for Child's sweater; cont until work measures 8cm (3⅛in) from beg, ending with a 1st rib row.

⊞ *Inc row* Rib 6 (8), [inc in next st, rib 14 (12)] 10 (12) times, inc in next st, rib 6 (8). 174 (186) sts. Change to larger needles and patt, dividing work at centre.

⊞ *1st row* With **A**, k 86 (92), inc in next st, turn and cont on these sts for right back, leaving rem sts on a spare needle. Cont on 88 (94) sts; this row counts as 1st row of Square No 1. Work rem row of this square, then work a Square No 2, the another Square No 1; cont until 65 (69) rows of this square have been worked, thus ending at centre.

⊞ **Neck Shaping** Cast off 18 sts at beg of next row and 7 (8) sts at same edge on next 2 alt rows. This completes the square. Cast off rem 56 (60) sts for shoulder edge.

⊞ With right side facing and using **B**, rejoin yarn to group of sts left unworked after welt, inc in 1st st, k to end. Cont on these 88 (94) sts for left back; work rem rows of Square No 2, then work a Square No 1, then another Square No 2. Begin neck shaping 1 row before that of right back and after last shaping row work 1 row on rem 56 (60) sts then cast off.

⊞ **Front** Work as for back, working squares in same positions; right back will thus be left front and vice versa. Cont until 49 (51) rows of third square are worked thus ending at centre.

⊞ **Neck Shaping** Cast off 12 sts at beg of next row, 4 sts at same edge on next 2 alt rows, 2 sts on next 4 (5) alt rows and 1 st on next 4 alt rows to complete square. Cast off rem 56 (60) sts for shoulder.

⊞ Work right front as for left back with squares in same order; begin neck shaping after 48 (50) rows of third square working as for left front. After last shaping row work 1 row on rem 56 (60) sts. Cast off.

⊞ **Sleeves** Both alike. With smaller needles and **A** cast on 71

(77) sts and work in rib as for Child's sweater; cont until work measures 7(9)cm, 2¾(3½)in, from beg, ending with a 1st rib row.

⊞ *Inc row* Rib 2 (5), [inc in next st, rib 2] 23 times, rib rem 0 (3) sts. 94 (100) sts. Change to larger needles and patt dividing work at centre; change to **B**.

⊞ *1st row* K 46 (49), inc in next st, turn and cont on these 48 (51) sts leaving rem sts on a spare needle. Cont working a Square No 2 but inc 1 st at side edge on every foll 6th row 5 (7) times then every foll 4th row 9 (7) times. Cont on 62 (65) sts until this square is completed then work a Square No 1 without shaping. Cast off. Return to sts left unworked, join on **A**, inc in 1st st, k 46 (49). Cont on these 48 (51) sts working a Square No 1 with incs at side edge as on first half of sleeve then work a Square No 2 without shaping. Cast off.

⊞ **Triangular Insertions** With larger needles and **B** cast on 3 sts and work in st st beg with a k row. Work 2 (4) rows then inc 1 st at beg of next row then at same edge on every foll 4th row 16 times more. Cont on 20 sts until 70 (74) rows have been worked. Cast off. Work another triangle in same way but using **A** and reversing shapings. Make two triangles per sleeve.

⊞ **Neck Border** With smaller needles and **A** cast on 157 (167) sts and work in rib for 10 rows. Cast off loosely in rib.

⊞ **Finishing** Join seam along centre back, centre front and centre of each sleeve making neat backstitch seams. Sew straight side edge of each triangle to side edge of the second square worked on each sleeve so that the triangle in **B** is joined to side of Square No 1 and triangle in **A** is joined to Square No 2. On each side edge of main part mark a point 27(28)cm, 10⅝(11)in, down from shoulder seam for armholes and sew cast-off edge of sleeves between markers. Join side and sleeve seams. Join ends of neck border; placing seam level with left shoulder seam sew cast-on edge of border to neck edges.

See instructions for arrangement of patt on squares. On Child's sweater work all 46 rows of chart.

On Man's sweater work all 46 rows then from 1st to 14th row again.

See instructions for arrangement of patt on the squares. On Child's sweater work all 41 rows of chart.

On Man's sweater work from 1st to 24th row twice, then from 1st to 17th rows again.

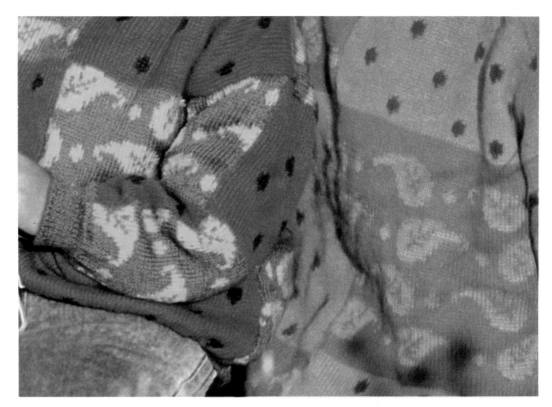

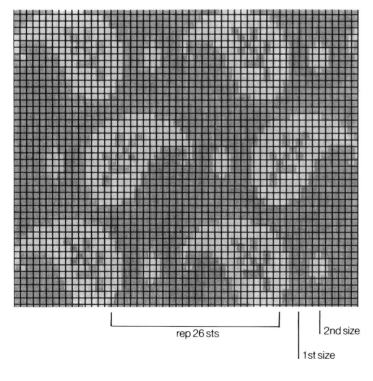

rep 26 sts

2nd size

1st size

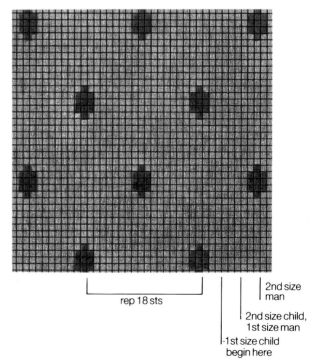

rep 18 sts

2nd size man

2nd size child, 1st size man

1st size child begin here

TWEEDY FAMILY

This family set is modelled on the British country style – all tweeds and casual elegance – but with that extra plus factor of French chic and colour sense. From a sweater for the youngest member of the family, to a cardigan for the head of the clan, all are worked in straightforward block designs, with edges and borders (apart from the girl's sweater) finished in contrast bands of crochet.

MAN'S CARDIGAN

CHECKLIST

Materials
La Droguerie Tweed: *350(400)g of green (**A**). Surnaturelle: 150(150)g of pale yellow (**B**), 60g of apricot and 30g of silver grey. Pair each of needles size 2¾mm and 4½mm; small size crochet hook; 4 buttons.*

Sizes
Two sizes, to fit 97/102(107/112)cm, 38/40(42/44)in chest. Actual measurements shown on diagram.

Stitches used
Single rib; st st; patt, worked from charts as explained below. Strand yarn not in use loosely across wrong side of work to keep fabric elastic and weave in only when working across 5 or more sts. Take great care to position patt correctly each time. Read k rows from right to left and p rows from left to right.

Tension
Over patt using 4½mm needles, 25 sts and 25 rows to 10cm (4in). Work a sample on 30 sts.

INSTRUCTIONS

▦ **Back** With smaller needles and **B**, cast on 137 (149) sts. Break off **B**, join in **A** and work in rib.
▦ *1st row* (right side) P 1, * k 1, p 1; rep from * to end.
▦ *2nd row* K 1, * p 1, k 1; rep from * to end. Rep these 2 rows until work measures 5cm (2in) from beg, ending with a 2nd rib row and inc one st in centre of last row. 138 (150) sts. Change to larger needles and beg with a k row work in st st. Cont in patt from Chart until work measures 37(39)cm, 14½(15⅜)in, from beg, ending with a p row.
▦ **Raglan Shaping** Keeping patt correct, dec one st at each end of next 43 (51) rows, then every foll alt row until 38 (40) sts rem, ending

with a p row. Cast off.

▦ **Pocket Linings** (make 2) With larger needles and **A** cast on 33 (35) sts. Beg with a k row cont in st st until work measures 9(10)cm, 3½(4)in, from beg, ending with a p row. Leave sts on a spare needle.

▦ **Left Front** With smaller needles and **B** cast on 69 (75) sts. Break off **B**, join in **A** and work in rib as on back welt for 5cm (2in), ending with a 2nd rib row. Change to larger needles and work in st st. Cont in patt from chart until work measures 14(15)cm, 5½(6)in, from beg, ending with a p row.
▦ **Place Pocket** *Next row* Patt 18 (20), slip next 33 (35) sts on to a holder, then with right side facing patt across sts of first pocket

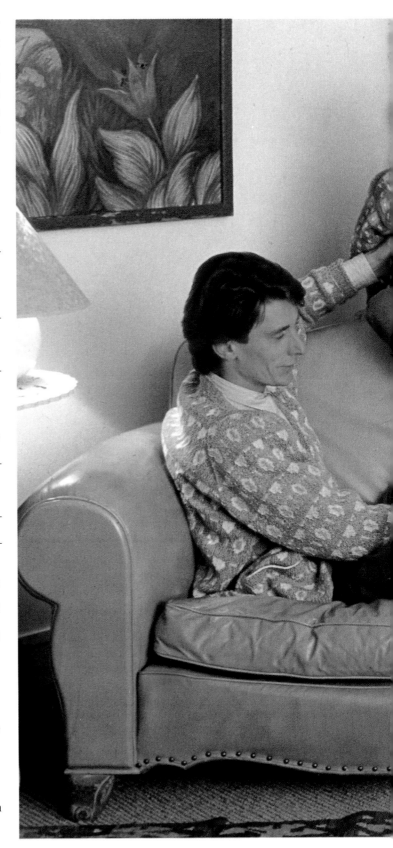

lining, patt to end. Cont until work measures 28(30)cm, 11(11¾)in, from beg, ending with a k row.

▦ **Front Shaping** Keeping patt correct, dec one st at beg of next and every foll 4th row until 17 (18) sts in all have been dec at front edge, *at the same time,* when work measures the same as back to armholes, ending with a p row, *for 2nd size only* cast off 3 sts at beg of next and foll 2 alt rows. *For both sizes* dec one st at armhole edge on every row until 2 sts rem. Cast off.

▦ **Right Front** Work to match left front, reversing all shaping and position of patt.

▦ **Right Sleeve** With smaller needles and **B** cast on 47 (53) sts. Break off **B** join in **A** and work in rib as on back welt for 3cm (1¼in) ending with a 2nd rib row and inc 5 sts evenly across the last row. 52 (58) sts. Change to larger needles and work in st st. Cont in patt from chart; inc one st at each end of the 3rd and every foll 3rd row until there are 120 (130) sts. Cont without shaping until work measures 47(49)cm, 18½(19¼)in, from beg, ending with a p row.

▦ **Top Shaping** *Next row* Cast off 1 (2) sts, patt to last 2 sts, k 2 tog.

▦ *Next row* P 2 tog, patt to last 2 sts, p 2 tog tbl. Rep these 2 rows twice more. Keeping patt correct, dec one st at both ends of next 37 (45) rows. *For first size* only, cont to dec at right hand edge (front) on every row and at left hand edge (back) on every foll alt row until 25 sts rem.

▦ *Next row* Patt to last 2 sts, p 2 tog tbl.

▦ *For both sizes, next row* Cast off 4 sts, patt to last 2 sts, k 2 tog.

▦ *Next row* Patt to end. Rep these 2 rows 3 times more. Cast off rem 4 sts.

▦ **Left Sleeve** Work to match right sleeve, reversing top shaping.

▦ **Button Band** Join raglan seams. With smaller needles and **A** cast on 12 sts and work in rib.

▦ *1st row* (right side) * K 1, p 1; rep from * to end.

▦ Rep this row until band, when slightly stretched, reaches up right front edge and around to centre back neck. Cast off in rib. Tack band in place; with pins mark position of buttons, 1st to come 1cm (½in) from cast on edge, 2nd to come just below beg of front shaping, with 2 more spaced evenly between these.

▦ **Buttonhole Band** Work as given for button band, making buttonholes to correspond with positions of pins as foll: (right side) rib 4, cast off next 4 sts, rib to end.

▦ *Next row* Rib to end, casting on 4 sts over the 4 cast off.

▦ **Pocket Tops** With smaller needles, **A** and right side facing, k to end across sts on holder working twice into first and last sts. 35 (37) sts. Beg with a 2nd row, work 2cm (¾in) in rib as on back welt. Cast off *loosely* in rib.

▦ **Finishing** Darn in loose ends. Join side and sleeve seams. Sew on front bands, joining ends at centre back neck. Sew down pocket tops and pocket linings. With right side facing and **B** crochet 1 slip-st row at pocket tops and edge of front bands. Sew on buttons.

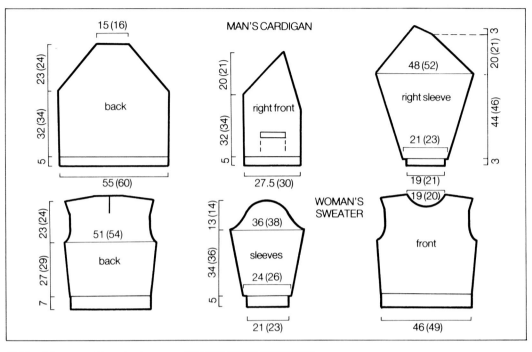

MAN'S CARDIGAN

back — 15 (16) — 23 (24) — 32 (34) — 5 — 55 (60)

back — 23 (24) — 51 (54) — 27 (29) — 7

right front — 20 (21) — 32 (34) — 5 — 27.5 (30)

WOMAN'S SWEATER

sleeves — 13 (14) — 36 (38) — 34 (36) — 24 (26) — 5 — 21 (23)

right sleeve — 20 (21) — 3 — 48 (52) — 44 (46) — 21 (23) — 3 — 19 (21)

front — 19 (20) — 46 (49)

WOMAN'S SWEATER

CHECKLIST

Materials
La Droguerie Tweed: *320(350)g of rose* (**A**)*, and 40 g each of orange and green. Surnaturelle: 20g of rose* (**B**)*. Pair each of needles size 2¾mm and 4½mm; small size crochet hook; 2 pink buttons.*

Sizes
Two sizes, to fit 87/92 (97/102)cm, 34/36 (38/40)in, bust. Actual measurements shown on diagram.

Stitches used and tension
As for Man's cardigan.

INSTRUCTIONS

▦ **Back** With smaller needles and **A**, cast on 115 (123) sts and work in rib as on back welt of Man's cardigan until work measures 7cm (2¾in) from beg, ending with a 2nd rib row. Change to larger needles and beg with a k row work in st st. Cont in patt from chart, inc 1 st at both ends of the 9th and every foll 10th row until there are 127 (135) sts. Cont without shaping until work measures 34(36)cm, 13⅜(14¼)in, from beg, ending with a p row.

▦ **Armhole Shaping** Keeping patt correct, cast off 4 sts at beg of next 2 rows, 3 sts at beg of next 2 rows, 2 sts at beg of next 2 rows, then 1 st at beg of next 2 rows. Work 2 rows straight. Dec 1 st at both ends of next and foll 4th row. 103 (111) sts. Cont without shaping until work measures 47(50)cm, 18½(19¾)in, from beg, ending with a p row. **.

▦ Inc 1 st at both ends of next and foll 4th row. Work 3 rows straight.

▦ **Divide for Opening** *Next row* Inc in first st, patt 52 (56) and leave these sts of right back on a spare needle, cast off 1 st, patt to last st, inc in last st. Cont on 54 (58) sts now rem on needle for left back. Cont as set, inc 1 st at armhole edge on every 4th row until there are 57 (61) sts. Cont without

BABY'S SWEATER

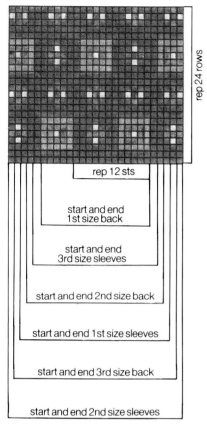

rep 24 rows

rep 12 sts

start and end
1st size back

start and end
3rd size sleeves

start and end 2nd size back

start and end 1st size sleeves

start and end 3rd size back

start and end 2nd size sleeves

MAN'S CARDIGAN

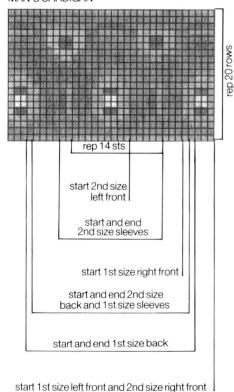

rep 20 rows

rep 14 sts

start 2nd size
left front

start and end
2nd size sleeves

start 1st size right front

start and end 2nd size
back and 1st size sleeves

start and end 1st size back

start 1st size left front and 2nd size right front

WOMAN'S SWEATER

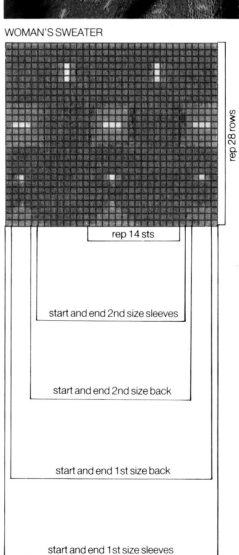

rep 28 rows

rep 14 sts

start and end 2nd size sleeves

start and end 2nd size back

start and end 1st size back

start and end 1st size sleeves

BOY'S SWEATER

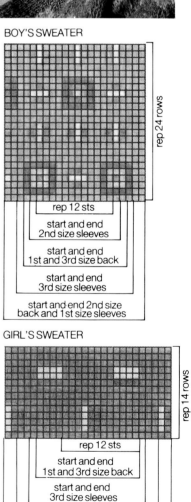

rep 24 rows

rep 12 sts

start and end
2nd size sleeves

start and end
1st and 3rd size back

start and end
3rd size sleeves

start and end 2nd size
back and 1st size sleeves

GIRL'S SWEATER

rep 14 rows

rep 12 sts

start and end
1st and 3rd size back

start and end
3rd size sleeves

start and end 2nd size
back and 1st size sleeves

start and end 2nd size sleeves

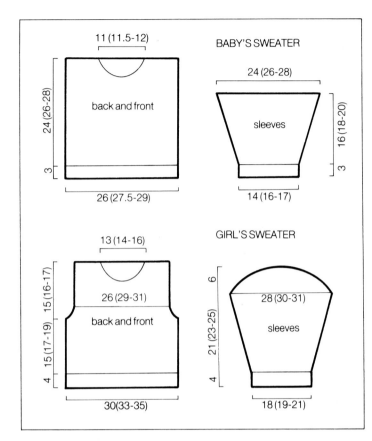

BABY'S SWEATER

11 (11.5-12)

24 (26-28)

back and front

24 (26-28)

sleeves

16 (18-20)

3

3

26 (27.5-29)

14 (16-17)

GIRL'S SWEATER

13 (14-16)

26 (29-31)

15 (16-17)

15 (17-19)

back and front

4

30(33-35)

6

28 (30-31)

sleeves

21 (23-25)

4

18 (19-21)

shaping until work measures 57(60)cm, 22½(23⅝)in, ending with a k row.

◼ **Shoulder Shaping** Cast off 11 sts at beg of next and foll alt row, then 12 (15) sts at beg of foll alt row. Leave rem 23 (24) sts on a holder for neckband. Rejoin yarn to centre back edge of right back sts and patt to end. Cont to match first side, reversing all shaping.

◼ **Front** Work as given for back to **. Inc 1 st at both ends of next and foll 4th row. Work 1 row straight.
◼ **Neck Shaping** *Next row* Patt 46 (49), turn and leave rem sts on a spare needle. Cont on these 46 (49) sts now rem on needle for left front; cast off at neck edge 3 sts at beg of next and 2 foll alt rows, 2 sts at beg of foll 3 alt rows, then 1 st at beg of foll alt row; *at the same time* inc 1 st at armhole edge on every 4th row as set to match back until 6 sts in all have been inc at this edge. 34 (37) sts. Cont without shaping until work measures the same as back to shoulders,

ending with a p row.
◼ **Shoulder Shaping** Cast off 11 sts at beg of next and foll alt row. Work 1 row straight, then cast off rem 12 (15) sts. Return to sts on spare needle, slip first 15 (17) sts on to a holder for neckband, rejoin yarns to neck edge of right front sts, cast off 3 sts and patt to end. Cont to match first side, reversing all shaping.

◼ **Sleeves** With smaller needles and **A** cast on 53 (57) sts and work in rib as on back welt for 5cm(2in), ending with a 2nd rib row and inc 8 sts evenly across the last row. 61 (65) sts. Change to larger needles. Beg with a k row work in st st. Cont in patt from chart, inc 1 st at both ends of the 5th and every foll 6th row until there are 83 (93) sts, then every foll 4th row until there are 91 (95) sts. Cont without shaping until work measures 39(41)cm, 15⅜(16⅛)in, from beg, ending with a p row.
◼ **Top Shaping** Keeping patt correct, cast off 4 sts at beg of next 2 rows, 3 sts at beg of next 4 rows,

2 sts at beg of next 12 rows, 1 st at beg of next 10 (12) rows, then 2 sts at beg of next 4 rows. Cast off rem 29 (31) sts.

◼ **Neckband** Join shoulder seams. With smaller needles, **A** and right side facing, pick up and k 92 (96) sts evenly round neck edge including sts on holders. Beg with a p row, work in st st. Work 2 rows, dec 6 sts evenly across the last row. 86 (90) sts. Work 7 more

rows in **A**, 1 row in **B**, then 7 rows in **A**. Cast off *loosely*.

◼ **Finishing** At this stage darn in all loose ends. Sew in sleeves. Join side and sleeve seams. Fold neckband to inside on contrast line and sew in place.
◼ With crochet hook, **B** and right side facing, work 1 row in slip st along back neck opening, making 2 button loops. Fasten off. Sew on buttons.

BABY'S SWEATER

CHECKLIST

Materials
La Drouguerie Tweed: *100(100-100)g of rose* (**A**). Surnaturelle: *20g each of rose* (**B**), *apricot and pale green. Pair each of needles size 2¾mm and 4½mm; small size crochet hook; 1 pink button.*

Sizes
Three sizes, to fit a baby aged 12 (18-24) months. Actual measurements shown on diagram.

Stitches used and tension
As for Man's cardigan.

INSTRUCTIONS

◼ **Back** With smaller needles and **A**, cast on 65 (69-73) sts and work in rib as on back welt of Man's cardigan until work measures 3cm (1¼in) from beg, ending with a 2nd rib row. Change to larger needles and beg with a k row work in st st. Cont in patt from chart until work measures 27(29-31)cm, 10⅝(11⅜-12¼)in, from beg, ending with a p row. Cast off.

◼ **Front** Work as given for back until front measures 23(25-27)cm, 9(9⅞-10⅝)in, from beg, endig with a p row.
◼ **Neck Shaping** *Next row* Patt 27 (28-29) and leave these sts of left front on a spare needle, cast off next 11 (13-15) sts, patt to end. Cont on 27 (28-29) sts now rem on needle for right front; work 1 row straight. Cast off at neck edge 3 sts at beg of next row and foll alt row, then 2 sts at beg of foll alt row. 19 (20-21) sts.
◼ Cont without shaping until work measures the same as back to shoulders, ending with a p row.

Cast off. Rejoin yarns to sts of left front, cast off 3 sts and patt to end. Cont to match first side, reversing shaping.

◼ **Sleeves** With smaller needles and **A** cast on 35 (39-43) sts and work in rib as on back welt for 3cm (1¼in), ending with a 2nd rib row. Change to larger needles and beg with a k row work in st st. Cont in patt from chart, inc 1 st at both ends of the 3rd and every foll alt row until there are 61 (65-69) sts. Cont without shaping until work measures 19(21-23)cm, 7½(8¼-9)in, from beg, ending with a p row. Cast off *loosely*.

◼ **Neckband** Join left shoulder seam. With smaller needles, **A** and right side facing, pick up and k 89 (95-101) sts evenly round neck edge. Beg with a 2nd row, work 2cm (¾in) in rib as on back welt. Cast off in rib.

◼ **Finishing** At this stage darn in all loose ends. Join right shoulder seam, leaving an opening at neck edge. On each side edge mark a

point 12(13-14)cm, 4¾(5⅛-5½)in, down from shoulder seams for armholes and sew cast-off edge of sleeves between marked points. Join side and sleeve seams.

▦ With crochet hook, **B** and right side facing, work 1 row in slip st along neck opening, making a button loop. Sew on button to match.

GIRL'S SWEATER

CHECKLIST

Materials
La Droguerie Tweed: *130(140-150)g of orange (***A***), and 20g of green.*
Surnaturelle: *20g of pale yellow. Pair each of needles size 2¾mm and 4½mm.*

Sizes
Three sizes, to fit ages 1/2 (2/3-4/5) years. Actual measurements shown on diagram.

Stitches used and tension
As for Man's cardigan.

INSTRUCTIONS

▦ **Back** With smaller needles and **A** cast on 75 (81-87) sts and work in rib as on back welt of Man's cardigan for 4cm (1½in), ending with a 2nd rib row and inc 1 st in centre of last row. 76 (82-88) sts. Change to larger needles and beg with a k row work in st st. Cont in patt from chart until work measures 19(21-23)cm, 7½(8¼-9)in, from beg, ending with a p row.

▦ **Armhole Shaping** Keeping patt correct, cast off 2 sts at beg of next 4 rows, then 1 st at beg of next 2 rows. 66 (72-78) sts. Cont without shaping until work measures 34(37-40)cm, 13⅜(14½-15¾)in, from beg, ending with a p row. Cast off.

▦ **Front** Work as given for back until front measures 29(32-35)cm, 11⅜(12⅝-13¾)in, from beg, ending with a p row.

▦ **Neck Shaping** *Next row* Patt 26 (27-28) and leave these sts of left front on a spare needle, cast off next 14 (18-22) sts, patt to end. Cont on 26 (27-28) sts now rem on needle for right front; work 1 row straight. Cast off at neck edge 3 sts at beg of next and foll alt row, 2 sts at beg of foll alt row, then 1 st at beg of foll alt row. 17 (18-19) sts.

▦ Cont without shaping until work measures the same as back to shoulders, ending with a p row. Cast off. Rejoin yarns to neck edge of left front sts, cast off 3 sts and patt to end. Cont to match first side, reversing shaping.

▦ **Sleeves** With smaller needles and **A** cast on 45 (49-53) sts and work in rib as on back welt for 4cm (1½in) ending with a 2nd rib row and inc 1 st in centre of last row. 46 (50-54) sts. Change to larger needles and beg with a k row work in st st. Cont in patt from chart, inc 1 st at both ends of the 3rd and every foll 4th row until there are 70 (74-78) sts. Cont without shaping until work measures 25(27-29)cm, 9⅞(10⅝-11⅜)in, from beg, ending with a p row.

▦ **Top Shaping** Keeping patt correct, cast off 4 sts at beg of next 4 rows, 2 sts at beg of next 6 rows,

BOY'S SWEATER

CHECKLIST

Materials
La Droguerie Tweed: *170(190-200)g of blue* (**A**). Surnaturelle: *20g each of apricot, pale yellow* (**B**) *and pale green. Pair each of needles size 2¾mm and 4½mm; small crochet hook; 2 green buttons.*

Sizes
As for Girl's sweater.

Stitches used and tension
As for Man's cardigan.

then 3 sts at beg of next 6 rows. Cast off rem 24 (28-32) sts.

▦ **Neckband** Join left shoulder seam. With smaller needles, **A** and right side facing, pick up and k 99 (107-115) sts evenly along neck edge. Beg with a 2nd row, work 2cm (¾in) in rib as on back welt. Cast off *loosely* in rib.

▦ **Finishing** At this stage darn in all loose ends. Join right shoulder and neckband seam. Sew in sleeves. Join side and sleeve seams.

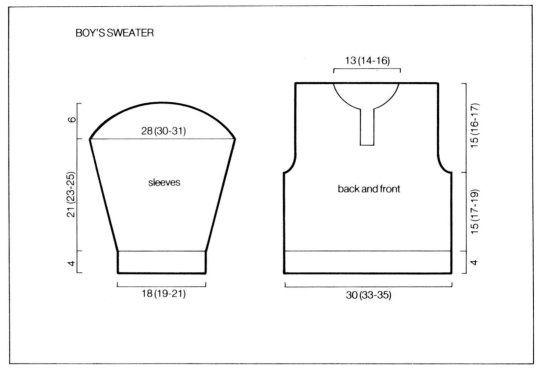

BOY'S SWEATER

sleeves
6
21 (23-25)
4
28 (30-31)
18 (19-21)

back and front
13 (14-16)
15 (16-17)
15 (17-19)
4
30 (33-35)

INSTRUCTIONS

▦ **Back and Sleeves** Work as given for Girl's sweater.

▦ **Front** Work as given for back until front measures 23(25-27)cm, 9(9⅞-10⅝)in, from beg, ending with a p row.

▦ **Divide for Opening** *Next row* Patt 30 (33-36) and leave these sts of left front on a spare needle, cast off next 6 sts, patt to end. Cont on 30 (33-36) sts now rem on needle for right front; cont until work measures 29(32-35)cm, 11⅜(12⅝-13¾)in, from beg, ending with a p row.

▦ **Neck Shaping** Keeping patt correct, cast off at neck edge 4 (6-8) sts at beg of next row, 4 sts at beg of foll alt row, 3 sts at beg of foll alt row, then 2 sts at beg of foll alt row. 17 (18-19) sts. Cont without shaping until work measures the same as back to shoulders, ending with a p row. Cast off. Rejoin yarns to left front sts and patt to end. Cont to match first side, reversing shaping.

▦ **Collar** With smaller needles and **A** cast on 99 (107-115) sts and work in rib as on back welt

until work measures 6cm (2⅜in) from beg. Cast off *loosely* in rib.

▦ **Button Band** With smaller needles and **A** cast on 11 sts and work in rib as on back welt until band, when slightly stretched, reaches up front opening. Cast off in rib. Tack band in place, with pins mark position of buttons, first to come 2cm (¾in) from cast on edge and 2nd to come 1cm (⅜in) from cast off edge.

▦ **Buttonhole Band** Work as given for button band, making buttonholes to correspond with positions of pins as foll: (right side) rib 4, cast off next 3 sts, rib 4.

▦ *Next row* Rib to end, casting on 3 sts over the 3 cast off.

▦ **Finishing** At this stage darn in all loose ends. Join shoulder seams. Sew in sleeves. Join side and sleeve seams. Sew on front bands, sewing cast on edges to cast off sts at centre front. Sew cast on edge of collar to neck edge, beginning and ending in centre of front bands. With crochet hook, **B** and right side facing, slip st along edges of front bands and collar. Fasten off. Sew on buttons.

4
FASHION &
FLAIR

MING JERSEY

Oriental artefacts are a perfect source of patterns for handknitting; their symmetry and geometry lend themselves to interpretation in simple stitches. The glowing colours of priceless porcelains can be well matched in the richness of wool, as in this design inspired by a Ming vase. Here, a geometric background is cut through by a band with a leaf pattern.

CHECKLIST

Materials
*Bouton d'Or yarns: Superwash (100% laine) 7 (8) balls noir (**B**); Cordonnet (acrylique) 5 (6) balls bleu cobalt (**A**). Pair each of needles size 2¾mm and 3mm.*
Note *If the above yarn is unobtainable, please refer to page 192.*

Sizes
Two sizes, to fit bust 87/92 (97/102) cm; 34/36 (38/40) in. Actual measurements shown on diagram.

Stitches used
Single rib; st st; patt, *worked from charts as explained below.*

Tension
Over patt using 3mm needles, 28 sts and 32 rows to 10 cm (4 in). Work a sample on 38 sts beg and ending 2 sts from edge of Chart 1.

INSTRUCTIONS

BACK
▦ With 2¾mm needles and **B** cast on 137 (145) sts and work in rib.
▦ ** *1st row* (right side). P 1, * k 1, p 1; rep from * to end.
▦ *2nd row* K 1, * p 1, k 1; rep from * to end. Rep these 2 rows until work measures 6 cm (2½ in) from beg, ending with a 1st rib row. **

▦ *Inc row* Rib 3 (5), [inc in next st, rib 9 (8)] 13 (15) times, inc in next st, rib 3 (4). 151 (161) sts. Change to 3 mm needles and working in st st work patt from Chart 1.
▦ *1st row 1st size* K 3 **B**, * 3 **A**, 4 **B**, 3 **A**, 3 **B**, 3 **A**, 5 **B**, 3 **A**, 3 **B**; * rep from * to * 4 times more, 3 **A**, 4 **B**, 3 **A**, 3 **B**.
▦ *2nd size* K 2 **B**, 3 **A**, 3 **B**, then rep from * to * in 1st size row 5 times, 3 **A**, 4 **B**, 3 **A**, 3 **B**, 3 **A**, 2 **B**.

▦ *Both sizes* Cont in patt as now set without shaping until work measures 56 (59) cm, 22¼ (23⅜) in from beg, ending with a wrong-side row.
Neck Shaping *Next row* Patt 60 (63) and leave these sts of right back on a spare needle, cast off next 31 (35) sts, patt to end. Cont on 60 (63) sts now rem on needle for left back and work 1 row straight.
▦ Cast off at neck edge 5 sts at beg of next row and next alt row and dec 1 st at same edge on foll row. Work 1 row on rem 49 (52) sts then cast off these sts for shoulder.
▦ Rejoin yarns to neck edge of right back sts, cast off 5, patt to end. Cast off 5 sts at neck edge on next alt row, dec 1 st at same edge on foll row then work 2 rows straight. Cast off rem 49 (52) sts.

FRONT
▦ Work as for back until the inc row at end of welt has been worked. Change to 3 mm needles and patt.
▦ *1st row 1st size* K 3 **B**, then rep from * to * in 1st row of back twice, 3 **A**, 4 **B**, 3 **A**, 3 **B**, 3 **A**, 2 **B**, then working from Chart 2 work all the sts shown in 1st row, then k 1 **B**, 3 **A**, 3 **B**, 3 **A**, 5 **B**, 3 **A**, 3 **B**, 3 **A**, 4 **B**, 3 **A**, 3 **B**.
▦ *2nd size* K 2 **B**, 3 **A**, 3 **B**, then rep from * in 1st row of back twice, 3 **A**, 4 **B**, 3 **A**, 3 **B**, 3 **A**, 2 **B**, then working from Chart 2 work all the sts shown in 1st row, then 1 **B**, 3 **A**, 3 **B**, 3 **A**, 5 **B**, 3 **A**, 3 **B**, 3 **A**,

4 **B**, 3 **A**, 3 **B**, 3 **A**, 2 **B**.
▦ *Both sizes* Cont in patt as now set working 75 (80) sts at left side of front and 34 (39) sts at right side from Chart 1 and working the 42 sts of Chart 2 in position established on 1st row. Cont without shaping until 19 rows less have been worked than on back to shoulder edge, thus ending with a p row.
Neck Shaping *Next row* Patt 64 (67) and leave these sts of left front on a spare needle, cast off next 23 (27) sts, patt to end. Cont on 64 (67) sts now rem on needle for right front and work 1 row straight. *** Cast off 4 sts at beg of next row, 2 sts at same edge on next 4 alt rows and 1 st on next 3 alt rows. Cont on rem 49 (52) sts until work matches back to shoulder, ending with same patt row. Cast off these sts. Rejoin yarns to neck edge of left front sts and complete as for right front from *** to end.

SLEEVES
▦ With 2¾mm needles and **B**, cast on 61 (65) sts and work as for back welt from ** to **.
▦ *Inc row* Rib 2, [inc in next st, rib 6 (5)] 8 (10) times, inc in next st, rib 2. 70 (76) sts. Change to 3 mm needles and working in st st work patt from Chart 1.
▦ *1st row 1st size* K 3 **B**, then rep from * to * in 1st patt row of back twice, 3 **A**, 4 **B**, 3 **A**, 3 **B**.
▦ *2nd size* K 3 **A**, 3 **B**, then rep from * to * in 1st patt row of back twice, 3 **A**, 4 **B**, 3 **A**, 3 **B**, 3 **A**.

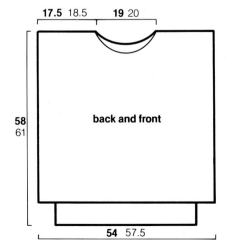

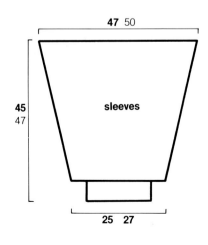

Blue and black or blue and white are natural combinations for this stunning jersey, but it could work equally well in other porcelain shades. Try fresh green and white for the background, for example, perhaps with splashes of rose pink in the main panel.

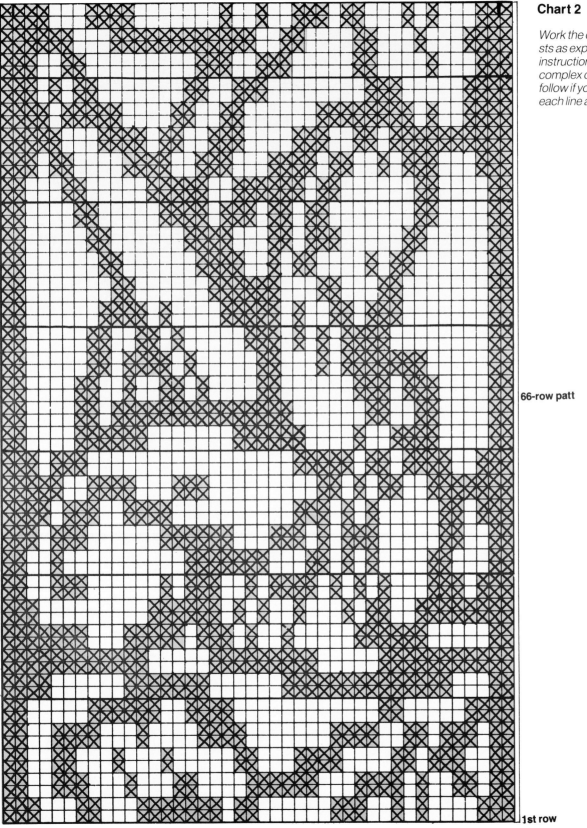

Chart 2

Work the complete panel of 42 sts as explained in the instructions for front. This complex chart will be easier to follow if you cross out or cover up each line after you have knitted it.

66-row patt

1st row

Chart 1

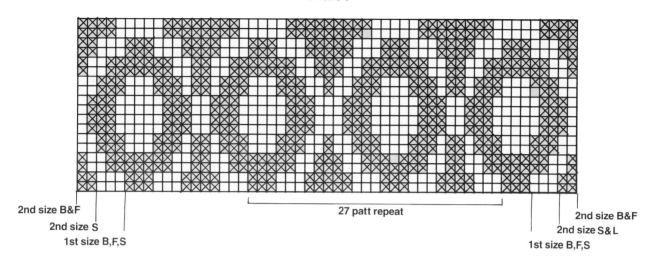

2nd size B&F
2nd size S
1st size B,F,S

27 patt repeat

2nd size B&F
2nd size S&L
1st size B,F,S

▦ *Both sizes* Cont in patt as now set and work 2 more rows straight then inc 1 st at both ends of next row, then every foll 4th row 27 (28) times, then every alt row 3 times, working extra sts into patt. Cont on 132 (140) sts until work measures 45 (47) cm, 17¾ (18½) in from beg. Cast off all sts.

NECK BORDER
▦ With 2¾ mm needles and **B**, cast on 231 (237) sts and work in rib as on back welt for 7 cm (2¾ in). Cast off loosely ribwise.

MAKING UP
▦ Join shoulder seams. Join ends of neck border. Placing seam level with left shoulder seam pin cast-on edge of neck border around neck edges placing it about 1 cm (⅜ in) below neckline. Sew in place as pinned then fold border in half to wrong side enclosing neck edges and slip-st cast-off edge in place. The band is intended to stand away from neckline. Pin cast-off edge of sleeves to sides of sweater placing centre of sleeves level with shoulder seams and ensuring that sides of sleeves reach to same position on patt at each side. Sew in place as pinned then join side and sleeve seams.

WOVEN ROSES

This summery design suggests a sunny trellis covered in climber roses. It is a perfect start to working with two colours as none of the threads are carried very far across the back of the knitting. The roses, too, are easy to work, as they are embroidered in plain panels once the sweater is made.

CHECKLIST

Materials
Berger du Nord yarns in the foll colours: Qualité Classique: *8 (9) balls beige No 7540 (**A**), and 5 (6) balls mais (**B**), yellow. For the flowers: 1 ball angora 70% in red No 8431 and 1 ball bordeaux No 8430. Pair each of needles size 2¾ mm and 3mm.*
Note *If the above yarn is unobtainable. please refer to page 192.*

Sizes
Two sizes, to fit bust 82/87 (92/97) cm; 32/34 (36/38) in. Actual measurements shown on diagram.

Stitches used
Single rib; st st; patt, *worked from chart, as explained below.*

Tension
Over patt using 3mm needles, 28 sts and 32 rows to 10cm (4 in). Work a sample on 41 sts beg at right-hand edge of chart.

INSTRUCTIONS

BACK
▦ With 2¾ mm needles and **A** cast on 131 (147) sts and work in rib.
▦ ** *1st row* (right side). P 1, * k 1, p 1; rep from * to end.
2nd row K 1, * p 1, k 1; rep from * to end. Rep these 2 rows until work measures 5 (6) cm, 2 (2⅜) in

from beg, ending with a 1st rib row. **
▦ *Inc row* Rib 7 (8), [inc in next st, rib 12 (9)] 9 (13) times, inc in next st, rib 6 (8). 141 (161) sts. Change to 3mm needles and working in st st work patt from chart.
▦ *1st row 1st size* * K 1 **A**, 9 **B**, [1 **A**, 1 **B**] 5 times; * rep from * to * 6 times more, 1 **A**.
▦ *2nd size* * K[1 **A**, 1 **B**] 5 times, 1

A, 9 **B**; * rep from * to * 7 times more, 1 **A**.
▦ *Both sizes* Cont as now set and after the 18th row has been worked cont to work the main patt sequence from 19th row to 98th row inclusive, throughout back.
At same time, after 60 rows have been worked from chart, work a plain square on which the motif will be embroidered.
▦ *61st row* Patt 70 (80), then k next 31 sts in **A**, join on another ball of **B**, patt rem 40 (50) sts of row. Cont as now set, twisting **B** around **A** at each side of the plain square; work 37 more rows in this way then cut off spare ball of **B** and cont in patt beg with 99th row. Cont until 186 (194) rows have been worked in patt.
Neck Shaping *Next row* Patt 55 (63) and leave these sts of right back on a spare needle, cast off next 31 (35) sts, patt to end. Cont on 55 (63) sts now rem on needle for left back; work 1 row straight then cast off at neck edge 5 sts at beg of next row and next alt row. Work 1 row then cast off rem 45 (53) sts for shoulder edge. Rejoin yarns to neck edge of right back sts, cast off 5, patt to end. Cast off 5 sts at neck edge on next alt row, work 2 rows on rem 45 (53) sts then cast off.

FRONT
▦ Work as for back until 20th row of patt has been worked then work a plain square for motif.

▦ *21st row* Patt 70 (80), then k next 31 sts in **A**, join on another ball of **B**, patt rem 40 (50) sts. Work 37 more rows as now set then resume patt. Cont until 140th row has been worked then work another square.
▦ *141st row* Patt 10 (20), k next 31 sts in **A**, join on another ball of **B**, patt 100 (110). Cont working this square in same way as before. *At same time* cont without shaping until 166 (174) rows have been worked in patt.
Neck Shaping *Next row* Patt 62 (70) still working the plain square, leave these sts of left front on a spare needle, cast off next 17 (21) sts, patt to end. Cont on 62 (70) sts now rem on needle for right front and work 1 row straight. ***
Cast off 4 sts at beg of next row, 3 sts at same edge on next alt row, 2 sts on next 2 alt rows and 1 st on next 6 alt rows. Cont on rem 45 (53) sts until 192 (200) rows have been worked in patt thus reaching same position as on back shoulder. Cast off.
▦ Rejoin yarns to neck edge of left front sts; cont with the plain square until it is completed then resume normal patt.
At same time, complete as for right front from *** to end.

LEFT SLEEVE
▦ With 2¾ mm needles and **A** cast on 61 (65) sts and work as for back welt from ** to **

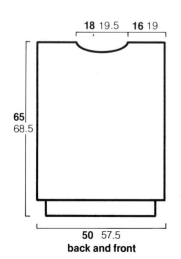

18 19.5 16 19

65
68.5

50 57.5
back and front

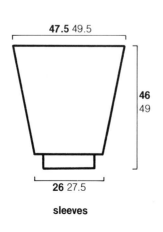

47.5 49.5

46
49

26 27.5
sleeves

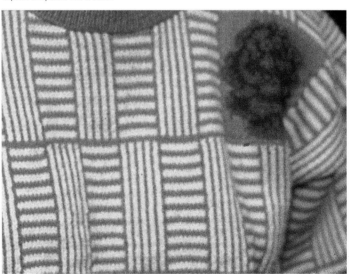

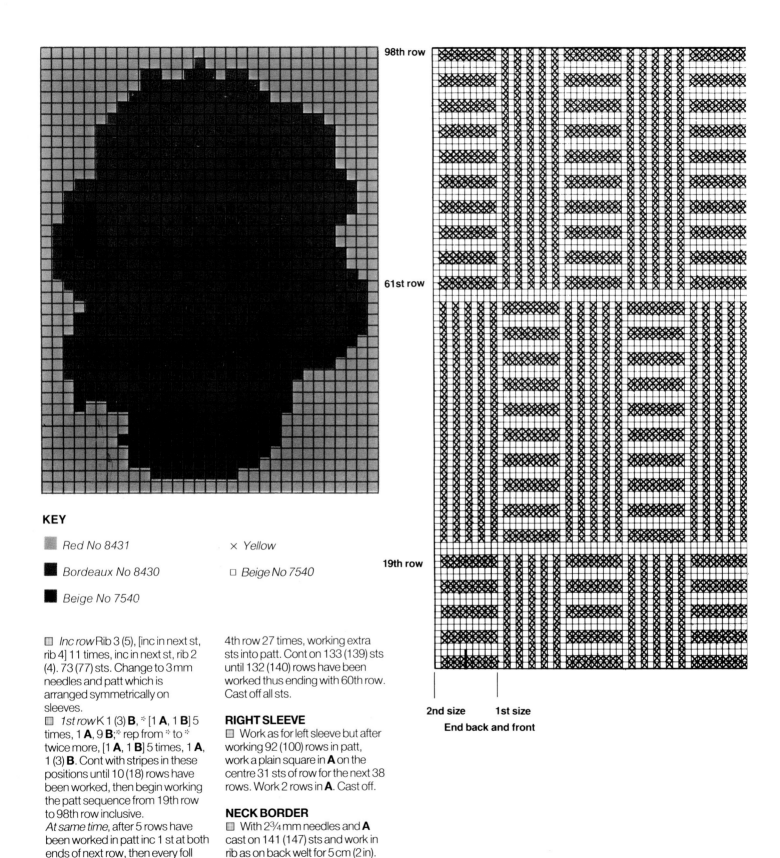

98th row

61st row

19th row

2nd size   1st size

End back and front

KEY

    Red No 8431   ✕ *Yellow*

    Bordeaux No 8430   ☐ *Beige No 7540*

    Beige No 7540

▦ *Inc row* Rib 3 (5), [inc in next st, rib 4] 11 times, inc in next st, rib 2 (4). 73 (77) sts. Change to 3 mm needles and patt which is arranged symmetrically on sleeves.

▦ *1st row* K 1 (3) **B**, ✳ [1 **A**, 1 **B**] 5 times, 1 **A**, 9 **B**;✳ rep from ✳ to ✳ twice more, [1 **A**, 1 **B**] 5 times, 1 **A**, 1 (3) **B**. Cont with stripes in these positions until 10 (18) rows have been worked, then begin working the patt sequence from 19th row to 98th row inclusive.

At same time, after 5 rows have been worked in patt inc 1 st at both ends of next row, then every foll 6th row 2 (3) times, then every foll

4th row 27 times, working extra sts into patt. Cont on 133 (139) sts until 132 (140) rows have been worked thus ending with 60th row. Cast off all sts.

RIGHT SLEEVE

▦ Work as for left sleeve but after working 92 (100) rows in patt, work a plain square in **A** on the centre 31 sts of row for the next 38 rows. Work 2 rows in **A**. Cast off.

NECK BORDER

▦ With 2¾ mm needles and **A** cast on 141 (147) sts and work in rib as on back welt for 5 cm (2 in). Cast off loosely ribwise.

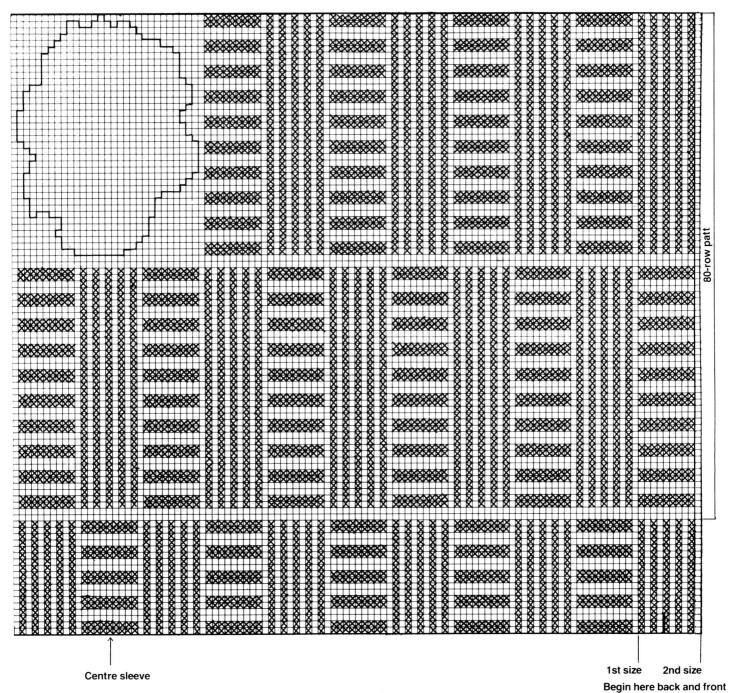

Centre sleeve

1st size   2nd size
Begin here back and front

80-row patt

MAKING UP
▦ Embroider the rose motif in the plain squares using the Swiss Darning method described on page 6. Join shoulder seams. Join ends of neck border. Placing seam at left shoulder pin cast-on edge of border around neck edges placing it a little below the neck edges. Sew in place then fold border in half to wrong side and slip-st cast-

off edge in place, enclosing neck edges. Pin cast-off edge of sleeves to sides of sweater placing centre of sleeve level with shoulder seam and ensuring that sides of sleeves reach to same position on patt at each side. Sew in place as pinned then join side and sleeve seams. On side seams take care to match patt changes so that patt appears continuous.

Work the stripes on back, front and sleeves as indicated on the chart. The rose motifs are embroidered on the large plain squares. The position for the back square is shown on the chart; see instructions for the correct placing of the two squares on the front and the one on the right sleeve.

SILKEN SHIMMER

The 'crackle glaze' effect on this superb silk sweater is an evocative reminder of heat in faraway places and makes a luxurious summer cover-up. Bands of black and blue are chic, and in addition they help you to achieve half the design before the patterning begins!

CHECKLIST

Materials

Anny Blatt Silk Anny: *13 balls blue/black No 1731* (**A**), *3 balls light blue No 1729* (**B**), *and 2 balls grey No 1967* (**C**). *Pair each of needles size 4 mm and 5 mm.*

Sizes

Two sizes, to fit bust 82/87 (92/97) cm; 32/34 (36/38) in. Actual measurements shown on diagram.

Stitches used

Single rib; st st; patt, worked from charts as explained below. When working the patt cut off short lengths of **C** *yarn using a separate length for each line so that the yarns are not carried across more than 2 or 3 sts; for larger motifs wind off a small ball of* **C**. *Always twist* **C** *around* **A** *when beg each line or motif in* **C**.

Tension

Over st st using 5 mm needles, 18 sts and 24 rows to 10 cm (4 in). Work a sample on 24 sts.

INSTRUCTIONS

BACK

▦ With 4 mm needles and **A** cast on 85 (91) sts and work in rib.

▦ *1st row* (right side). P 1, * k 1, p 1; rep from * to end.

▦ *2nd row* K 1, * p 1, k 1; rep from * to end. Rep these 2 rows until work measures 5 cm (2 in) from beg, ending with a 1st rib row.

▦ *Inc row* Rib 6 (9), [inc in next st, rib 11] 6 times, inc in next st, rib 6 (9). 92 (98) sts. Change to 5 mm needles and beg with a k row work in st st. Work 2 (6) rows **A**, then [12 rows **B**, 12 rows **A**] twice, 12 rows **B**. ** Now begin motifs from Chart 1, on left back, joining on 2 short lengths of **C** as explained above.

▦ *1st row* K 44 (50) **A**, then working from chart k 24 **A**, 5 **C**, 12 **A**, 1 **C**, 6 **A**. Cont working from chart as now set, without shaping until 52nd row has been worked.

Neck Shaping *53rd row* K 36 (38) **A** and leave these sts of right back on a spare needle, then with **A** cast off next 20 (22) sts, then patt to end. Cont on 36 (38) sts now rem on needle for left back keeping patt correct; work 1 row straight. Cast off at neck edge 6 sts on next row and 2 sts on next 2 alt rows. Work 60th row of chart to complete patt. Using **A**, k 1 row on rem 26 (28) sts then cast off for shoulder edge. Rejoin **A** to neck edge of right back sts, cast off 6, p to end. Cast off 2 sts at neck edge on next 2 alt rows, then work 3 rows on rem 26 (28) sts. Cast off.

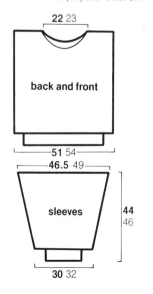

22 23	
back and front	
51 54	
46.5 49	
sleeves	**44** 46
30 32	

FRONT

Work as for back to ** then begin motifs from Chart 2 on left front.

1st row Working from chart, k 20 **A**, 2 **C**, 8 **A**, 3 **C**, 5 **A**, 2 **C**, 9 **A**, then k rem 43 (49) sts in **A**. Cont working from chart as now set, without shaping until 46th row of chart has been worked.

Neck Shaping *47th row* Patt 39 (41) and leave these sts of left front on a spare needle, cast off next 14 (16) sts, then using **A**, k to end. Cont on 39 (41) sts now rem on needle for right front using **A** only; work 1 row straight. *** Cast off 4 sts at beg of next row, 3 sts at same edge on next alt row, 2 sts on next 2 alt rows and 1 st on next 2 alt rows. *** Work 2 rows on rem 26 (28) sts then cast off for shoulder edge.

Rejoin yarn to neck edge of left front sts and keeping patt correct cont as for right front from *** to ***. Cont on rem 26 (28) sts and work 2 rows to complete the chart then k 1 row in **A**. Cast off.

LEFT SLEEVE

With 4 mm needles and **A** cast on 47 (51) sts and work in rib as on back welt for 5 cm (2 in), ending with a 1st rib row.

Inc row Rib 5 (7), [inc in next st, rib 5] 6 times, inc in next st, rib 5 (7). 54 (58) sts. Change to 5 mm needles and beg with a k row work 4 (6) rows in st st then begin patt from Chart 3.

1st row K 8 (10) **A**, 2 **C**, 4 **A**, 2 **C**, 2 **A**, 2 **C**, 1 **A**, 2 **C**, 3 **A**, 3 **C**, 18 **A**, 1 **C**, 6 (8) **A**. Cont from chart as now set but inc 1 st at both ends of 5th, 11th, 15th, 21st rows and so on at intervals of 4 rows and 6 rows alternately as shown on chart. When the last incs have been worked on 75th row of chart cont on 84 (88) sts until the 88th row of chart has been worked. Work 2 (4) rows in **A** then cast off all sts.

RIGHT SLEEVE

Work as for left sleeve but working entirely in **A**.

NECK BORDER

Join right shoulder seam. With right side of work facing and using 4 mm needles and A, pick up and k 55 (57) sts round front neck edge and 46 (48) sts across back neck. Beg with 2nd row work in rib as on welt for 5 rows then cast off loosely ribwise.

MAKING UP

At this stage it is advisable to darn in all the ends of yarn used for the motifs to prevent the yarn slipping through. Join left shoulder seam and ends of neck border. On each side edge mark a point 23 (24) cm, 9 (9½) in down from shoulder seam for armholes and sew cast-off edge of sleeves between marked points. Join side and sleeve seams matching stripes at sides.

FRONT

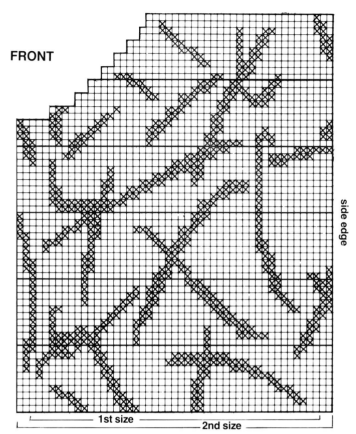

side edge

1st size

2nd size

BACK

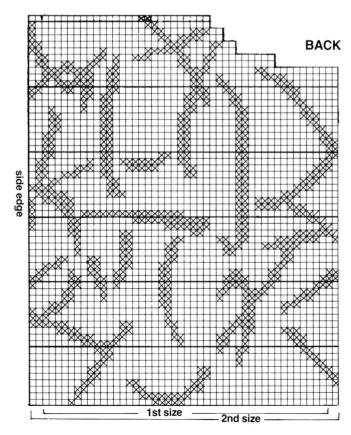

side edge

1st size

2nd size

SLEEVE

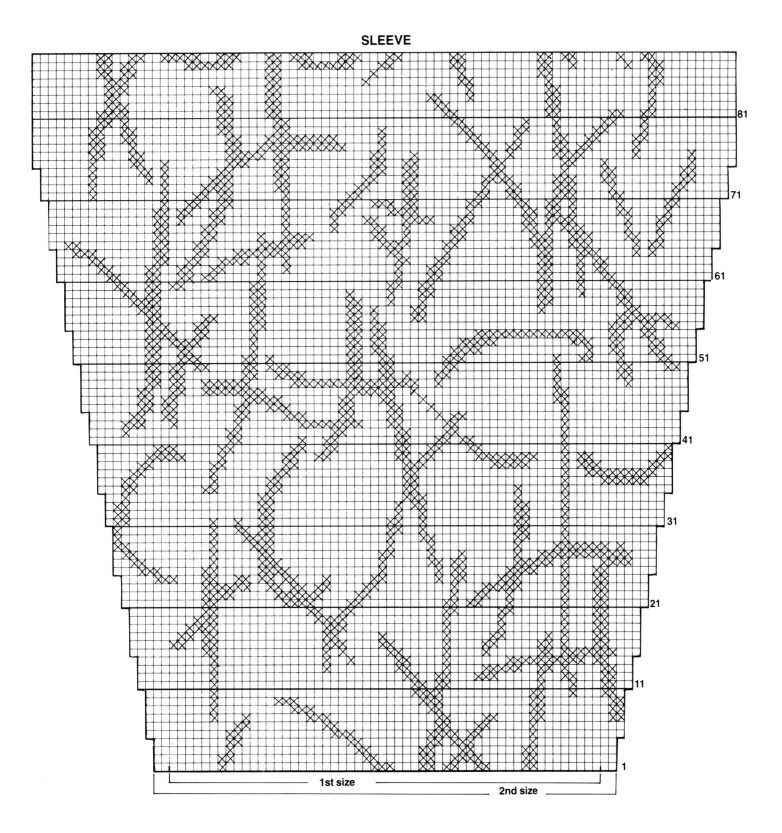

1st size · 2nd size

139

WISTERIA CARDIGAN

This floral cardigan with a 1940s, romantic look has a tie-neck, and set-in sleeves emphasized with padded shoulders for a flattering, contemporary line. The trails of wisteria are knitted in, using simple stocking stitch, but the leaves are embroidered on afterwards to enrich the surface. The front borders and the ties are knitted in a moss stitch to give a raised effect.

CHECKLIST

Materials
Georges Picaud Georges Swing: *10 (11) balls No 1 (grey); quality* Orient Express, *3 balls No 8 (mauve); quality* Feu Vert, *1 ball No 66 (green). Pair each of needles size 2¾mm, 3mm and 3¼mm; 4 buttons; pair of shoulder pads.*
Note *If the above yarn is unobtainable, refer to page 192.*

Sizes
Two sizes, to fit bust 82/87 (92/97) cm; 32/34 (36/38) in. Actual measurements shown on diagram in centimetres.

Stitches used
Single rib; st st; m st. *For the motifs work from charts as explained below. Wind off a small ball of* **B** *for each flower motif.*

Tension
Over st st using 3¼mm needles, 24 sts and 32 rows to 10 cm (4 in). Work a sample on 30 sts.

INSTRUCTIONS

BACK
▨ With 2¾mm needles and **A** cast on 111 (119) sts and work in rib.

▨ ** *1st row* (right side). P 1, * k 1, p 1; rep from * to end.
▨ *2nd row* K 1, * p 1, k 1; rep from * to end. Rep these 2 rows until work measures 3 cm (1¼ in) from beg, ending with a 2nd rib row and inc 1 st in centre of last row. *** 112 (120) sts. Change to 3¼mm needles and working in st st begin motifs from charts.

▨ *1st row* K 0 (2) **A**, now working from Chart No 1, k 31 **A**, join on a ball of **B** and k 1 **B**, then k 23 **A** to complete chart; k the centre 2 (6) sts, then working from Chart No 2, k 23 **A**, join on another ball of **B**, k 1 **B**, then k 31 **A** to complete the chart k 0 (2) **A**. Cont in patt as now set working only the flower motifs; the leaves are embroidered later. *At same time*, when 10 rows have been worked in st st inc 1 st at both ends of next row, then every foll 10th row 7 times more, keeping these extra sts at sides in **A**; after incs are completed there are 8 (10) sts in **A** outside the charts. Cont on 128 (136) sts until work measures 33 (34) cm, 13 (13⅜) in, from beg, ending with a p row.

▨ **Armhole Shaping** Cast off 4 sts at beg of next 2 rows, 2 sts at beg of next 8 rows and 1 st at beg of next 4 (6) rows. 100 (106) sts. Now inc 1 st at both ends of every foll 6th row 6 times then cont on 112 (118) sts until work measures 52 (54) cm, 20½ (21¼) in from beg, ending with a p row. For 1st size a few rows rem to be worked from charts; (for 2nd size charts should be completed).

▨ **Shoulder and Neck Shaping** *1st row* Cast off 9, k until there are 36 (38) sts on right needle, leave these for right back, cast off next 22 (24) sts, k to end. Cont on 45 (47) sts now rem at end of needle for left back and cast off 9 sts at beg of next row. *** Cast off 3 sts at neck edge on next row and 9 sts at shoulder edge on foll row; rep last 2 rows once. Cast off 3 sts at neck edge on foll row then cast off rem 9 (11) sts to complete shoulder slope. Rejoin yarn to neck edge of right back sts and complete as for left back from *** to end.

LEFT FRONT
▨ With 2¾mm needles and **A** cast on 55 (59) sts and work as for back welt from ** to ***. 56 (60) sts. Change to 3¼mm needles and working in st st work patt from Chart No 1.

▨ *1st row* K 0 (2) **A**, then working from chart k 31 **A**, join on **B** and k 1 **B**, then k 23 **A** to complete chart, k 1 (3) **A**. Cont in patt as now set and work 9 more rows without shaping. For side shaping inc 1 st at beg of next row then at same edge on every foll 10th row 7 times more keeping these extra sts at side in **A**. Cont on 64 (68) sts until work matches back to armhole, ending at side edge.

▨ **Armhole Shaping** Cast off 4 sts at beg of next row, 2 sts at same edge on next 4 alt rows and 1 st on next 2 (3) alt rows. 50 (53)

15 15.5   16.5 17.5

19.5 20

53 56.5

back

33 34

46.5 50

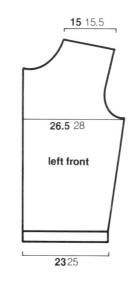

15 15.5

26.5 28

left front

23 25

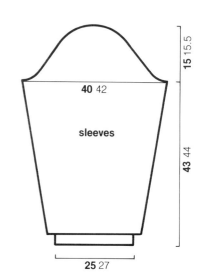

15 15.5

40 42

sleeves

43 44

25 27

sts. Now inc 1 st at same edge on every foll 6th row 6 times.

At same time, keep front edge straight until work measures 46 (48)cm, 18⅛ (18⅞)in, from beg, ending at front edge.

▦ **Shoulder and Neck Shaping**
Cast off 5 (6) sts at beg of next row, 2 sts at same edge on next 6 alt rows and 1 st on next 3 alt rows; *at same time*, after last inc at armhole edge, keep this edge straight until work matches back to shoulder, ending at this edge. Cast off 9 sts at beg of next row and next 2 alt rows, work 1 row then cast off rem 9 (11) sts.

RIGHT FRONT

▦ Work as for left front until welt is completed then change to 3¼mm needles and cont on 56 (60) sts in st st working patt from Chart No 2.

▦ *1st row* K 1 (3) **A**, then working from chart k 23 **A**, join on **B** and k 1 **B**, k 31 **A** to complete chart, k 0 (2) **A**. Cont as now set and using Chart No 2 throughout, complete as for left front reversing shapings.

LEFT SLEEVE

▦ With 2¾mm needles and **A** cast on 57 (61) sts and work in rib for same number of rows as on back welt but working 4 incs evenly spaced along last row. 61 (65) sts. Change to 3¼mm needles and beg with a k row work in st st; inc 1 st at both ends of every foll 8th row twice then work 0 (2) rows on these 65 (69) sts. ✳✳✳✳
Now work in patt from Chart No 1.

▦ *1st row* K 5 (7) **A** then working from chart k 31 **A**, join on **B**, k 1 **B**, then k 23 **A** to complete chart, then 5 (7) **A**. Cont as now set and work 6 (4) rows without shaping then inc at both ends of next row, then every foll 8th row 3 (4) times, then every foll 6th row 12 (11) times keeping all extra sts at sides in **A**. Cont on 97 (101) sts until work measures 43 (44)cm, 17 (17⅜)in, from beg.

▦ **Top Shaping** Cast off 2 sts at beg of next 10 rows, 1 st at beg of next 24 (26) rows, 2 sts at beg of next 12 rows and 3 sts at beg of next 2 rows. Cast off rem 23 (25) sts.

RIGHT SLEEVE

▦ Work as for left sleeve to ✳✳✳✳ then work in patt from Chart No 2.

▦ *1st row* K 5 (7) **A**, then working from chart k 23 **A**, join on **B** and k 1 **B**, then k 31 **A** to complete chart then 5 (7) **A**. Cont as now set and complete to match left sleeve but using Chart No 2 throughout.

FRONT BORDERS

▦ With 3mm needles and **A** cast on 11 sts and work in m st.

▦ *1st row* K 1, ✳ p 1, k 1; rep from ✳ to end; this row forms m st and all rows are alike. Cont until work measures 3cm (1¼in) from beg, then make buttonhole.

▦ *Next row* M st 4, cast off 3, m st to end. On foll row cast on 3 sts over buttonhole. Cont in m st making 3 more buttonholes each 13.5 (14)cm, 5⅜ (5½)in, above lower edge of previous one then cont until border when slightly stretched fits along front edge of right front. Cast off. Make similar border for left front omitting buttonholes.

NECK BORDER

▦ With 3mm needles and **A** cast on 11 sts and work in m st for 84 (86)cm, 33 (33¾)in. Cast off.

MAKING UP

▦ First complete the motifs by working the leaves in the Swiss Darning method described on page 6. Join shoulder seams. Sew in sleeves gathering in fullness at the top. Join side and sleeve seams. Sew on front borders stretching them slightly to fit. Matching centre of neck border to centre back sew border around neck edges beg and ending halfway across front borders leaving same length free at each end to tie. Sew on buttons to correspond with buttonholes.

To achieve the authentic 1940s look, with wide shoulders to accentuate the cinched-in waist and demure tie neck, you should ideally insert shoulder pads, though these may be omitted if preferred. If you are using them, choose soft pads to avoid a rigid outline, catch-stitching them in place around the seams.

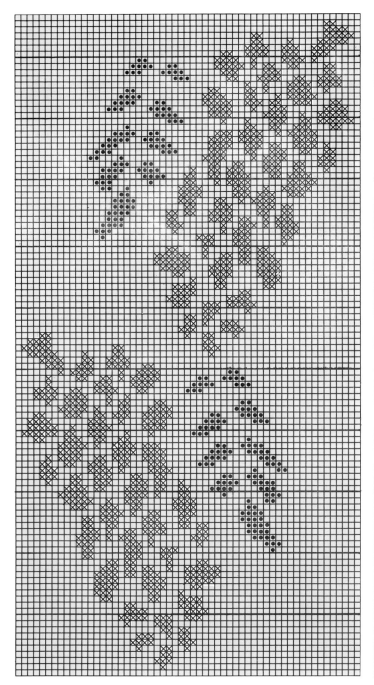

KEY

× Mauve

● Green

□ Grey

Chart 1 is used for the back, left front and left sleeve. Chart 2, which is a mirror image of Chart 1, is used for the right front and right sleeve. The mauve wisteria flowers are knitted in with the pattern while the leaves are added on later in Swiss darning (see page 8) Although the contrast between the knitted and embroidered areas of the motifs adds subtly to the texture of the pattern, you could knit the entire cardigan in the background shade and embroider the flowers as well as the leaves.

ETHNIC AFRICA

Tribal patterns and sizzling tropical colours are used for two sweaters based on traditional African textile designs. Every decorative surface in a tribal culture has a symbolic significance. This feeling has been echoed in the knitting by enriching the shapes with long straight stitch, in black, and little knots of bright yellow in the black borders. Both sweaters are generous in fit, in line with the bold colouring and distinctive designs.

CHECKLIST

Materials

Pernelle Touareg: *for Style 1, yellow as main colour, 9 balls No 252 (**Y**), and 4 balls noir No 207 (**B**),. For Style 2, black as main colour, 8 balls noir No 207 (**B**), and 5 balls No 252 (**Y**),. Pair each of needles size 3 mm and 3¼ mm.*
Note *If the above yarn is unobtainable, refer to page 192.*

Sizes

One size, to fit bust 92/102 cm (36/40 in), fitting very loosely. Actual measurements shown on diagram.

Stitches used

Single rib; st st; patt, *worked from charts. Separate balls are used for the various sections; take care always to twist them around each other when changing colour.*
Style 1 *Use a separate ball for each of the large diamonds and triangles and small balls for the small triangles in **Y**; for the small triangles in **B** at top of chart wind a short length onto a piece of card for each motif. The darning is worked afterwards.*
Style 2 *Use separate balls of **B** and **Y** for the vertical panels and small balls of each for the elongated diamonds. The ball of **B** used for the large diamond is also used for the small centre diamond. Join on short lengths of **B** for each of the small triangles; the spot in **Y** is worked afterwards. The single vertical lines in **B** are worked afterwards as is the darning.*

Tension

Over st st using 3¼ mm needles, 24 sts and 32 rows to 10 cm (4 in). Work a sample on 30 sts.

INSTRUCTIONS: STYLE 1

BACK

▦ With 3 mm needles and **Y** cast on 135 sts and work in rib.
▦ *1st row* (right side). P 1, * k 1, p 1; rep from * to end.
▦ *2nd row* K 1, * p 1, k 1; rep from * to end. Rep these 2 rows until work measures 8 cm (3⅛ in) from beg, ending with a 1st rib row.
▦ *Inc row* Rib 9, [inc in next st, rib 12] 9 times, inc in next st, rib 8. 145 sts. Change to 3¼ mm needles and beg with a k row work in st st. Cont until work measures 21 cm (8¼ in) from beg, ending with a p row. Begin working from Chart 1.
▦ *1st row* K 42 **Y**, join on a ball of **B**, k 1 **B**, then k 59 **Y**, join on another ball of **B**, k 1 **B**, then k 42 **Y**. Cont with colours as now set for 2 more rows.
▦ *4th row* P 41 **Y**, 3 **B**, 57 **Y**, 3 **B**, 41 **Y**. Cont with colours as now set for 2 more rows. Now join on separate balls of **Y** for the sections on each side of the triangles.
▦ *7th row* K 40 **Y**, 5 **B**, join on another ball of **Y**, k 55 **Y**, 5 **B**, join on another ball of **Y**, k 40 **Y**. Cont with colours as now set for 2 more rows. Now join on small balls of **Y** for centres of the triangles.

▥ *10th row* P 39 **Y**, 3 **B**, join on small ball of **Y**, 1 **Y**, 3 **B**, 53 **Y**, 3 **B**, join on small ball of **Y**, 1 **Y**, 3 **B**, 39 **Y**. Cont as now set for 2 more rows.

▥ *13th row* K 12 **Y**, rep from * to * on chart twice, joining on balls of **B** as required, 1 **B**, 12 **Y**. Cont working from chart, without shaping until 58th row of chart has been worked.

▥ **Armhole Shaping** Keeping patt correct cast off 4 sts at beg of next 2 rows, 3 sts at beg of next 4 rows and 2 sts at beg of next 2 rows then dec 1 st at both ends of every alt row 5 times. Cont on rem 111 sts until chart is completed then cont with **Y** only until work measures 66 cm (26 in) from beg, ending with a p row.

▥ **Neck Shaping** *1st row* K 40 and leave these sts of right back on needle, cast off 31, k to end. Cont on 40 sts now rem at end of needle for left back and work 1 row. Cast off 5 sts at beg of next row and next alt row, p 1 row on rem 30 sts, then cast off these sts for shoulder edge. Rejoin yarn to neck edge of right back sts, cast off 5, p to end. Cast off 5 sts at neck edge on next alt row, work 2 rows straight. Cast off rem 30 sts.

FRONT

▥ Work as for back until work measures 60 cm (23⅝ in) from beg, ending with a p row.

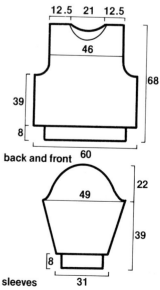

back and front

sleeves

▦ **Neck Shaping** *1st row* K 45 and leave these sts of left front on a spare needle, cast off next 21 sts, k to end. Cont on 45 sts now rem on needle for right front and work 1 row straight. ✳✳ Cast off 4 sts at beg of next row, 2 sts at same

edge on next 2 alt rows and 1 st on next 7 alt rows. Cont on rem 30 sts until work matches back to shoulder edge. Cast off. Rejoin yarn to neck edge of left front sts and complete as for right front from ✳✳ to end.

SLEEVES
▦ With 3 mm needles and **Y** cast on 65 sts and work in rib as on back welt for 8 cm (3⅛ in) ending with a 1st rib row.
▦ *Inc row* Rib 5, [inc in next st, rib 5] 10 times. 75 sts. Change to

3¼ mm needles and beg with a k row work in st st but inc 1 st at both ends of every foll 6th row 8 times, then every foll 4th row 11 times. *At same time*, when 40 rows have been worked in st st and there are 87 sts, begin working from chart.
▦ *1st row of chart* K 13 **Y**, join on a ball of **B**, k 1 **B**, then 59 **Y**, join on another ball of **B**, 1 **B**, then 13 **Y**. Cont working from chart as now set and cont with incs until all are completed taking extra sts into patt. Cont on 113 sts until 58th row has been worked from chart.
▦ **Top Shaping** Keep patt correct until chart is completed then cont with **Y** only; cast off 4 sts at beg of next 2 rows, 3 sts at beg of next 4 rows and 2 sts at beg of next 2 rows; dec 1 st at both ends of every alt row 26 times, then cast off 2 sts at beg of next 10 rows and 3 sts at beg of next 2 rows. Cast off rem 11 sts.

EMBROIDERY
▦ Using a length of **B** threaded in a tapestry needle complete the patt by working vertical sts as shown on chart, taking care to alternate the positions of sts in each row to give the effect of darning.

MAKING UP AND NECK BORDER
▦ Join right shoulder seam. With right side of work facing and using 3 mm needles and **Y**, pick up and k 78 sts round front neck edge and 55 sts across back neck. Beg with 2nd row work in rib for 9 rows then cast off loosely ribwise. Join left shoulder seam and ends of neck border. Sew in sleeves then join side and sleeve seams matching patt.

INSTRUCTIONS: STYLE 2

BACK
▦ Using **B** instead of **Y**, work as for Style 1 until work measures 21 cm (8¼ in) from beg, ending with a p row then begin working from Chart 2.
▦ *1st row* K 16 **Y**, * join on a ball of **B**, k 5 **B**, join on another ball of **Y**, k 31 **Y**;* rep from * to * twice more, join on a ball of **B**, k 5 **B**, join

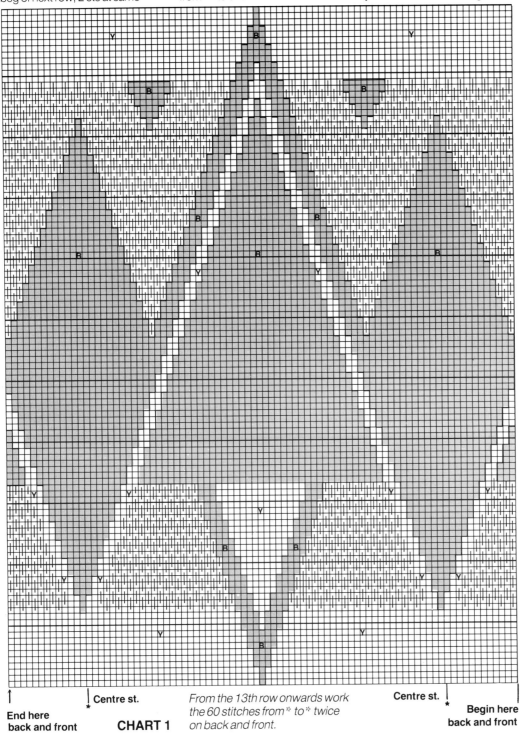

End here back and front | Centre st. | From the 13th row onwards work the 60 stitches from * to * twice on back and front. | Centre st. | Begin here back and front

CHART 1

on a ball of **Y**, k 16 **Y**. Now begin the small triangles in **B** joining on a short length of **B** for each, using the balls previously joined on for remainder of row.

⊞ *2nd row* P 12 **Y**, join on short length of **B**, p 1 **B**, then p 3 **Y**, * 5 **B**, 3 **Y**, join on short length of **B**, p 1 **B**, then 23 **Y**, join on short length of **B**, p 1 **B**, then 3 **Y**, * rep from * to * twice more, 5 **B**, 3 **Y**, join on short length of **B**, p 1 **B**, then 12 **Y**. Cont working from chart as now set and when 58th row has been worked, work armhole shaping as for Style 1. Cont on rem 111 sts until chart is completed then cont with **B** only and complete back as for Style 1.

FRONT
⊞ Work as for back until chart is completed then cont with **B** only until work measures 60 cm (23⅝ in) from beg, ending with a p row. Complete as for front of Style 1.

SLEEVES
⊞ Using **B** instead of **Y** work as for Style 1 until 40 rows have been worked in st st and there are 87 sts. Now begin working from Chart 2.

⊞ *1st row of chart* K 23 **Y**, rep from * to * in 1st row given for back once, join on a ball of **B**, k 5 **B**, join on a ball of **Y**, k 23 **Y**. Cont in patt as now set and cont with incs until all are completed. Cont on 113 sts until 58th row has been worked from chart.

⊞ **Top Shaping** Keep patt correct until chart is completed then cont with **B**, only.
At same time shape top as for Style 1.

EMBROIDERY
⊞ Using **Y** make a French knot in centre of each of the small **B** triangles. Using a length of **B** threaded into a tapestry needle work the vertical sts as shown on chart to form the darning effect. Using **B** work the single vertical lines; on each side of the 5 sts in **B**, miss the next st in **Y** then cover the next st with a line of **B** using the Swiss Darning method.

MAKING UP
⊞ As Style 1, using, **B** for neck.

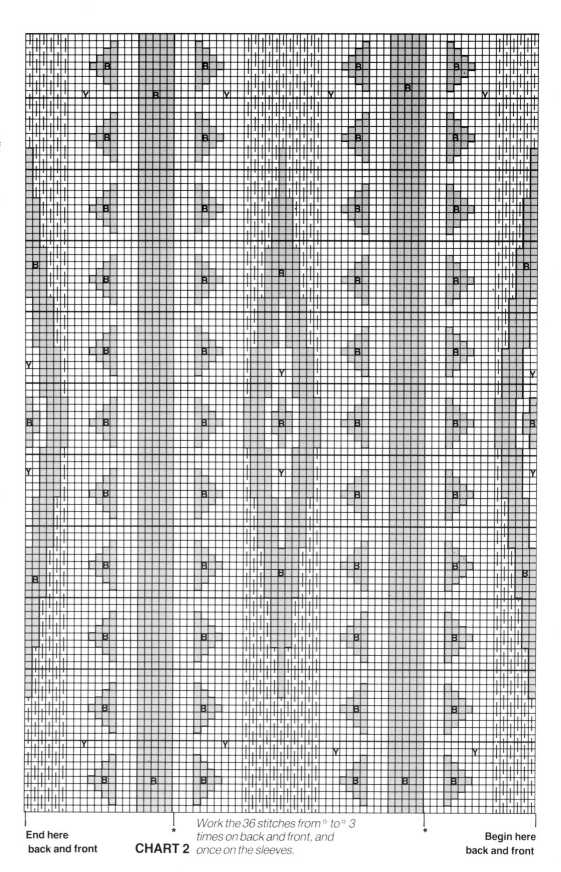

End here
back and front

CHART 2

*Work the 36 stitches from * to * 3 times on back and front, and once on the sleeves.*

Begin here
back and front

CINEMASCOPE JERSEY

Cinemascope colours on a black background give great style to this big, loose-cut jersey, with raglan shaping. The two designs on the front of the sweater are knitted in, but the one on the sleeve is appliquéd on top of the finished sleeve seam for a neater effect. Filmic sprocket holes are embroidered on the stocking stitch after making up, a witty detail that is simplicity itself to achieve, and if you do not enjoy jacquard knitting you could Swiss darn all details.

CHECKLIST

Materials
La Droguerie quality Surnaturelle *in the foll colours: 9 (10) balls noir (**A**) and 1 ball chaudron (**5**), a dark tan shade; for the rem colours only small amounts are needed and in each case we give the shade name and also the actual colour. Small amounts in anis (pale green), abricot (light orange), ocre (ochre), bleu ocean (deep blue), porcelaine (lighter blue), gris argent (silvery grey), saumon (salmon pink), bois de rose (deep pink), mangue (orange), jaune (yellow) and blanc (white). Pair each of needles size 2¼mm and 3mm.*
Note *If the above yarn is unobtainable, refer to page 192.*

Sizes
Two sizes, to fit bust 82/87 (92/97) cm; 32/34 (36/38) in, fitting very loosely. Actual measurements shown on diagram.

Stitches used
*Single rib; st st; for the motifs work from charts as explained below. Use a separate ball of **A** for the sts on each side of the motifs and when **A** is used during the motif join on a short length to avoid carrying it across. Always twist yarns around each other when changing colour. Join on the other colours as required. The short vertical lines around the yoke are embroidered on afterwards.*

Tension
Over st st using 3mm needles, 30 sts and 38 rows to 10 cm (4 in). Work a sample on 36 sts.

INSTRUCTIONS

BACK
▦ With 2¼mm needles and **A** cast on 159 (175) sts and work in rib.
▦ *1st row* (right side). P 1, * k 1, p 1; rep from * to end.
▦ *2nd row* K 1, * p 1, k 1; rep from * to end. Rep these 2 rows 7 times more then change to **5** and work 3 more rows. Change back to **A**.
▦ *Inc row* Rib 4 (2), [inc in next st, rib 9] 15 (17) times, inc in next st, rib 4 (2). 175 (193) sts. Change to 3mm needles and beg with a k row work in st st. Cont until work measures 14 (16) cm, 5½ (6¼) in, from beg, ending with a p row then begin motif from Chart A.

▦ *1st row* K 16 (22) **A**, join on white and k 1, then k rem 74 sts of this chart in **A**, then k rem sts of row in **A**. On foll row join on a ball of pale green for background of chart leaving the first ball of **A** hanging at side of motif, joining on another ball of **A** for sts at other side. Remember always to twist **A** around the colour being used for motif at beg and end of motif. When this motif is completed cont with **A** only until work measures 36 (39) cm, 14⅛ (15⅜) in, from beg, ending with a p row.
▦ **Raglan Shaping** Cast off 2 sts at beg of next 2 rows. ** K 1 row without shaping, dec at both ends of next 2 rows, p 1 row without shaping then dec at both ends of

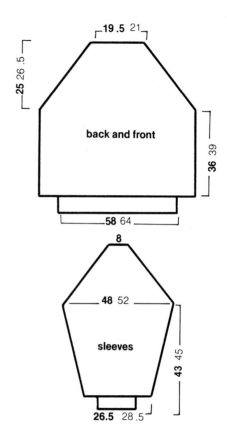

back and front

sleeves

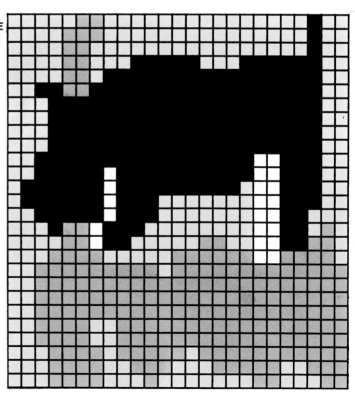

E

148

foll 2 rows. ✳✳ Rep from ✳✳ to ✳✳ 8 (12) times more. Now dec at both ends of every alt row 20 (11) times. Cast off rem 59 (63) sts for back neck.

FRONT

▦ Work as for back until work measures 10 (12) cm, 4 (4¾) in, from beg, ending with a p row. Now begin motif from Chart B.

▦ 1st row K 19 (25) **A**, then working from chart k 24 **A**, join on deep blue and k 11 sts with this, join on another ball of **A** and k rem 11 sts of motif then k rem sts of row in **A**. Cont working from chart as now set until motif is completed then work 4 rows in **A**. Now work motif from Chart C.

▦ 1st row K 93 (105) **A**, join on pale green and k 41 with this, join on a short length of **A** and k 3, k 1 with the green, 3 **A**, then with green k rem 8 sts of motif, join on another ball of **A**, k 26 (32) **A**. Cont with this motif as now set and when it is completed cont with **A** only. Work as given for back, beg raglan shaping in same way and cont until 84 (90) rows of raglan shaping have been worked ending

with a p row. 71 (75) sts.

▦ **Neck Shaping** 1st row K 26 and leave these sts of left front on a spare needle, cast off next 19 (23) sts, k to end. Cont on 26 sts now rem on needle for right front. ✳✳✳ Cont to dec at raglan edge on next row and next 5 alt rows; at same time cast off at neck edge on alt rows 4 sts twice and 3 sts 3 times. After last raglan dec cast off rem 3 sts. Rejoin yarn to neck edge of left front sts and complete as for right front from ✳✳✳ to end.

LEFT SLEEVE

▦ With 2¼ mm needles and **A** cast on 69 (73) sts and work in rib as on back welt working 16 rows in **A** then 3 rows in **5**. Change back to **A**.

▦ Inc row Rib 4 (6), [inc in next st, rib 5 (4)] 10 (12) times, inc in next st, rib 4 (6). 80 (86) sts. Change to 3 mm needles and beg with a k row work in st st using **A**. Inc 1 st at both ends of every foll 6th row 4 (2) times, then every foll 4th row 28 (33) times.

At same time, when work measures 38 (40) cm, 15 (15¾) in, from beg, ending with a p row,

begin motif from Chart D on the centre 24 sts of row. When side incs are completed cont on 144 (156) sts until work measures 43 (45) cm, 17 (17¾) in, from beg, ending with a p row.

▦ **Raglan Shaping** Cont with motif until it is completed then cont in **A** and at same time, cast off 2 sts at beg of next 2 rows then rep from ✳✳ to ✳✳ as on back raglan 10 (13) times, then dec 1 st at both ends of every alt row 17 (11) times. Cast off rem 26 sts.

RIGHT SLEEVE

▦ Work as for left sleeve but omitting the motif which is worked separately. For the motif cast on 25 sts using yellow and p 1 row then cont in st st working from Chart E with colours as shown.

MAKING UP AND NECK BORDER

▦ Join front raglan seams and right back seam. With right side of work facing and using 2¼ mm needles and **A**, pick up and k 25 sts across top edge of left sleeve, 71 (75) sts round front neck edge, 24 sts across top of right sleeve

and 59 (63) sts across back neck. Beg with 2nd row work in rib as on welt working 13 rows in **A**, 3 rows in **5** and 16 rows in **A**. Cast off loosely ribwise. Join left shoulder seam and ends of neck border. Now using white work the short vertical lines beg on front. Mark the centre st of work at a position 8 cm (3⅛ in) above start of raglan and using the Swiss Darning method explained on page 6, cover this st in white and work 9 more sts above this in a vertical line. Miss next 9 sts to one side and work a similar line, then cont in this way to raglan edge. Work similar lines on other side of centre and cont the lines across each sleeve forming a neat angle where the lines meet on raglan.

▦ Join side and sleeve seams. Slip-st motif worked from Chart E to right sleeve with lower edge 13 (15) cm, 5⅛ (5⅞) in, from beg of sleeve and placing it exactly centred over sleeve seam. Fold neck border in half to wrong side and slip-st cast-off edge to back of picked-up sts.

A *Back*
B *Left front*
C *Right front*
D *Left sleeve*
E *(see page 148) Right sleeve*
A, B, C and **D** *are knitted in with the pattern.* **E** *is Swiss darned (see page 8) after the sleeve seam has been sewn.*

KEY

1 *Pale green*

2 *Apricot/orange*

3 *Ochre*

4 *Deep blue*

5 *Tan*

6 *Porcelain/mid-blue*

7 *Silvery grey*

8 *Salmon*

9 *Old rose*

10 *Peachy-sand*

11 *Golden yellow*

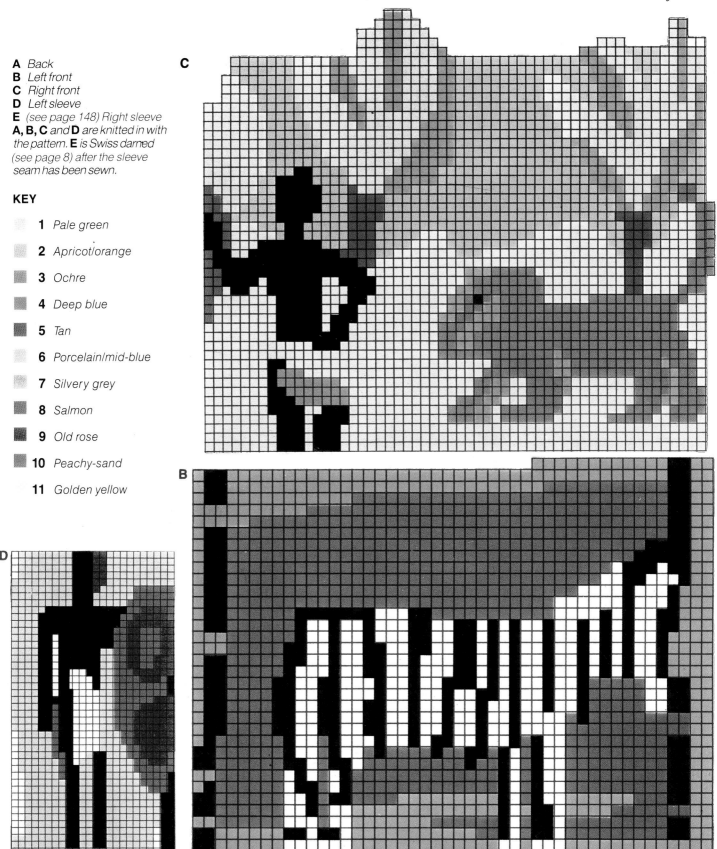

TECHNICOLOUR MOHAIR

This beautiful drop-sleeve coat uses all the colours of the primary palette to give drama to plain black. The main sections are worked with a strand each of thick yarn and mohair twined together, for thickness and luxury. Under the mohair coat is a dazzling red mini dress with a huge roll collar and turnback cuffs in a different, thick, fluffy yarn. The main parts are in a wide rib, with a fisherman's rib for the collar and cuffs. Big needle sizes make both quick to knit.

MULTICOLOURED COAT

CHECKLIST

Materials
La Droguerie Mohair: *500g noir* (**A**). Surnaturelle: *350g noir* (**B**). Benjamine: *160g rouge vermillon* (**C**), *bright red; 50g blue dur* (**E**), *bright blue; 50g jaune* (**J**), *yellow; 50g violet* (**G**); *50g vert vif* (**H**), *bright green; 100g fuchsia* (**D**), *and 50g orange* (**F**). *Pair each of needles size 4mm and 5mm; a cable needle; 2 buttons.*
Note *If the above yarn is unobtainable, refer to page 192.*

Sizes
Two sizes, to fit bust 82/87 (92/97) cm; 32/34 (36/38) in. Actual measurements shown on diagram; these measurements do not include the cable braids.

Stitches used
Rice st, *worked on an odd number of sts as folls:*
  1st row *(right side). K 1, * p 1, k 1; rep from * to end.*
  2nd row *K all sts. These 2 rows form one patt.*
  Cable patt *worked over 13 sts for the braids.*
  1st row *(right side). P 2, k 9, p 2.*
  2nd row *P all sts.*
  3rd row *P 2, slip next 3 sts on cable needle, leave at back, k 3, then k 3 from cable needle, k next 3 sts, p 2.*
  4th row *P.*
  5th row *P 2, k 3, slip next 3 sts on cable needle, leave at front, k 3, then k 3 from cable needle, p 2.*
  6th row *P. The last 4 rows from 3rd to 6th inclusive, form one patt.*

Tensions
Over rice st using 5mm needles and a strand each of **A** *and* **B** *tog, 18 sts and 24 rows to 10cm (4 in). The braid worked on 4mm needles using Pingofrance, measures 4cm (1½in) wide.*

INSTRUCTIONS

BACK
▦ With 5mm needles and using **A** and **B** tog cast on 91 (103) sts and work in rice st; cont until work measures 70 (75) cm, 27½ (29½) in from beg, ending with a 2nd patt row. Cast off all sts in patt. On cast-off edge mark the centre 33 (37) sts for neckline leaving 29 (33) sts on each side for shoulders.

LEFT FRONT
▦ With 5mm needles and using **A** and **B** tog, cast on 49 (55) sts and work in rice st; cont until work measures 62 (67) cm, 24⅜ (26⅜) in, from beg, ending with a 1st patt row.
▦ **Neck Shaping** Cast off 12 (14) sts at beg of next row, 2 sts at same edge on next 2 alt rows and 1 st on next 4 alt rows. ** Cont on rem 29 (33) sts until work

measures 70 (75) cm, 27½ (29½) in, from beg, ending with a 2nd patt row. Cast off in patt.

RIGHT FRONT

▦ With 5 mm needles and using **A** and **B** tog, cast on 57 (63) sts and work in rice st; cont until work measures 62 (67) cm, 24⅜ (26⅜) in, from beg, ending with a 2nd patt row.

▦ **Neck Shaping** Cast off 20 (22) sts at beg of next row, 2 sts at same edge on next 2 alt rows and 1 st on next 4 alt rows. Complete as for left front from ✴✴ to end.

SLEEVES

▦ Each sleeve is worked in two halves. For one half cast on 17 (19) sts using 5 mm needles and **A** and **B** tog. Work 4 rows in patt then to shape side edge inc 1 st at beg of next row, then at same edge on every foll 4th row 6 times more, then on every alt row 34 (36) times working extra sts into patt. Cont on 58 (62) sts until work measures 43 (45) cm, 17 (17¾) in, from beg, ending with a 2nd patt row.
▦ Cast off in patt. Work other half of sleeve in same way but working shapings at opposite edge – end of right-side rows.

POCKET

▦ Make one only. With 5 mm needles and using **A** and **B** tog, cast on 39 (41) sts and work in patt for 23 (24) cm, 9 (9½) in, ending with a 2nd patt row. Cast off in patt.

BRAIDS

▦ These are all worked with 4 mm needles; cast on 13 sts for each braid and work in cable patt using colours as folls: using **C** work a braid 38 (41) cm, 15 (16⅛) in long for sewing between right front and back and a similar braid using **D** for sewing between left front and back. Using **H** work a braid 43 (45) cm, 17 (17¾) in long for centre of left sleeve and a similar braid using **J** for centre of right sleeve. Using **H** work a braid 16 (18) cm, 6¼ (7) in long for left shoulder and a similar braid using **J** for right shoulder. Using **D** work a braid 67 (71) cm, 26⅜ (30) in long for left armhole and a similar braid using

C for right armhole. Using **F** work a braid 62 (67) cm, 24⅜ (26⅜) in long for left front border and a similar braid using **E** for right front border. Using **G** work a braid 57 (62) cm, 22½ (24⅜) in long for neck border; leave the sts of this braid on a safety pin for adjustment if necessary without cutting yarn. Using **F** work a braid long enough to fit across top of pocket.

MAKING UP

▦ Sew shoulder braids between shoulder edges of back and front; for all the braids lap edge of braid over edge of main part and sew in place with small neat sts in the purl edging. Assemble the two halves of each sleeve by sewing the braids between them. Sew armhole borders to upper edges of each sleeve ensuring that when seen from the front the braid patt will run vertically on each armhole. Pin other edge of armhole borders to sides of coat matching centre of sleeve to centre of shoulder braid and ensuring that 38 (41) cm, 15 (16⅛) in, is left free on each side edge. Sew armhole borders in place; join sleeve seams and cont seams along half the width of armhole borders. Now sew side braids between side edges of back and fronts and sew rem edges of armhole borders to top edge of side braids. Sew pocket braid to top of pocket and slip-st pocket to right front in desired position. Sew on front borders. Starting at right front neck edge pin neck border all round neck edges; adjust length if necessary so that it ends at left front neck edge and cast off sts. Sew neck border in place. Lap right front over left, sew a button to left front neck border and make a buttonhole loop on right front edge to correspond. Make another loop on front edge of left front border and sew rem button to wrong side of right front neck to correspond.

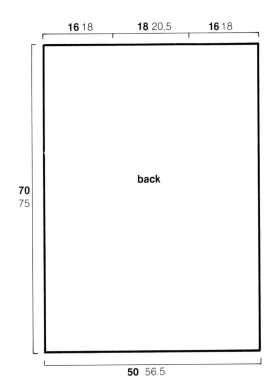

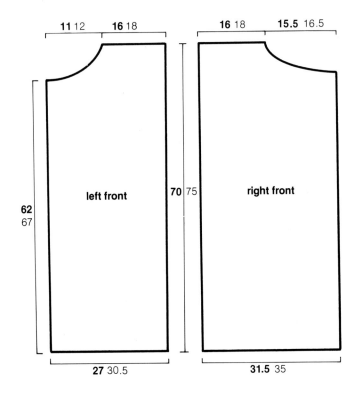

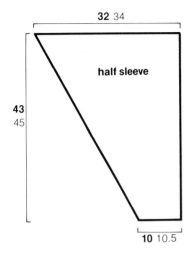

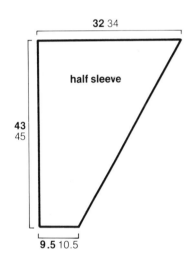

The measurements given above do not include the 4cm (1½in) wide cable pattern braids. These are used to join the back to fronts at the shoulders and down the sides, to join the two halves of each sleeve down the top seam and to attach the sleeves to the body of the coat. Braids are also used to give a decorative edging to the fronts, neck and pockets.

ROLL COLLAR DRESS

CHECKLIST

Materials

La Droguerie Mohair: 650g rouge. Pair each of needles size 4 mm and 5 mm.
Note *If the above yarn is unobtainable, refer to page 192.*

Sizes

Two sizes, to fit bust 82/87 (92/97) cm; 32/34 (36/38) in. Actual measurements shown on diagram.

Stitches used

Wide rib patt, *worked on a multiple of 10 sts plus 3 as folls:*
 1st row *(right side). P 4, * p 5, k 5; rep from * to last 9 sts, p 5, k 4.*
 2nd row k 4, * p 5, k 5; rep from * to last 9 sts, p 5, k 4. These 2 rows form patt. Fisherman rib, *worked on an even number of sts as folls:*
 1st row *(right side). K all sts; this row forms a foundation and is not worked again.*
 2nd row K 1, * k next st but in row below, inserting needle through work from front to back and allowing st above to drop off needle, k next st normally; rep from * to last st, k 1. This row forms patt; cont to rep 2nd row throughout. The rib effect does not appear until several rows have been worked.

Tensions

Over wide rib patt using 5 mm needles and flattening work slightly when measuring, 19 sts and 22 rows to 10 cm (4 in). Over Fisherman rib patt using 4 mm needles, 15 sts and 32 rows to 10 cm (4 in). When counting rows in this patt each k rib which you can see counts as 2 rows.

INSTRUCTIONS

MAIN PART

▦ Beg at lower edge of back cast on 103 (113) sts and work in wide rib patt. Cont until work measures 53 (57) cm, 20⅞ (22½) in, from beg, ending with a 2nd patt row.

▦ **Sleeve Shaping** Cast on 2 sts at beg of next 10 (6) rows and 3 sts at beg of next 36 (40) rows taking extra sts into patt. 231 (245) sts. The right-side rows will now begin and end k 3 (5) and wrong-side rows p 3 (5). At this point it may be more convenient to use a circular needle still working in rows as usual. Cont in patt and work 12

(13) cm, 4¾ (5⅛) in, without shaping ending with a wrong-side row.

▦ **Neck Shaping** *1st row* Patt 100 (106) and leave these sts of right back on a spare needle, cast off next 31 (33) sts in patt, then patt to end.

Cont on 100 (106) sts now rem on needle for left back. ** Dec 1 st at neck edge on next 4 rows. The shoulder line has now been reached so place a marker loop of contrast yarn at side edge and cont on same sts for left front. Work 5 cm (2 in) without shaping on rem 96 (102) sts ending at neck edge. Inc 1 st at beg of next row

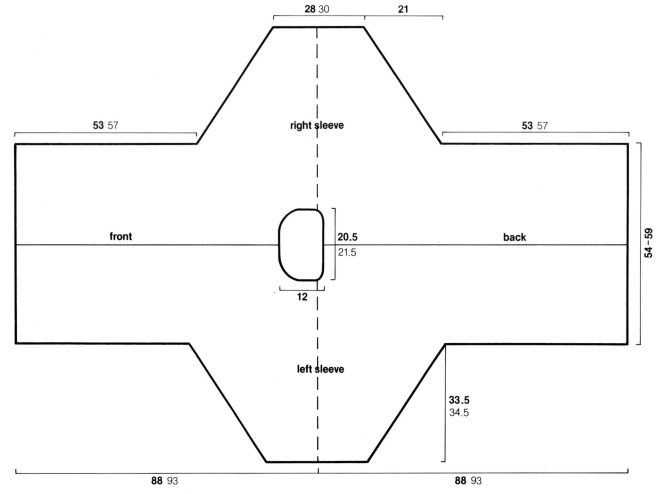

and next 2 alt rows then cast on 2 sts at same edge on next 2 alt rows and 4 sts on next alt row. ✳✳ Work 1 row on these 107 (113) sts thus ending at neck edge then cut yarn and leave these sts on a spare needle.

▦ Rejoin yarn to neck edge of right back sts and cont as for left back and front from ✳✳ to ✳✳ ending at side edge after last shaping row.

▦ *Next row* Patt across these 107 (113) sts, turn, cast on 17 (19) sts, turn, then work in patt across sts of left front. 231 (245) sts. Cont in patt across all sts until work measures 14 (15) cm, 5½ (5⅞) in from shoulder markers, ending with a wrong-side row.

▦ **Sleeve Shaping** Cast off 3 sts at beg of next 36 (40) rows and 2 sts at beg of next 10 (6) rows. Cont on rem 103 (113) sts and work 53 (57) cm, 20⅞ (22½) in, in patt. Cast off loosely in patt.

COLLAR
▦ With 4 mm needles cast on 126 (130) sts and work in Fisherman rib; cont until work measures 24 cm (9½ in) from beg. Cast off very loosely.

CUFFS
▦ Make 2 alike. With 4 mm needles cast on 42 (44) sts and work in Fisherman rib patt until work measures 17 cm (6⅝ in) from beg. Cast off very loosely.

MAKING UP
▦ With right side of cuff to wrong side of dress sew cast-off edges of cuffs to side edges of sleeve sections of main part. Join side and sleeve seams reversing seams on cuffs. Join sides of collar. With right side of collar to wrong side of dress, placing seam at centre back, sew cast-off edge of collar to neck edges easing in collar to fit.

The roll collar dress is the perfect partner for the coat featured on the previous page, but you could easily shorten the pattern to make a chunky sweater. The dress is knitted in one piece, like a poncho but with added cuffs and collar.

JAPANESE WAVE

Inspired by the Japanese artist, Hokusai, this all-weather jumper can be worn with winter woollens or over lighter-weight summer skirts. The back of the design is worked in stripes to echo the colours of the waves and foam. It's much less complicated than it first appears – graphs give you all the decorative details, and stocking stitch is easy to maintain.

CHECKLIST

Materials

*Laine Marigold 4 fils using the foll colours: 5 balls marine No 8601 (**1**), blue black; 3 balls ecru No 8627 (**7**); 2 balls mélé gris moyen No 8650 (**4**), mid grey; 2 balls mélé gris No 8607 (**3**), light grey; 2 balls granit bleu No 8691 (**2**), blue grey; 1 ball or part-ball in each of the foll, berlingot No 8798 (**5**), pink; terre No 8804 (**6**), mid brown; hussard No 8739 (**11**), light blue; ciel No 8097 (**12**), darker blue; opaline No 8811 (**13**), light green; bleu roi No 8616 (**9**), royal blue; porcelaine No 8693 (**8**), bright blue, and marmara No 8674 (**10**), dark blue green. Pair each of needles size 3mm and 3¾ mm.*
Note *If the above yarn is unobtainable, refer to page 192.*

Size

One size to fit bust 82 to 92 cm (32 to 36 in). Actual measurements given on diagram.

Stitches used

Single rib; st st; patt, worked from charts on front and sleeves. Use separate balls or short lengths of yarn for each of the sections shown on chart taking care to wind yarns around each other when changing colour. Any very small sections can be embroidered on afterwards using the Swiss Darning method described on page 6. Back is worked in stripes to coincide with some of the colour changes on the front.

Tension

Over st st using Laine Marigold *and 3¾ mm needles or* Pingouin *yarns and 3¼ mm needles, 24 sts and 32 rows to 10 cm (4 in). Work a sample on 28 sts. Take care to use the stated sizes for the correct yarn.*

INSTRUCTIONS

BACK

▦ With smaller needles and **1** cast on 115 sts and work in rib.
▦ *1st row* (right side). P 1, * k 1, p 1; rep from * to end.
▦ *2nd row* K 1, * p 1, k 1; rep from * to end. Rep these 2 rows until work measures 8 cm (3⅛ in) from beg, ending with a 1st rib row.
▦ *Inc row* Rib 9, [inc in next st, rib 15] 6 times, inc in next st, rib 9. 122 sts. Change to larger needles and beg with a k row work in st st. Work 74 rows in **1**, 6 rows in **4**, 32 rows in **3** and 24 rows in **2**, then cont with **1**.
At same time, cont until 98 rows have been worked in st st.
▦ **Armhole Shaping** Cast off 4 sts at beg of next 2 rows, 2 sts at beg of next 6 rows and 1 st at beg of next 4 rows. Cont on rem 98 sts and when the stripe in **2** has been completed cont with **1** until 156th row has been worked in st st.
▦ **Neck and Shoulder Shaping** *157th row* K 36 and leave these sts of right back on spare needle, cast off next 26 sts, k to end. Cont on 36 sts now rem on needle for left back and work 1 row straight.
** Cast off 3 sts at beg of next row and 10 sts at side edge on foll row; rep last 2 rows once. Work 1 row straight then cast off rem 10 sts to complete shoulder slope. Rejoin

yarn to neck edge of right back sts and complete as for left back from ** to end.

FRONT
▦ Work as for back until the inc row has been completed at end of welt. Change to larger needles and beg with a k row work in st st working patt from Chart 1. Work armhole shaping as given for back beg on 99th row of chart. Cont on rem 98 sts until 137th row has been worked from chart.

▦ **Neck and Shoulder Shaping**
138th row Patt 43 and leave these sts of right front on a spare needle, cast off next 12 sts, patt to end. Cont on 43 sts now rem on needle for left front and work 1 row straight. *** Cast off 3 sts at beg of next row, 2 sts at same edge on next 2 alt rows and 1 st on next 6 alt rows. *** Cont on rem 30 sts and work 2 rows straight then cast off for shoulder 10 sts at beg of next row and next alt row, work 1 row then cast off rem 10 sts.
▦ Rejoin yarn to neck edge of right front sts and keeping patt correct cont as for left front from *** to ***. Cont on rem 30 sts until 159th row has been worked from chart thus ending at side edge. Shape shoulder as for left front.

RIGHT SLEEVE
▦ With smaller needles and **1** cast on 53 sts and work in rib as on

back welt for 7 cm (2¾ in), ending with a 1st rib row.
▦ *Inc row* Rib 1, [inc in next st, rib 4] 10 times, inc in next st, rib 1. 64 sts. Change to larger needles and beg with a k row work in st st working patt from Chart 2. Inc 1 st at both ends of 5th row, then every foll 4th row 3 times, then at both ends of every foll 6th row 7 times, then every foll 8th row 4 times. All these incs are shown on chart. Cont on 94 sts until 128 rows have been worked from chart.
▦ **Top Shaping** Cast off 4 sts at beg of next 2 rows and 2 sts at beg of next 8 rows; now dec 1 st at both ends of every alt row 8 times, then cast off 2 sts at beg of next 12 rows and 3 sts at beg of next 6 rows. Cast off rem 12 sts.

LEFT SLEEVE
▦ Work as for right sleeve but working patt from Chart 3.

NECK BORDER
▦ Join right shoulder seam. With right side of work facing and using smaller needles and **1**, pick up and k 57 sts around front neck edge and 42 sts across back neck. Beg with 2nd row work in rib for 6 rows then cast off loosely ribwise.

MAKING UP
▦ Join left shoulder seam and ends of neck border. Sew in sleeves. Join remaining seams.

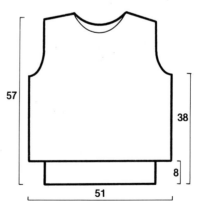

back and front

If you find the fine detail of the huge tsunami *wave too daunting to knit, many of the isolated splashes of foam could easily be Swiss darned after the larger-scale areas have been knitted.*

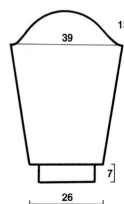

sleeves

Note that although the neck and shoulder shapings are shown on the chart as being at both ends of the same row, they are worked at the start of consecutive rows in the usual manner.

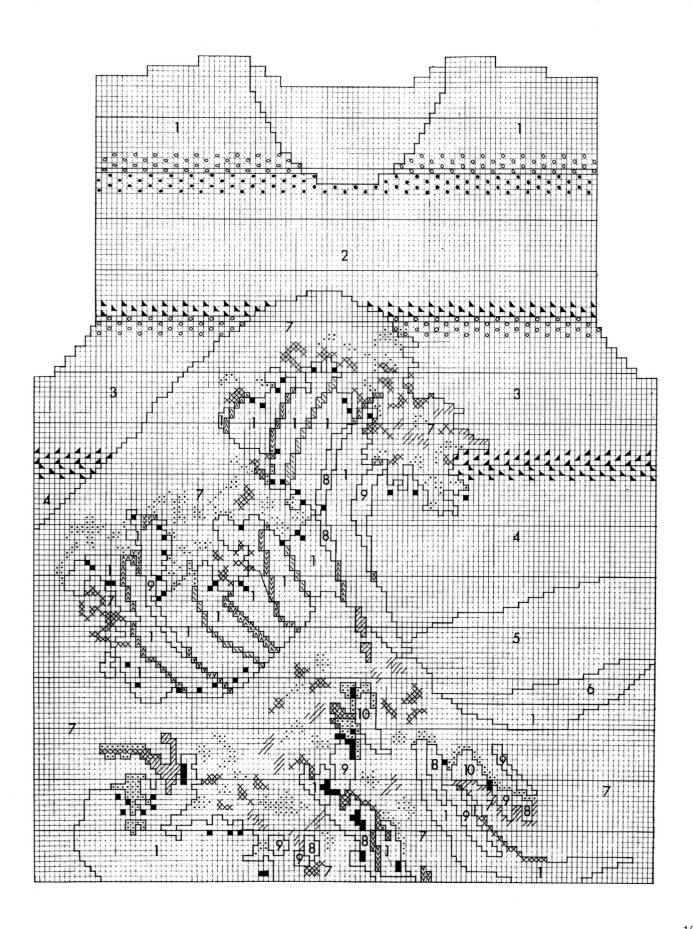

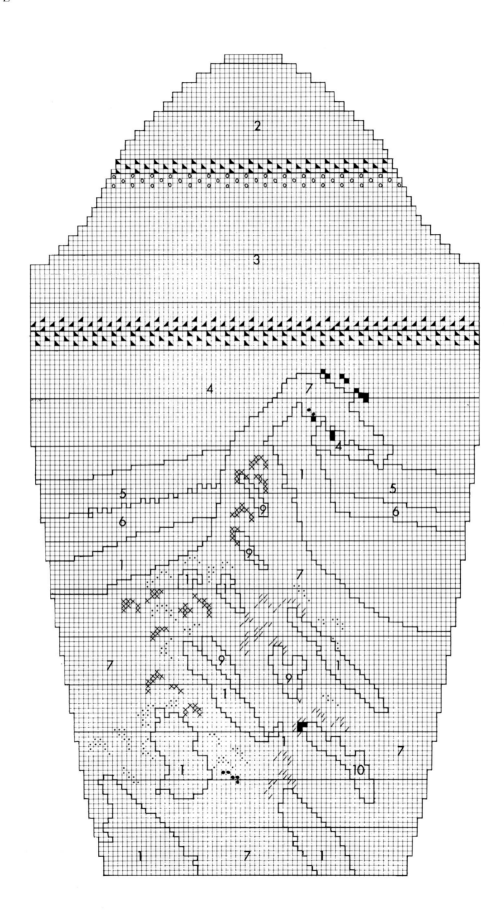

KEY

1 and ● *Blue black*
2 and ○ *Blue grey*
3 and ◤ *Light grey*
4 and ◥ *Mid grey*
5 *Pink*
6 *Mid brown*
7 and ■ *Ecru*
8 and ^ *Bright blue*
9 and ˅ *Royal blue*
10 and ` *Dark blue green*
11 and . *Light blue*
12 and × *Darker blue*
13 and / *Light green*

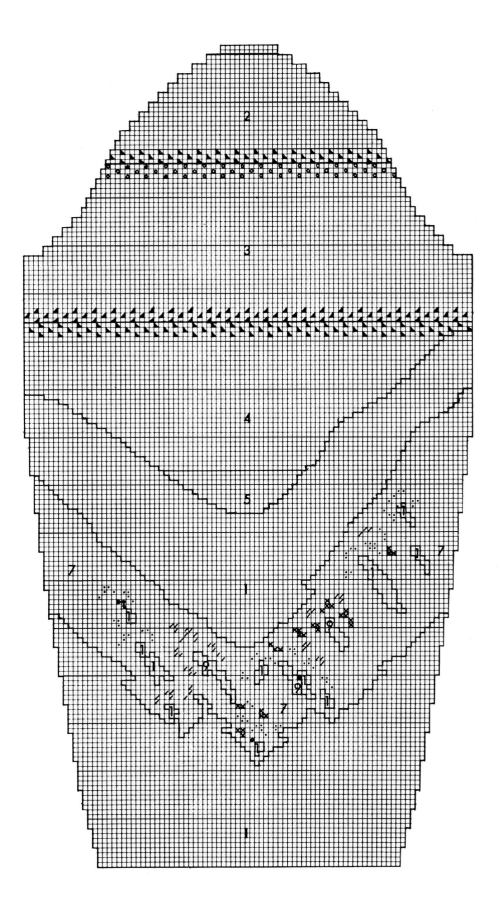

The subtle effect of the finished sweater is due in large part to the use of closely related shades in a limited colour range of blues, greys and neutrals, with just a touch of brown and green. The colours available in different yarns are constantly changing and it may not be possible for you to use exactly the same shades as the designer, but provided you keep to a similar palette of colours there is no reason why your sweater should not be just as successful as the original. As with the front, the sleeve top shapings are shown on the charts as being at both ends of the same row but they are made at the beginning of consecutive rows in the usual manner.

THIRTIES FAVOURITES

Make an echo of the past with 1930s lacy patterns in a classic T-shirt line. All four are the same shape and all are knitted in a pure cotton yarn for a cool, summery feel. You need a little experience for the laces, which are all delightfully old-fashioned in name. The first, in pale blue, is called the 'bunch of grapes' pattern. The second, in a darker blue, is known as 'the waffle', while the third, very French in ecru, is called a 'fantasy zig-zag lace'. The fourth, a nostalgic old-rose pink, is called 'dance of the little faun'. Intricate lace patterns can be time-consuming to knit, but these little T-shirts are worked on large needles so they do not take an age to make.

BUNCH OF GRAPES

CHECKLIST

Materials
Georges Picaud Akala *mercerized cotton: 8 (9-9) balls. Pair each of needles size 3 mm and 4 ½ mm.*

Sizes
Three sizes, to fit bust 76/82 (87-92/97) cm; 30/32 (34-36/38) in. Actual measurements shown on diagram in centimetres.

Stitches used
Single rib; g st; bunch of grapes patt, *worked on a multiple of 8 sts plus 2 as folls:*

   1st row *K 1, * yfd, k 1 tbl, yfd, SKPO, k 5; * rep from * to * ending k 1.*
   2nd row *P 1, * p 4, p 2 tog tbl, p 3; * rep from * to * ending p 1.*
   3rd row *K 1, * yfd, k 1 tbl, yfd, k 2, SKPO, k 3; * rep from * to *, ending k 1.*
   4th row *P 1, * p 2, p 2 tog tbl, p 5; * rep from * to * ending p 1.*
   5th row *K 1, * k 1 tbl, yfd, k 4, SKPO, k 1, yfd; * rep from * to *, ending k 1.*
   6th row *P 1, * p 1, p 2 tog tbl, p 6; * rep from * to * ending p 1.*
   7th row *K 1, * k 5, k 2 tog, yfd, k 1 tbl, yfd; * rep from * to * ending k 1.*
   8th row *P 1, * p 3, p 2 tog, p 4; * rep from * to * ending p 1.*
   9th row *K 1, * k 3, k 2 tog, k 2, yfd, k 1 tbl, yfd; * rep from * to * ending k 1.*
   10th row *P 1, * p 5, p 2 tog, p 2; * rep from * to * ending p 1.*
   11th row *K 1, * yfd, k 1, k 2 tog, k 4, yfd, k 1 tbl; * rep from * to * ending k 1.*
   12th row *P 1, * p 6, p 2 tog, p 1; * rep from * to * ending p 1.*

These 12 rows form one patt. This patt requires some care; where the patt rep ends with yfd as on 5th, 7th and 9th rows remember to work the yfd at end of row before the last k 1. On every right-side row an extra st is made in each patt rep and these are eliminated on the foll row. If counting sts after a right-side row count the sts of each rep as 8 sts; do not make an extra yfd in places where you will be casting off on foll row.

Tension
Over patt using 4 ½ mm needles, 20 sts and 24 rows to 10 cm (4 in). Work a sample on 26 sts; this should measure 13 cm (5 ⅛ in) wide.

INSTRUCTIONS

BACK

▦ With 3 mm needles cast on 90 (98-106) sts and work in g st for 3 rows then change to 4½ mm needles and work in patt as given above. Cont until work measures 41 (42-43) cm, 16⅛ (16½-17) in, from beg, ending with a wrong-side row.

▦ **Armhole Shaping** Cast off 4 sts at beg of next 2 rows and 2 sts at beg of next 2 rows then dec 1 st at both ends of next 2 alt rows. Cont on rem 74 (82-90) sts until work measures 62 (64-66) cm, 24⅜ (25¼-26) in from beg, ending with a wrong-side row.

▦ **Shoulder and Neck Shaping** Cast off 6 (7-8) sts at beg of next 2 rows.

▦ *Next row* Cast off 6 (7-8), patt until there are 11 (12-13) sts on right needle, leave these for right back, cast off next 28 (30-32) sts, patt to end. Cont on 17 (19-21) sts now rem at end of needle for left back. Cast off 6 (7-8) sts at beg of next row and 4 sts at neck edge on foll row. Cast off rem 7 (8-9) sts to complete shoulder slope. Rejoin yarn to neck edge of right back sts, cast off 4, patt to end. Cast off rem 7 (8-9) sts.

FRONT

▦ Work as for back until work measures 56 (58-60) cm, 22 (22⅞-23⅝) in, from beg, ending with a wrong-side row.

▦ **Neck and Shoulder Shaping** *Next row* Patt 32 (35-38) and leave these sts of left front on a spare needle, cast off next 10 (12-14) sts, patt to end.

Cont on 32 (35-38) sts now rem on needle for right front and work 1 row. ** Cast off 4 sts at beg of next row, 2 sts at same edge on next 3 alt rows and 1 st on next 3 alt rows. *At same time*, when work matches back to beg of shoulder, ending at side, cast off 6 (7-8) sts at beg of next row and next alt row, work 1 row then cast off rem 7 (8-9) sts.

▦ Rejoin yarn to neck edge of left front sts; complete as for right front from ** to end.

SLEEVES

▦ With 3 mm needles cast on 70 (74-78) sts and work 2 rows in g st then k 1 more row working 4 incs evenly spaced. 74 (78-82) sts. Change to 4½ mm needles and patt; for 1st and 3rd sizes work patt as given above. (For 2nd size work 2 extra sts in st st at each side; thus the right-side rows will begin and end k 3 and wrong-side rows p 3.)

Cont in patt until work measures 5 cm (2 in) from beg then inc 1 st at both ends of next row keeping this extra st at each side in st st. Cont on 76 (80-84) sts until work measures 8 (8-9) cm, 3⅛ (3⅛-3½) in, from beg, ending with a wrong-side row.

▦ **Top Shaping** Cast off 4 sts at beg of next 2 rows, 2 sts at beg of next 8 (10-12) rows, 4 sts at beg of next 6 rows and 8 sts at beg of next 2 rows. Cast off rem 12 sts.

NECK BORDER

▦ Join right shoulder seam. With right side of work facing and using 3 mm needles, pick up and k 57 (59-61) sts round front neck edge and 38 (40-42) sts across back neck.

▦ *1st row* (wrong side). K 1, * p 1, k 1; rep from * to end.

▦ *2nd row* P 1, * k 1, p 1; rep from * to end. Cast off loosely ribwise.

MAKING UP

▦ Join left shoulder seam and ends of neck border. Sew in sleeves then join side and sleeve seams.

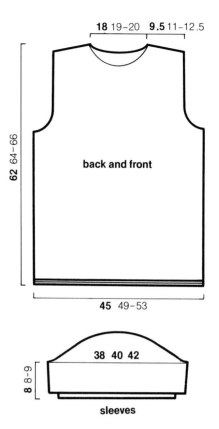

back and front

18 19-20 9.5 11-12.5

62 64-66

45 49-53

38 40 42

8 8-9

sleeves

THE WAFFLE

CHECKLIST

Materials

Filature de Paris Big Louisiana: *10 (11-11) balls gobelin, or colour of your choice. Pair each of needles size 3mm and 4½mm.*
Note *If the above yarn is unobtainable, refer to page 192.*

Sizes

Three sizes, to fit bust 82/87 (92-97) cm; 32/34 (36-38) in. Actual measurements shown on diagram.

Stitches used

Single rib; g st; cross 2 = *pass needle in front of 1st st, lift up 2nd st and k it leaving it on needle, then k 1st st and slip both off needle;* yo2 = *wind yarn twice around right needle;* k 2 in loop = *drop one loop of the yo2 to make a long st and k into front then into back of this st;* waffle patt, *worked on a multiple of 4 sts plus 2 as folls:*

1st row *(right side)*. K 1, yfd, * SKPO, k 2 tog, yo2; rep from * to last 5 sts, SKPO, k 2 tog, yfd, k 1.
2nd row K 2, * p 2, k 2 in loop; rep from * to last 4 sts, p 2, k 2.
3rd row K 1, p 1, * cross 2, p 2; rep from * to last 4 sts, cross 2, p 1, k 1.
4th row K 2, * p 2, k 2; rep from * to end.
5th row K 1, * k 2 tog, yo2, SKPO; rep from * to last st, k 1.
6th row K 1, p 1, * k 2 in loop, p 2; rep from * ending last rep p 1, k 1.
7th row K 2, * p 2, cross 2; rep from * to last 4 sts, p 2, k 2.
8th row K 1, p 1, * k 2, p 2; rep from * to last 4 sts, k 2, p 1, k 1.
These 8 rows form one patt.

Tension

Over patt using 4½ mm needles, 22 sts and 25 rows to 10 cm (4 in).
Work a sample on 26 sts.

INSTRUCTIONS

BACK

▦ With 3 mm needles cast on 102 (110-118) sts and work 3 rows in g st then change to 4½ mm needles and work in patt as given above. Cont until work measures 41 (42-43) cm, 16⅛ (16½-17) in, from beg, ending with a wrong-side row.

▦ **Armhole Shaping** Cast off 4 sts at beg of next 2 rows and 2 sts at beg of next 2 rows then dec 1 st at both ends of next 2 alt rows. Cont on rem 86 (94-102) sts until work measures 62 (64-66) cm, 24⅜ (25¼-26) in, from beg, ending with a wrong-side row.

▦ **Shoulder and Neck Shaping** Cast off 8 sts at beg of next 2 rows.

▦ *Next row* Cast off 8, patt until there are 11 (14-17) sts on right needle, leave these for right back, cast off next 32 (34-36) sts, patt to end. Cont on 19 (22-25) sts now rem at end of needle for left back. Cast off 8 sts at beg of next row

and 4 sts at neck edge on foll row. Cast off rem 7 (10-13) sts to complete shoulder slope. Rejoin yarn to neck edge of right back sts, cast off 4, patt to end. Cast off rem 7 (10-13) sts.

FRONT

▦ Work as for back until work measures 56 (58-60) cm, 22 (22⅞-26) in, from beg, ending with a wrong-side row.

▦ **Neck and Shoulder Shaping** *Next row* Patt 38 (41-44) and leave these sts of left front on a spare needle, cast off next 10 (12-14) sts, patt to end. Cont on 38 (41-44) sts now rem on needle for right front and work 1 row straight. ** Cast off 4 sts at beg of next row and next alt row, 2 sts at same edge on next 2 alt rows and 1 st on next 3 alt rows.

At same time, keep side edge straight until work matches back to shoulder, ending at side then cast off 8 sts at beg of next row and next alt row, work 1 row then

cast off rem 7 (10-13) sts. Rejoin yarn to neck edge of left front sts and complete as for right front from ** to end.

SLEEVES

▦ With 3 mm needles cast on 77 (81-85) sts and work 2 rows in g st then k 1 more row working 5 incs evenly spaced. 82 (86-90) sts. Change to 4½ mm needles and work in patt; cont until work measures 5 cm (2 in) from beg then inc 1 st at both ends of next row. Keep extra st at each side in st st still with border st in g st as before. Cont on 84 (88-92) sts until work measures 8 (8-9) cm, 3⅛ (3⅛-3½) in, from beg, ending with a wrong-side row.

▦ **Top Shaping** Cast off 4 sts at beg of next 2 rows, 3 sts at beg of next 2 rows, 2 sts at beg of next 8 (10-12) rows, 4 sts at beg of next 6 rows and 8 sts at beg of next 2 rows. Cast off rem 14 sts.

NECK BORDER

▦ Join right shoulder seam backstitching this and all seams. Press all seams lightly on wrong side with warm iron and damp cloth avoiding ribbing and g st.

With right side of work facing and using 3 mm needles, pick up and k 57 (59-61) sts round front neck edge and 38 (40-42) sts across back neck.

▦ *1st row* (wrong side). K 1, * p 1, k 1; rep from * to end.

▦ *2nd row* P 1, * k 1, p 1; rep from * to end. Cast off loosely ribwise.

MAKING UP

▦ Join left shoulder seam and ends of neck border. Sew in sleeves then join side and sleeve seams.

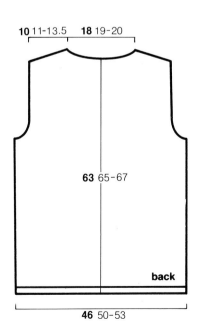

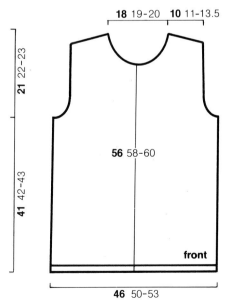

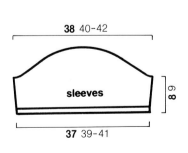

DANCE OF THE LITTLE FAUN

CHECKLIST

Materials
Georges Picaud Akala *mercerized cotton: 8 (9) balls. Pair each of needles size 3 mm and 4½ mm.*

Sizes
Two sizes, to fit bust 76/82 (87/92) cm; 30/32 (34/36) in. Actual measurements shown on diagram.

Stiches used
Single rib; g st; dance of the little faun patt, *worked on a multiple of 12 sts plus 3 as folls:*

1st row *K 2, * SKPO, k 3, yfd, k 1, yfd, k 3, k 2 tog, k 1;* rep from * to * ending k 1.*
2nd row *P 2, * p 2 tog, p 2, yrn, p 3, yrn, p 2, p 2 tog tbl, p 1;* rep from * to * ending p 1.*
3rd row *K 2, * SKPO, k 1, yfd, k 5, yfd, k 1, k 2 tog, k 1;* rep from * to * ending k 1.*
4th row *P 2, * yrn, p 2 tog, p 7, p 2 tog tbl, yrn, p 1;* rep from * to * ending p 1.*
5th row *K 2, * yfd, k 3, k 2 tog, k 1, SKPO, k 3, yfd, k 1;* rep from * to * ending k 1.*
6th row *P 3, * yrn, p 2, p 2 tog tbl, p 1, p 2 tog, p 2, yrn, p 3;* rep from * to *.*
7th row *K 4, * yfd, k 1, k 2 tog, k 1, SKPO, k 1, yfd, k 5;* rep from * to * but ending last rep k 4 instead of k 5.*
8th row *P 5, * p 2 tog tbl, yrn, p 1, yrn, p 2 tog, p 7;* rep from * to * but ending last rep k 5, instead of k 7.*
These 8 rows form one patt.

Tension
Over patt using 4½ mm needles, 20 sts and 26 rows to 10 cm (4 in). Work a sample on 27 sts.

INSTRUCTIONS

BACK
▦ With 3 mm needles cast on 87 (99) sts and work 4 rows in g st then change to 4½ mm needles and work in patt. Cont until work measures 41 (43) cm, 16⅛ (17) in, from beg, ending with a wrong-side row.
▦ **Armhole Shaping** Cast off 3 sts at beg of next 2 rows and 2 sts at beg of next 2 rows then dec 1 st at both ends of next alt row. 75 (87) sts. A half-patt has been taken off at each side; if the next row to be worked is a 1st patt row then the 5th row should be worked and this will fit correctly, if the next row is a 3rd row then the 7th row will fit correctly and so on. Cont thus in patt until work measures 62 (65) cm, 24⅜ (25⅝) in, from beg, ending with a wrong-side row.

Shoulder and Neck Shaping
▦ Cast off 6 sts at beg of next 2 rows.
▦ *Next row* Cast off 6, patt until there are 11 (15) sts on right needle, leave these for right back, cast off next 29 (33) sts, patt to end. Cont on 17 (21) sts now rem at end of needle for left back. Cast off 6 sts at beg of next row and 4 sts at neck edge on foll row. Cast off rem 7 (11) sts to complete shoulder slope.
▦ Rejoin yarn to neck edge of right back sts, cast off 4, patt to end. Cast off rem 7 (11) sts.

FRONT
▦ Work as for back until work measures 56 (59) cm, 22 (23¼) in, from beg, ending with a wrong-side row.
▦ **Neck and Shoulder Shaping**
Next row Patt 32 (36) and leave these sts of left front on a spare

needle, cast off next 11 (15) sts, patt to end. Cont on 32 (36) sts now rem on needle for right front and work 1 row. ✷✷ Cast off 4 sts at beg of next row 2 sts at same edge on next 3 alt rows and 1 st at same edge on next 3 alt rows.
At same time, when work matches back to beg of shoulder, ending at side, cast off 6 sts at beg of next row and next alt row, work 1 row then cast off rem 7 (11) sts.
▦ Rejoin yarn to neck edge of left front sts; complete as for right front from ✷✷ to end.

SLEEVES
▦ With 3 mm needles cast on 70 (74) sts and work 3 rows in g st then k 1 more row working 5 incs evenly spaced. 75 (79) sts. Change to 4½ mm needles and work in patt; for 1st size work rows as given above. (For 2nd size work 2 extra sts in st st at each side; thus the 1st patt row will begin and end k 4, the 2nd row will begin and end p 4, and so on).
Cont in patt until work measures 5 cm (2 in) from beg then inc 1 st at both ends of row keeping the extra st each side in st st.
Cont on 77 (81) sts until work measures 8 (9) cm, 3⅛ (3½) in, from beg, ending with a wrong-side row.
▦ **Top Shaping** Cast off 3 sts at beg of next 2 rows, 2 sts at beg of next 10 (12) rows, 4 sts at beg of

next 6 rows and 6 sts at beg of next 2 rows. Cast off rem 15 sts.

NECK BORDER
▦ Join right shoulder seam. With right side of work facing and using 3 mm needles, pick up and k 58 (62) sts round front neck edge and 39 (43) sts across back neck.
▦ *1st row* (wrong side). K 1, * p 1, k 1; rep from * to end.
▦ *2nd row* P 1, * k 1, p 1; rep from * to end. Rep these 2 rows once then cast off loosely ribwise.

MAKING UP
▦ Join left shoulder seam and ends of neck border. Sew in sleeves then join side and sleeve seams.

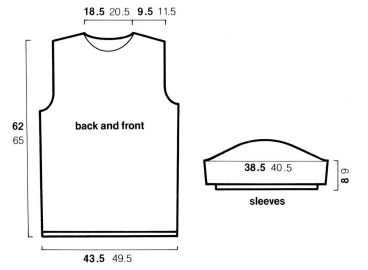

back and front

18.5 20.5   9.5 11.5

62
65

43.5   49.5

38.5 40.5

8 9

sleeves

FANTASY ZIG-ZAG LACE

CHECKLIST

Materials
Pingouin Coton Naturel 8 fis: *10 (11) balls. Pair each of needles size 3 mm and 4½ mm.*

Sizes
Two sizes, to fit bust 82/87 (92/97) cm; 32/34 (36/38) in. Actual measurements shown on diagram.

Stitches used
Single rib; g st; zig-zag lace patt, *worked over a multiple of 9 sts plus 4 as folls:*

1st row *(right side)*. K 3, * yfd, k 1, yfd, k 2, k 2 tog tbl, k 2 tog, k 2; rep from * to last st, k 1.
2nd row P.
3rd to 10th rows *Rep 1st and 2nd rows 4 times more.*
11th row *K 3, * k 2 tog tbl, k 2 tog, k 2, yfd, k 1, yfd, k 2; rep from * to last st, k 1.*
12 row P.
13th to 20th rows *Rep 1st and 2nd rows 4 times more. These 20 rows form one patt.*

Tension
Over patt using 4½ mm needles, 19 sts and 28 rows to 10 cm (4 in). Work a sample on 22 sts, changing needle size if necessary as explained on page 6.
Note The zig-zag patt causes the side edges to assume an irregular shape; to correct this, before making up garment pin out the sections onto an ironing board, gently pulling the sides so that they are straight and parallel. Lay a damp cloth on the work and press very lightly with a warm iron avoiding g st edgings. Leave in place until they are quite dry; this should be done before working neck border.

INSTRUCTIONS

BACK
With 3 mm needles cast on 94 (103) sts and work 3 rows in g st. Change to 4½ mm needles and work in patt as given above. Cont until work measures 41 (43) cm, 16⅛ (17) in, from beg, ending with a p row.

Armhole Shaping Cast off 4 sts at beg of next 2 rows and 2 sts at beg of next 2 rows then dec 1 st at both ends of next 3 alt rows. Cont on rem 76 (85) sts until work measures 62 (65) cm, 24⅜ (25⅝) in, from beg, ending with a p row.

Shoulder and Neck Shaping
Cast off 6 sts at beg of next 2 rows.
Next row Cast off 6, patt until there are 18 (21) sts on right needle, leave these for right back, cast off next 16 (19) sts, patt to end.

Cont on 24 (27) sts now rem at end of needle for left back. Cast off 6 sts at beg of next row and 9 sts at neck edge on foll row. Cast off rem 9 (12) sts to complete shoulder slope.
Rejoin yarn to neck edge of right back sts, cast off 9, p to end. Cast off rem 9 (12) sts.

FRONT
Work as for back until armhole shaping is completed then cont until work measures 56 (59) cm, 22 (23¼) in, from beg, ending with a p row.

Neck and Shoulder Shaping
Next row Patt 32 (35) and leave these sts of left front on a spare needle, cast off next 12 (15) sts, patt to end.
Cont on 32 (35) sts now rem on needle for right front and work 1 row straight. ** Cast off 4 sts at beg of next row, 2 sts at same

edge on next 2 alt rows and 1 st on next 3 alt rows.
Work a few rows on rem 21 (24) sts until work matches back to shoulder, ending at side edge.
Cast off 6 sts at beg of next row and next alt row, work 1 row then cast off rem 9 (12) sts.
Rejoin yarn to neck edge of left front sts and complete as for right front from ** to end.

SLEEVES
With 3 mm needles cast on 67 (71) sts and work 2 rows in g st then k 1 more row working 5 incs evenly spaced. 72 (76) sts. Change to 4½ mm needles and work in patt.
For 1st size, rows will read as folls: On either 1st or 11th patt row begin k 1, then rep from * in correct patt row ending last rep with k 1 instead of k 2.
For 2nd size, work the normal patt rows. Cont in patt without shaping until work measures 8 (9) cm, 3⅛ (3½) in, from beg, ending with a p row.
Top Shaping Cast off 4 sts at beg of next 2 rows, 3 sts at beg of next 2 rows, 2 sts at beg of next 6 rows, 3 sts at beg of next 8 rows and 6 sts at beg of next 2 rows. Cast off rem 10 (14) sts.

NECK BORDER
Before working border press parts as explained above. Join right shoulder seam; press all seams in same way avoiding rib and g st. With right side facing and using 3 mm needles, pick up and k 57 (60) sts round front neck edge and 38 (41) sts across back neck.
1st row (wrong side). K 1, * p 1, k 1; rep from * to end.
2nd row P 1, * k 1, p 1; rep from * to end. Rep these 2 rows once then cast off loosely ribwise.

MAKING UP
Join left shoulder seam and ends of neck border. Sew in sleeves. Join side and sleeve seams.

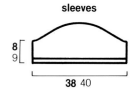

AT THE RUSSIAN BALLET

Leon Bakst set Paris on fire with his designs for the Russian Ballet in the 1910s. This gorgeous evening sweater is based on his distinctive ideas. The main blocks of the pattern are worked in glittering yarns and soft, fine wools, used double. Embroidery on top adds a brocaded opulence. The entire garment, front, sleeves and back, is knitted in one piece.

CHECKLIST

Materials

*Berger du Nord Douceur: 8 balls noir No 8521 (**1**); 3 balls pinede No 8545 (**6**), jade; 3 balls rouge No 8532 (**4**), red; 2 balls lavande No 8539 (**5**), blue; 1 ball rosée No 8529, old rose, and 1 ball paille No 8532, pale yellow. Moonlight: 6 balls or No 6422 (**2**), gold, and 10 balls champagne No 7466 (**3**), pinky gold. Pair each of needles size 4 mm and 4½ mm.*
Note *If the above yarns are unobtainable, refer to page 192.*

Sizes

Two sizes, to fit bust 82/87 (92/97) cm; 32/34 (36/38) in. Actual measurements shown on diagram.

Stitches used

Single rib; st st; patt, worked from chart. The various sections indicated by numbers should be worked in the appropriate colors as shown in the key to chart. All unnumbered areas should be embroidered on after the knitting is complete, using the Swiss Darning method described on page 8.
Note *Yarns are used double throughout; take a ball of the color, wind it into 2 equal balls then wind these tog to form a double thickness ball which is easier to use.*

Tension

Over st st using 4½ mm needles and yarn double, 19 sts and 28 rows to 10 cm (4 in). Work a sample on 24 sts.

INSTRUCTIONS

MAIN PART

Beg at lower edge of front cast on 79 (83) sts using 4 mm needles and **1**. Work in rib as folls:

1st row (right side). P 1, * k 1, p 1; rep from * to end.

2nd row K 1, * p 1, k 1; rep from * to end. Rep these 2 rows until work measures 6 cm (2⅜ in) from beg, ending with a 2nd rib row.

Inc row Rib 4 (3), [inc in next st, rib 2, inc in next st, rib 3] 10 (11) times, inc in next st, rib 4 (2). 100 (106) sts. Change to 4½ mm needles and p 1 row on wrong side.

Now work in st st beg with a k row and work from chart; join on balls of the various colours indicated for the backgrounds on which the motifs will be embroidered and always twist yarns around each other when changing colour. Cont until 68 rows have been worked.

Sleeve Shaping Cast on 3 sts at beg of next 4 (0) rows and 6 sts at beg of next 26 (30) rows; begin working the small squares and triangles during these rows. When shapings are completed cont on these 268 (286) sts and work 42 rows without shaping; 140 rows have been worked from chart.

Neck Opening *141st row* Patt 106 (115) and leave these sts of left shoulder section on a spare needle, now with **2**, p next 56 sts to make a ridge on right side for fold-line, turn and leave rem 106 (115) sts of right shoulder section on a spare needle. Cont on centre

a gala knit for great scenes

56 sts and beg with another p row work 6 rows in st st using **2** then cast off loosely. For back neck facing cast on 56 sts using **2**; beg with a k row work 6 rows in st st.

▦ *Next row* P these sts to make a ridge for foldline then onto same needle with right side facing work the 106 (115) sts which were left unworked thus competing 141st row.

▦ *142nd row* Patt 162 (171) then cont in patt across the first group of 106 (115) sts. Cont in patt across all sts for back; work 42 rows without shaping.

▦ **Sleeve Shaping** Cast off 6 sts at beg of next 26 (30) rows and 3 sts at beg of next 4 (0) rows. 100 (106) sts. Working patt to correspond with front work 68 rows without shaping. Cont with **1** only and k 1 row.

▦ *Dec row* P 4 (3), [p 2 tog, p 2, p 2 tog, p 3] 10 (11) times, p 2 tog, p 4 (2). Cont on rem 79 (83) sts; change to 4 mm needles and work in rib as on front welt for 6 cm (2⅜ in). Cast off loosely ribwise.

MAKING UP AND CUFFS

▦ First embroider the various motifs as shown on chart. With right side of work facing and using 4 mm needles and **2**, pick up and k 43 sts along outer edge of one sleeve. Beg with 2nd row work in rib for 6 cm (2⅜ in) then cast off loosely ribwise. Work other cuff in same way. Join entire side and sleeve seams. Fold neck facings to wrong side along the fold-lines and slip-st in place.

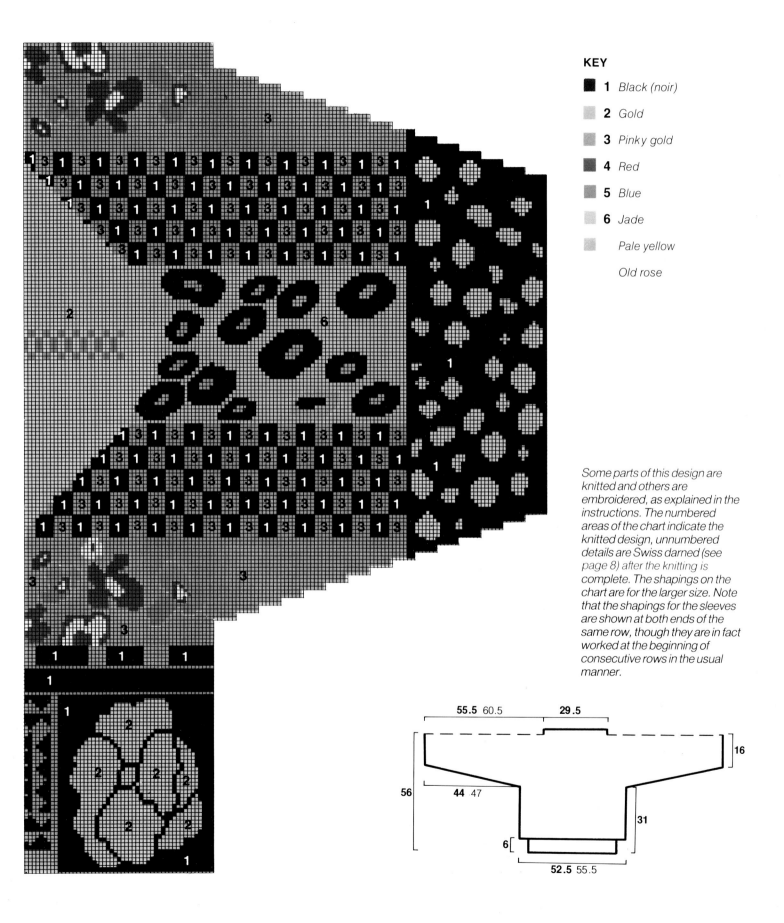

KEY

■ **1** *Black (noir)*

  2 *Gold*

  3 *Pinky gold*

  4 *Red*

  5 *Blue*

  6 *Jade*

  Pale yellow

  Old rose

Some parts of this design are knitted and others are embroidered, as explained in the instructions. The numbered areas of the chart indicate the knitted design, unnumbered details are Swiss darned (see page 8) after the knitting is complete. The shapings on the chart are for the larger size. Note that the shapings for the sleeves are shown at both ends of the same row, though they are in fact worked at the beginning of consecutive rows in the usual manner.

SHE SELLS SCALLOP SHELLS

These stunning summer cotton sweaters both use reverse stocking stitch. The first has chunky cables in white and scallop shells. The second design is knitted in one piece – only the frilled edgings and the shells are knitted separately then hand sewn in place.

SCALLOP SHELL SWEATER

CHECKLIST

Materials
Fil a tricoter Plassard, *quality Coton 6 fils: 17 balls in ecru* (**E**) *and 4 balls in white* (**W**). *Quality Coton 3 fils: 3 balls in white. Pair each of needles size 3¼ mm, 3¾ mm and 4½ mm; a cable needle.*
Note *If the above yarn is unobtainable, refer to page 192.*

Size
One size, to fit bust 87/97 cm (34/38 in). Actual measurements given on diagram.

Stitches used
Rev st st; cable patt as explained below.

Tension
Over main patt using 4½ mm needles, 21 sts and 26 rows to 10 cm (4 in). Work a sample on 30 sts using just one colour of the main yarn and working a cable in centre with 12 sts in rev st st at each side.
Change needle size if necessary as explained on page 8.
Note *Separate balls are needed for each cable and each panel of rev st st. For each cable wind off about half a ball onto a piece of cardboard.*

INSTRUCTIONS

BACK
With 3¾ mm needles and **E** cast on 119 sts and work in scalloped rib as foll:
1st row (right side). K 1, * [k 1, p 1] 3 times, k 1, p 3; rep from * to last 8 sts, [k 1, p 1] 3 times, k 2.
2nd row K 1, * [p 1, k 1] 3 times, p 1, then keeping yarn at front slip next 3 sts p-wise; rep from * to last 8 sts, [p 1, k 1] 4 times.
Rep these 2 rows 9 times more but working 3 incs evenly spaced along last row. 122 sts. Change to 4½ mm needles and patt; cut **E** and join on **W** at beg, then join on other colours along the row.
1st row K 4 **W**, * p 24 **E**, k 6 **W**; rep from * twice more, p 24 **E**, k 4 **W**. The panels of **W** at each end will form cables after side incs have been worked.
2nd row P 4 **W**, * twist yarns and take **E** to back, k 24 **E**, bring **E** to front and twist yarns, then p 6 **W**; rep from * twice more, twist yarns and take **E** to back, k 24 **E**,

bring **E** to front and twist yarns then p 4 **W**. Now begin shortened rows to form the curved shape.
3rd row Patt 114, turn leaving 8 sts unworked at side.
4th row Patt 106, turn leaving 8 sts unworked at this side also.
5th row P 20 **E**, twist yarns then with **W** work the cable, slip next 3 sts on cable needle, leave at front, k 3, then k 3 from cable needle (referred to as cable 6 front), * twist yarns, p 24 **E**, twist yarns then with **W** cable 6 front; rep from * once, twist yarns, p 10 **E**, turn thus leaving 10 extra sts unworked.
6th row Patt 86, turn. Cont to leave 10 extra sts unworked at end of next 4 rows; thus the last row was worked on centre 46 sts. Cut off the last ball of **E** used and rejoin this when needed. Slip all sts onto one needle so that right side will be facing for next row.
11th row K 4 **W**, * twist yarns, p 24 **E**, twist yarns then with **W** cable 6 front; rep from * twice more, twist yarns, p 24 **E**, twist yarns, k 4 **W**. Cont working across all sts and

cross each of the 3 cables at 6-row intervals for remainder of work. When work measures 12 cm (4¾ in) from beg, measuring along side edge, inc 1 st at both ends of next row then every foll 8th row twice more; keep these extra sts in st st using **W** and when incs are completed begin working a cable with 1 border st at each edge. Cont on these 128 sts: work measures 49 cm (19¼ in) from beg, measuring down the side, ending with wrong-side row.
Shoulder Shaping Cast off 30 sts at beg of next 2 rows then cont on rem 68 sts working shortened rows to shape centre section. On next row patt 58 turn; on foll row patt 48, turn. Cont working 10 sts less before turning on each of next 4 rows, turn after last row and work to end. Work 1 row on wrong side across all sts but working a dec in centre of each cable. Change to 3¾ mm needles and using **E** only work in scalloped rib on rem 65 sts.
1st row (right side). K 1, p 1, k 1, * p 3, [k 1, p 1] twice, k 1; rep from * to last 6 sts, p 3, k 1, p 1, k 1.
2nd row K 2, p 1, * keeping yarn at front slip 3 sts p-wise, [p 1, k 1] twice, p 1; rep from * to last 6 sts, keeping yarn at front slip 3 p-wise, then p 1, k 2. Rep last 2 rows 5 times more then cast off ribwise.

FRONT
Work as for back.

SLEEVES
With 3¾ mm needles and **E** cast on 63 sts and work in scalloped rib.
1st row K 1, * [k 1, p 1] twice, k 1, p 3; rep from * to last 6 sts, [k 1, p 1] twice, k 2.
2nd row K 1, * [p 1, k 1] twice, p 1, then keeping yarn at front, slip 3 p-wise; rep from * to last 6 sts, [p 1, k 1] 3 times. Rep these 2 rows 10 times more then 1st row again.
Inc row K 3, kfb, k 3, * [pfb] 3 times, [k 3, kfb] 4 times, k 4; rep from * once, [pfb] 3 times, k 3, kfb, k 3. This row sets position for patt and must be followed exactly. Change to 4½ mm needles and work in patt on 82 sts.
1st row P 8 **E**, * k 6 **W**, p 24 **E**;

rep from * once, k 6 **W**, p 8 **E**. Work 2nd row of patt as now set then begin shortened rows to form the double curve.
3rd row Patt 38, turn leaving rem 44 sts on a spare needle. Cont on this group of sts.
4th row Patt 34, turn.
5th row P 4 **E**, cable 6 front using **W**, p 20 **E**, turn.
6th row Patt 26, turn.
7th row Patt 22, turn.
8th row K 16 **E**, turn.
9th row P 10 **E**, turn. K 1 row in **E** on these 10 sts then cut this ball of yarn, turn. With right side facing slip the next 18 sts of this side section onto right-hand needle, then slip the next 6 sts which are the sts of centre cable and leave these 44 sts on a spare needle, now patt rem 38 sts to complete 3rd row of patt on this section.
4th row Patt 34, turn.
5th row P 20 **E**, cable 6 front using **W**, p 4 **E**, turn. Work from 6th row to 9th row as on first section, turn and k 1 row in **E** on these 10 sts. Now slip all the 82 sts of sleeve onto one needle so that right side will be facing.
11th row P 8 **E**, * using **W** cable 6 front, then p 24 **E**; rep from * once, using **W** cable 6 front, p 8 **E**. Cont in patt across all sts working cables at 6-row intervals and *at same time* inc 1 st at both ends of every foll 8th row 8 times then every foll 6th row 4 times keeping extra sts at sides in rev st st using **E**. Cont on 106 sts until work measures 47 cm (18½ in) from beg. Cast off all sts.

SHELL MOTIFS
Work these before making up garment. Work first motif in first panel of rev st st on back, beg on 7th row of patt. Mark the centre 10 sts of panel then with right side of work facing and using 3¼ mm needles and the thinner cotton yarn, pick up and k 10 sts along these sts by passing the needle under the horizontal thread of each st; this counts as 1st row.
2nd row (wrong side). K 1, p 6, p 2 tog, k 1.
3rd row [K 2, p 1] twice, k 2 tog, k 1.
4th row K 1, p 1, kfb, p 2, kfb, p 1, k 1.

cool summer sweaters

▣ *5th row* K 2, pfb, p 1, k 2, p 1, pfb, k 2.

▣ *6th row* K 1, p 1, kfb, k 2, p 2, k 2, kfb, p 1, k 1.

▣ *7th row* K 2, pfb, p 3, k 2, p 3, pfb, k 2.

▣ *8th row* K 1, p 1, kfb, k 4, p 2, k 4, kfb, p 1, k 1.

▣ *9th row* K 2, pfb, p 1, k 2, pfb, p 1, k 2 (the centre 2 sts), p 1, pfb, k 2, p 1, pfb, k 2. 22 sts.

▣ *10th row* K 1, p 1, [k 3, p 2] 3 times, k 3, p 1, k 1.

▣ *11th row* [K 2, p 3] 4 times, k 2.

▣ *12th row* As 10th.

▣ *13th row* [K 2, pfb, p 2] twice, [k 2, p 2, pfb] twice, k 2. 26 sts.

▣ *14th row* K 1, p 1, [k 4, p 2] 3 times, k 4, p 1, k 1.

▣ *15th row* [K 2, p 4] 4 times, k 2.

▣ *16th row* As 14th.

▣ Keeping patt correct as now set cast off 3 sts at beg of next 4 rows and 4 sts at beg of next 2 rows. Cast off rem 6 sts. Slip-st shell motif in place so that it covers a total of 14 rows at centre. Miss

next 10 rows then work another motif; work 2 more motifs in same panel leaving 10 rows between them. Work motifs in same way in each of the rem 3 panels of rev st st on back. Work similar motifs on front. Work motifs in same way on sleeves on the 2 complete panels of rev st st but do not work any on the side panels.

MAKING UP

▣ Join shoulder seams and sides of neck border backstitching these and all seams. Press all seams lightly on wrong side with warm iron and damp cloth using point of iron on ribbed sections. Pin cast-off edge of sleeves to sides of sweater placing centre of sleeves level with shoulder seams and sides of sleeves approx 25 cm (9¾ in) down from shoulders; ensure that sides of sleeves are at same level on patt at each side. Sew in place as pinned then join side and sleeve seams.

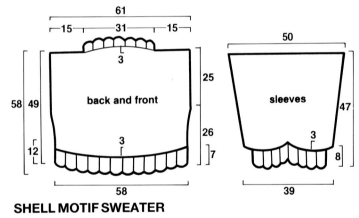

SHELL MOTIF SWEATER

Materials

Phildar Florenlin: 15 (16) balls No 3 (salmon). Pair each of needles size 3¼ mm and 3¾ mm; a circular needle size 3¾ mm in order to accommodate all sts for the full width of sweater.
Note *If the above yarn is unobtainable, refer to page 192.*

Sizes

Two sizes, to fit bust 82/87 (92/97) cm; 32/34 (36/38) in. Actual measurements shown on diagram.

Stitches used

Rev st st; g st; st st; m st.

Tension

Over rev st st using 3¾ mm needles, 21 sts and 30 rows to 10 cm (4 in). Work a sample on 27 sts and change needle size if necessary as explained on page 8.

INSTRUCTIONS

BACK

▣ With pair of 3¾ mm needles cast on 97 (105) sts for lower edge of front; frilled edging is worked later. Beg with a p row work in rev st st but inc 1 st at both ends of every foll 6th row 10 (11) times then every foll 4th row 3 (2) times. Cont on 123 (131) sts until work measures 26 (27) cm, 10¼ (10⅝) in, from beg. End with k row.

▣ **Sleeve Shaping** Cast on 3 sts at beg of next 4 rows, 5 sts at beg of next 20 (16) rows and 6 sts at beg of next 12 (16) rows; change to circular needle during these rows for ease of working and cont working backwards and forwards in rows as usual. Cont on 307 (319) sts until work measures 11 (12) cm, 4⅜ (4¾) in, along outer edge measured after last casting-on, ending with a k row.

▣ **Neck Shaping** *1st row* P 140 (146) and leave these sts of left front on circular needle, then using a straight needle, cast off next 27 sts, p to end. Cont on 140 (146) sts now rem on needle for right front and work 1 row straight. ✳✳ Cast off 4 sts at beg of next row and foll alt row, 2 sts at same edge on next alt row and 1 st on foll alt row. 129 (135) sts. ✳✳ Place a marker loop of contrast yarn at side edge to mark shoulder line and cont for right back. K 1 row then for back neck shaping cast on 6 sts at beg of next row and next alt row. K 1 row thus ending at neck edge then cut yarn and leave these 141 (147) sts on a spare needle. With wrong side facing rejoin yarn to neck edge of left front sts and work as for right front from ✳✳ to ✳✳. P 1 row without shaping thus reaching the shoulder line; place marker loop at side edge then cont for left back. Work 2 rows straight then for back neck cast on 6 sts at beg of next row and next alt row.

▣ *Next row* Using the circular needle p 141 (147) sts of left back, turn, cast on 25 sts, turn, then p 141 (147) sts of right back. 307 (319) sts. Cont across all sts until work measures 14 (15) cm, 5½ (5⅞) in from shoulder markers ending with a k row.

▣ **Sleeve Shaping** Cast off 6 sts at beg of next 12 (16) rows, 5 sts at beg of next 20 (16) rows and 3 sts at beg of next 4 rows. Cont on rem 123 (131) sts using pair of needles; work 6 (7) rows without shaping then dec 1 st at both ends of next row, then every foll 4th row twice (once), work 3 rows straight then dec 1 st at both ends of next row, then every foll 6th row 9 (10) times. Cont on rem 97 (105) sts until work measures 26 (27) cm, 10¼ (10⅝) in, from the last casting-off at end of sleeve shaping measured on the straight. Cast off.

LOWER BORDERS

▣ With 3¼ mm needles cast on 169 (183) sts for outer edge of border.

▣ *1st row* P 2, * k 11, p 3; rep from * to last 13 sts, k 11, p 2.

▣ *2nd row* K 2, * p 11, k 3; rep from * to last 13 sts, p 11, k 2.

▣ *3rd row* P 2, * k 3, k 2 tog, k 1, SKPO, k 3, p 3; rep from * to last 13 sts, k 3, k 2 tog, k 1, SKPO, k 3, p 2.

▣ *4th row* K 2, * p 9, k 3; rep from * to last 11 sts, p 9, k 2.

▣ *5th row* P 2, * k 9, p 3; rep from * to last 11 sts, k 9, p 2.

▣ *6th row* As 4th.

▣ *7th row* P 2, * k 2, k 2 tog, k 1, SKPO, k 2, p 3; rep from * to last 11 sts, k 2, k 2 tog, k 1, SKPO, k 2, p 2.

▣ *8th row* K 2, * p 7, k 3; rep from * to last 9 sts, p 7, k 2.

▣ *9th row* P 2, * k 7, p 3; rep from * to last 9 sts, k 7, p 2.

▣ *10th row* As 8th.

▣ *11th row* P 2, * k 1, k 2 tog, k 1, SKPO, k 1, p 3; rep from * to last 9 sts, k 1, k 2 tog, k 1, SKPO, k 1, p 2.

▣ *12th row* K 2, * p 5, k 3; rep from * to last 7 sts, p 5, k 2.

▣ *13th row* P 2, * k 5, p 3; rep from * to last 7 sts, k 5, p 2. Rep last 2 rows once. Cast off rem 97 (105) sts. Work another border in same way.

SLEEVE BORDERS

▣ With 3¼ mm needles cast on 113 (127) sts and work as for lower border; when the 15th row has been worked cast off rem 65 (73) sts. Work another border in same way.

COLLAR

▦ With 3¼ mm needles cast on 265 sts for upper edge of collar.

▦ *1st row* (right side). K 1, * k 11, p 3; rep from * to last 12 sts, k 12.

▦ *2nd row* K 1, * p 11, k 3; rep from * to last 12 sts, p 11, k 1. The patt is thus arranged in same way as on lower border but with 1 st in g st at each side instead of p 2 rib.

▦ *3rd row* K 1, * k 3, k 2 tog, k 1, SKPO, k 3, p 3; rep from * to last 12 sts, k 3, k 2 tog, k 1, SKPO, k 4. Cont to dec on the st st panels in same way as on lower border on 7th and 11th rows, always keeping the edge st in g st at each side. Work 1 row on rem 151 sts then shape for neck edge.

▦ *13th row* (right side). Cast off 34, patt to end.

▦ *14th row* Cast off 56, patt to end. Cast off 4 sts at beg of next 6 rows then cast off rem 37 sts.

SCALLOP SHELL

▦ Beg at lower edge cast on 59 sts using 3¼ mm needles.

▦ *1st row* (right side). K 1, * k 7, p 3; rep from * to last 8 sts, k 8.

▦ *2nd row* K 1, * p 7, k 3; rep from * to last 8 sts, p 7, k 1. Rep these 2 rows 4 times more.

▦ *11th row* K 1, * k 1, k 2 tog, k 1, SKPO, k 1, p 2 tog, p 1; rep from * to last 8 sts, k 1, k 2 tog, k 1, SKPO, k 2. 42 sts.

▦ *12th row* K 1, * p 5, k 2; rep from * to last 6 sts, p 5, k 1.

▦ *13th row* K 1, * k 5, p 2; rep from * to last 6 sts, k 6. Rep last 2 rows 3 times more, then 12th row again.

▦ *21st row* K 1, * k 2 tog, k 1, SKPO, p 2 tog; rep from * to last 6 sts, k 2 tog, k 1, SKPO, k 1. 25 sts.

▦ *22nd row* K 1, * p 3, k 1; rep from * to end.

▦ *23rd row* K 1, * k 3, p 1; rep from * to last 4 sts, k 4. Rep last 2 rows 3 times more, then 22nd row again. Cast off.

▦ Upper section cast on 42 sts.

▦ *1st row* As 13th row of upper section.

▦ *2nd row* As 12th row of upper section. Rep these 2 rows once.

▦ *5th row* K 1, * k 2 tog, k 1, SKPO, p 2; rep from * to last 6 sts, k 2 tog, k 1, SKPO, k 1. 30 sts.

▦ *6th row* K 1, * p 3, k 2; rep from * to last 4 sts, p 3, k 1.

▦ *7th row* K 1, * k 3, p 2; rep from * to last 4 sts, k 4.

▦ *8th row* K 1, * p 3, k 2 tog; rep from * to last 4 sts, p 3, k 1. Rep 23rd and 22nd rows of main part of motif then cast off.

COCKLE SHELLS

▦ With 3¼ mm needles cast on 3 sts and p these sts; now work in st st and shape as folls:

▦ *1st row* K 1, kfb, k 1.

▦ *2nd row* P 4.

▦ *3rd row* K 1, [kfb] twice, k 1.

▦ *4th row* P 6.

▦ *5th row* K 1, [kfb] 4 times, k 1.

▦ *6th row* P 10.

▦ *7th row* K 2, [kfb, k 1] twice, kfb, k 3. Cont on these 13 sts and work 3 rows in st st then cont in g st and work 2 rows without shaping.

▦ *13th row* K 3, [kfb, k 2] 3 times, k 1. Work 3 rows in g st on these 16 sts.

▦ *17th row* [K 2, kfb] 5 times, k 1. Cont on these 21 sts and work 7 rows in g st. Cast off. Make 5 more shells in same way.

WINKLE SHELLS

▦ Each shell consists of 3 triangles of different length. For 1st triangle cast on 12 sts and work in st st; k 1 row then dec 1 st at *end* of next row, then at same edge on every alt row until 3 sts rem. Cast off. For 2nd triangle cast on 10 sts and work in same way. For 3rd triangle cast on 8 sts and work in same way. Join the 3 triangles to form the shape as shown in photo. Make 6 more shells in same way.

SEAWEED

▦ For one strip cast on 3 sts using 3¼ mm needles and work in m st.

▦ *1st row* (count this as right side for 1st strip). K 1, p 1, k 1. *2nd row* As 1st. Keeping m st correct cont working from chart working incs at beg of wrong-side rows where shown and casting off 7 sts at beg of 48th, 68th and 88th rows and 5 sts at beg of 104th row. Complete as shown on chart. Work second strip in same way but counting 1st row as wrong side thus reversing the shape.

MAKING UP

▦ With right sides tog sew cast-off edge of one lower border to lower edge of front easing in front slightly to fit. Sew other border to lower edge of back. Sew cast-off edge of sleeve borders to outer edges of sleeves. Pin cast-off edge of collar to neck edges as folls: first mark centre of front neck. The edge where the first group of sts was cast off should be placed 4 sts beyond the centre towards the right front; pin cast-on edge around neck towards the left shoulder, then around back neck and right front and the remainder of border overlaps first section to end close to left front shoulder edge. Sew in place as pinned.

▦ Now sew on the motifs, padding each motif slightly with a few oddments of the yarn. Backstitch cast-off edges of upper and lower sections of scallop shell tog drawing in the seam slightly. Slip-st shell to centre front with upper edge about 4 cm (1½ in) below neckline. Slip-st a winkle shell to centre front below the scallop as shown, then on either side of this alternate a cockle shell and a winkle shell in a curved line up to each shoulder. Sew the seaweed on each side of neck as shown. Lastly join side and sleeve seams with backstitch.

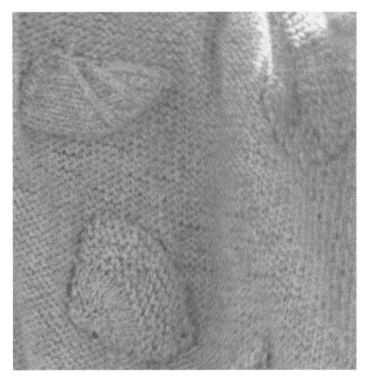

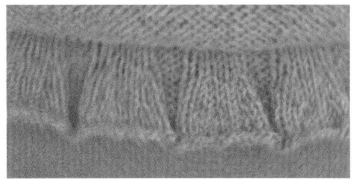

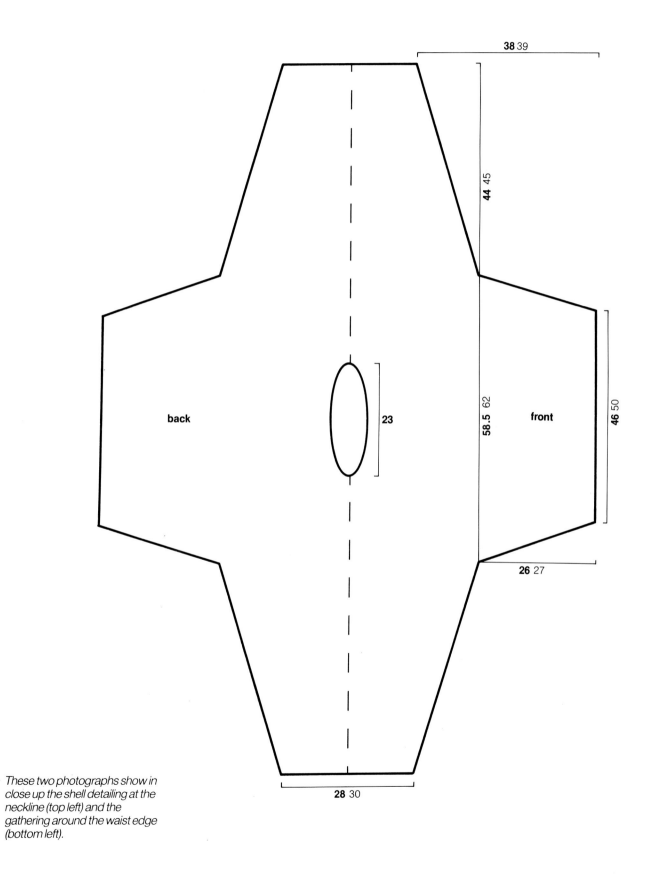

38 39

44 45

23

58.5 62

back

front

46 50

26 27

28 30

These two photographs show in close up the shell detailing at the neckline (top left) and the gathering around the waist edge (bottom left).

ARAN BEAUTY

The softest, subtlest greens of an Irish landscape are chosen for this original variation of an Aran sweater. Cotton yarns in two shades are knitted together to reflect the variety of nature. The sweater opens at the back, with a V-shaped neck and three big buttons. Picot edgings are worked on the ribs for a delicate finishing touch.

CHECKLIST

Materials

Pingouin Fil d'Ecosse No 5: *8 balls céleste ondine No 48 and 8 balls buvard No 33. Pair each of needles size 3¾ mm, 4 mm and 4½ mm; a cable needle; an extra pair of needles size 4 mm for neck border; 3 buttons.*

Size

One size, to fit bust 87/97 cm (34/38 in). Actual measurements shown on diagram.

Stitches used

Single rib; rev st st; cable 6 back (or front) = *slip next 3 sts on cable needle, leave at back (or front), k 3, then k 3 from cable needle;* C 4 R = *cross 4 right thus, slip next st on cable needle, leave at back, k 3, then p 1 from cable needle;* C 4 L = *cross 4 left thus, slip next 3 sts on cable needle, leave at front, p 1, then k 3 from cable needle;* C 3 R= *cross 3 right thus, slip next st on cable needle, leave at back, k 2, then p 1 from cable needle;* C 3 L = *cross 3 left thus, slip next 2 sts on cable needle, leave at front, p 1, then k 2 from cable needle;* MB = *make bobble thus, into next st p into front then [k into back then into front of same st] twice;* CB = *complete bobble thus, with yarn at back slip the 5 sts onto right needle, yarn over needle and pass the 5 sts one at a time over the made loop;* T 2 = *twist 2 thus, pass needle in front of 1st st, lift up 2nd st and k it, leaving it on needle, then k 1st st and slip both off needle.*
The various panels of patt are worked as folls:
Twist rib, *worked over 2 sts.*
   1st row *T 2.*
   2nd row *P 2. Rep these 2 rows throughout.*
Chain cable *worked over 14 sts as folls:*
   1st row *P 4, k 6, p 4.*
   2nd row *K 4, p 6, k 4.*
   3rd row *P 4, cable 6 back, p 4.*
   4th row *As 2nd.*
   5th to 8th rows *Rep 1st and 2nd rows twice more.*
   9th row *As 3rd.*
   10th row *As 2nd.*
   11th row *P 3, C 4 R, C 4 L, p 3.*
   12th row *K 3, p 3, k 2, p 3, k 3.*
   13th row *P 3, k 3, p 2, k 3, p 3.*
   14th to 24th rows *Rep 12th and 13th rows 5 times more, then 12th row again.*
   25th row *P 3, C 4 L, C 4 R, p 3.*
   26th row *As 2nd. These last 24 rows from 3rd to 26th inclusive, form one patt.*
Lobster Claw, *worked over 9 sts as folls:*
   1st row *K 9.*
   2nd row *P 9.*
   3rd row *Slip 3 sts on cable needle, leave at back, k 1, then k 3 from cable needle, k next st, now slip foll st on cable needle, leave at front, k 3, then k 1 from cable needle.*

4th row *P 9. These 4 rows form one patt.*
Zig-zag panel 1 *(moving to the left first). Worked over 14 sts as folls:*
   1st row *P 3, k 2, p 9.*
   2nd row *K 9, p 2, k 3.*
   3rd row *P 3, C 3 L, p 8.*
   4th row *K 8, p 2, k 4.*
   5th row *P 4, C 3 L, p 7.*
   6th row *K 7, p 2, k 5.*
   7th row *P 5, C 3 L, p 6.*
   8th row *K 6, p 2, k 6.*
   9th row *P 6, C 3 L, p 5.*
   10th row *K 5, p 2, k 7.*
   11th row *P 7, C 3 L, p 4.*
   12th row *K 4, p 2, k 8.*
   13th row *P 5, MB, p 2, C 3 L, p 3.*
   14th row *K 3, p 2, k 3, p 5, k 5.*
   15th row *P 5, CB, p 2, C 3 R, p 3.*
   16th row *As 12th.*
   17th row *P 7, C 3 R, p 4.*
   18th row *As 10th.*
   19th row *P 6, C 3 R, p 5.*
   20th row *As 8th.*
   21st row *P 5, C 3 R, p 6.*
   22nd row *As 6th.*
   23rd row *P 4, C 3 R, p 7.*
   24th row *As 4th.*
   25th row *P 3, C 3 R, p 2, MB, p 5.*
   26th row *K 5, p 5, k 3, p 2, k 3.*
   27th row *P 3, C 3 L, p 2, CB, p 5.*
   28th row *As 4th.*
These last 24 rows from 5th to 28th inclusive, form one patt for this panel.
Zig-zag panel 2 *(moving to the right first). Worked over 14 sts as folls:*
   1st row *P 9, k 2, p 3.*
   2nd row *K 3, p 2, k 9.*
   3rd row *P 8, C 3 R, p 3.*
   4th row *K 4, p 2, k 8.*
   5th to 16th rows *Rep from 17th row to 28th row of zig-zag panel 1.*
   17th to 28th rows *Rep from 5th row to 16th row of zig-zag panel 1.*
These last 24 rows from 5th to 28th inclusive, form one patt. Note that the sts of each panel must always be counted as 14 sts. Do not make a bobble in a place where you will shortly be working a dec.
Plaited cable, *worked over 24 sts as folls:*
   1st row *K 24.*
   2nd row *P 24.*
   3rd row *[Cable 6 back] 4 times.*
   4th row *P 24.*
   5th and 6th rows *As 1st and 2nd.*
   7th row *K 3, [cable 6 front] 3 times, k 3.*
   8th row *P 24. These 8 rows form one patt.*
Single cable, *worked over 6 sts as folls:*
   1st row *K 6.*
   2nd row *P 6.*
   3rd and 4th rows *As 1st and 2nd.*
   5th row *Cable 6 back.*
   6th row *P 6. These 6 rows form one patt.*

Tensions

Over rev st st using 4½ mm needles and the yarn double, 22 sts and 27 rows to 10 cm (4 in). Overall tension measured over a combination of patts, 24 sts and 27 rows to 10 cm (4 in).

INSTRUCTIONS

Throughout work use a strand of each colour tog.

FRONT

▦ With 3¾ mm needles cast on 90 sts. ** Beg with a p row work 2 rows in st st.

▦ *Next row* P 1, * yrn, p 2 tog; rep from * to last st, p 1. Work 2 more rows in st st. ** This completes picot edging; (after a few more rows have been worked fold up the cast-on edge to wrong side, folding along centre of line of holes and slip-st in place on wrong side so that measurements can be taken from lower edge.) Change to 4 mm needles and work in rib.

▦ *1st row* (right side). K 2, * p 2, k 2; rep from * to end.

▦ *2nd row* P 2, * k 2, p 2; rep from * to end. Rep these 2 rows until work measures 7 cm (2¾ in) from lower edge, ending with a 1st rib row.

▦ *Inc row* * K 4, p 2, [kfb] twice, p 6, [kfb] twice, p 2, kfb, k 1, [pfb, p 1] 3 times, kfb, k 1, p 2, [kfb, k 1] 3 times, * p 1, [pfb, p 2] 5 times, pfb, p 1, [kfb, k 1] 3 times, p 2, kfb, k 1, [pfb, p 1] 3 times, kfb, k 1, p 2, [kfb] twice, p 6, [kfb] twice, p 2, k 4. This row sets positions for patt and must be followed very carefully.

Change to 4½ mm needles and work in patt on 120 sts as folls:

▦ *1st row* P 4, T 2, work 1st row of chain cable, T 2, p 3, work 1st row of lobster claw, work 1st row of zig-zag panel 1, work 1st row of plaited cable, work 1st row of zig-zag panel 2, work 1st row of lobster claw, p 3, T 2, work 1st row of chain cable, T 2, p 4. Cont in patt as now set for 3 more rows then inc 1 st at both ends of next row, then every foll 6th row 9 times more keeping extra sts at sides in rev st st. Cont on 140 sts until work measures 32 cm (12⅝ in) from lower edge; place marker loops of contrast yarn at each end to indicate beg of armholes. Cont without shaping until work measures 44 cm (17⅜ in) from lower edge, ending with a wrong-side row.

▦ **Neck Shaping** *Next row* Patt 56 and leave these sts of left front on a spare needle, cast off next 28 sts, patt to end. Cont on 56 sts now rem on needle for right front and work 1 row straight. *** Cast off 3 sts at beg of next row and foll alt row, 2 sts at same edge on next 4 alt rows and 1 st on foll 5 alt rows. Cont on rem 37 sts until work measures 54 cm (21¼ in) from lower edge. Cast off all sts for shoulder edge.

▦ Rejoin yarns to neck edge of left front sts and complete as for right front from *** to end.

LEFT BACK

▦ With 3¾ mm needles cast on 48 sts and work as for front from ** to **; complete picot edging later, as on front.

▦ Change to 4 mm needles and rib.

▦ *1st row* * P 2, k 2; rep from * to end. Rep this row until same number of rows have been worked as on front thus ending with a right-side row.

▦ *Inc row* Rep from * to * in the inc row of front, p 6, kfb, k 1, p 2, k 2. 61 sts. Change to 4½ mm needles and patt.

▦ *1st row* P 2, T 2, p 3, work 1st row of single cable, work 1st row of zig-zag No 2, work 1st row of lobster claw, p 3, T 2, work 1st row of chain cable, T 2, p 4. Cont in patt as now set for 3 more rows then to shape side, inc 1 st at *end* of next row, then at same edge on every foll 6th row 9 times more, keeping extra sts at side in rev st st. Cont on 71 sts until work measures 32 cm (12⅝ in) from lower edge; place marker loop at side edge to indicate beg of armhole. Cont without shaping until work measures 34 cm (13⅜ in) from lower edge,

ending at the straight centre back edge.

▦ **Neck Shaping** Dec 1 st at beg of next row, then at same edge on next 2 rows, then work 1 row straight; rep last 4 rows 8 times more. Now dec 1 st at same edge on next 7 alt rows then cont on rem 37 sts until work matches front to shoulder edge. Cast off all sts.

RIGHT BACK

▦ Work as for left back but reversing the double rib, the inc row and arrangement of patt, also reverse all shapings.

SLEEVES

▦ With 3¾ mm needles cast on 54 sts and work from ** to ** as on front; complete picot edging later. Change to 4 mm needles and work in double rib as on front but beg with 2nd row which will be right side. Cont until work measures 7 cm (2¾ in) from lower edge, ending with a 2nd row.

▦ *Inc row* P 6, [kfb] twice, p 2, kfb, k 1, [pfb, p 1] 3 times, kfb, k 1, [pfb twice, p 1] 4 times, [pfb] twice, kfb, k 1, [pfb, p 1] 3 times, kfb, k 1, p 2, [kfb] twice, p 6. 78 sts. Change to 4½ mm needles and patt.

▦ *1st row* Working the last 10 sts of chain cable, k 6, p 4, then

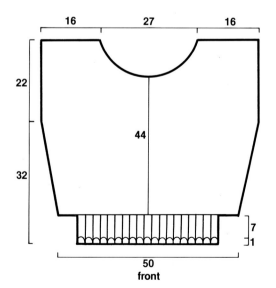

16   27   16

22

44

32

50
front

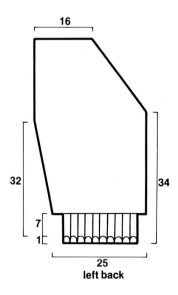

16

32   34

7
1

25
left back

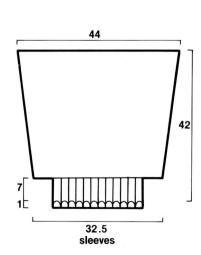

44

42

7
1

32.5
sleeves

T 2, p 3, work 1st row of lobster claw, p 3, work 1st row of plaited cable, p 3, work 1st row of lobster claw, p 3, T 2, then working first 10 sts of chain cable, p 4, k 6. Cont in patt as now set for 5 rows then inc 1 st at both ends of next row, then every foll 8th row 4 times, then every foll 6th row 8 times. The first 4 sts added each side will complete the chain cable, then the next 2 sts form a twist rib and the rem 7 sts should be worked in rev st st. Cont on 104 sts until work measures 42 cm (16½ in) from lower edge. Cast off all sts.

MAKING UP AND BORDERS

Join shoulder seams matching patt. With right side of work facing and using 3 of the 4 mm needles, pick up and k 81 sts along straight centre back edge of left back, 42 sts along sloping edge, 76 sts around front neck edge, 42 sts along sloping edge on right back and 81 sts along straight centre back edge. Using the 4th needle work in rows of double rib as on front welt but beg with 2nd row. After 4 rows have been worked make buttonholes.

Next row Beg at lower edge of right back, wrong side facing, rib 18, cast off 4, [rib until there are 24 sts on right needle after previous buttonhole, cast off 4] twice, rib to end. On foll row cast on 4 sts over each buttonhole. Work 4 more rows in rib then cast off ribwise.

With right side of work facing and using 3¾ mm needles, pick up and k 42 sts along cast-off edge of ribbed border on left back neck, 76 sts along edge of front neck border and 42 sts along corresponding edge on right back. Rep from ** to ** as on front. Cast off. Fold this cast-off edge to wrong side along centre of line of holes and slip-st in place. Sew cast-off edge of sleeves to sides of armholes between markers. Join side and sleeve seams. Sew buttons to right back to correspond with buttonholes.

1 Plaited Cable

2 Lobster Claw

3 Twist Rib

4 Zig Zag Panel

5 Chain Cable

6 Single Cable

LACY COTTON TOPS

Three simple tops are given a little luxury with satin ribbon woven through the lacy knitting. The centre and far right designs are based on the same slanted lace pattern. For the top on the right, the ribbon is threaded only on one diagonal, for the design in the middle, the ribbons are knotted where they cross, and the simpler knit on the left has vertical patterns.

CHECKLIST

Materials
Pingouin Coton Naturel 4 fils*: for each top, 3 (3) balls in white. Pair each of needles size 2¼ mm and 3 mm; approx 15 metres (16½ yd) of narrow ribbon.*

Sizes
Two sizes, to fit bust 82 (87/92) cm; 32 (34/36) in. Actual measurements shown on diagram.

Stitches used
Single rib; zig-zag lace patt, *used for No 1 and No 2, worked on a multiple of 24 sts plus 10 as folls:*

1st row *(right side)*. K 4, * yfd, SKPO, k 6; rep from * to last 6 sts, yfd, SKPO, k 4.

2nd and alt rows P.

3rd row K 3, * yfd, SKPO, yfd, k 2 tog, k 4; rep from * to last 7 sts, yfd, SKPO, yfd, k 2 tog, k 3.

5th row K 2, * yfd, SKPO, k 2, yfd, k 2 tog, k 2; rep from * to end.

7th row K 7, * yfd, k 2 tog, k 6; rep from * to last 3 sts, yfd, k 2 tog, k 1.

9th row K 8, * yfd, k 2 tog, k 6; rep from * to last 2 sts, k 2.

11th row K 1, * yfd, k 2 tog, k 4, yfd, SKPO, k 6, yfd, SKPO, yfd, k 2 tog, k 4, yfd, SKPO; rep from * to last 1 (9) sts, then for 1st size k 1, (for 2nd size yfd, k 2 tog, k 4, yfd, SKPO, k 1).

13th row K 1, * yfd, k 2 tog, k 3, yfd, SKPO, k 6, yfd, SKPO, k 2, yfd, k 2 tog, k 2, yfd, SKPO, k 1; rep from * to last 1 (9) sts, then for 1st size k 1, (for 2nd size yfd, k 2 tog, k 3, yfd, SKPO, k 2).

15th row K 5, * yfd, SKPO, k 6; rep from * to last 5 sts, yfd, SKPO, k 3.

16th row P. These 16 rows form one patt.

Vertical lace patt, *used for No 3 worked on a multiple of 8 sts plus 1 as folls:*

1st row *(right side)*. K 3, * k 2 tog, yfd, k 6; rep from * to last 6 sts, k 2 tog, yfd, k 4.

2nd row P 3, * p 2 tog, yrn, p 6; rep from * to last 6 sts, p 2 tog, yrn, p 4. These 2 rows form one patt.

Tensions
For either patt using 3 mm needles, 26 sts and 36 rows to 10 cm (4 in). For the zigzag patt work a sample on 34 sts working as for 2nd size on 11th and 13th rows. For the vertical lace patt work a sample on 33 sts.

INSTRUCTIONS

STYLE 1
BACK
▦ With 2¼ mm needles cast on 117 (125) sts and work in single rib.

▦ *1st row* (right side). P 1, * k 1, p 1; rep from * to end.

▦ *2nd row* K 1, * p 1, k 1; rep from * to end. Rep these 2 rows until work measures 6 cm (2⅜ in) from beg, ending with a 1st rib row. **
Change to 3 mm needles and p 1

row on wrong side working 5 incs evenly spaced. 122 (130) sts. Now work in zig-zag lace patt as given above; cont until work measures 32 (34) cm, 12⅝ (13⅜) in from beg, ending with a p row.

▦ **Armhole Shaping** Cast off 4 sts at beg of next 6 rows. Cont on rem 98 (106) sts keeping patt correct as far as possible; any sts at sides which cannot be fitted into patt should be worked in st st. Cont until work measures 40 (43) cm, 15¾ (17) in from beg, ending with a p row.

▦ **Neck Shaping** *Next row* Patt 43 (45) sts and leave these on a spare needle for one side of neck, cast off next 12 (16) sts, patt to end. Cont on 43 (45) sts now rem on needle and work 1 row straight. ✲✲✲ Cast off 4 sts at beg of next row and foll alt row, 3 sts at same edge on next 2 alt rows, 2 sts on next 2 alt rows and 1 st on foll 9 alt rows. Cont on rem 16 (18) sts until work measures 52 (55) cm, 20½ (21⅝) in from beg. Cast off these sts for shoulder edge. ✲✲✲ With wrong side facing rejoin yarn to neck edge of other group of sts and complete as for first side of neck from ✲✲✲ to ✲✲✲

FRONT
▦ Work exactly as for back.

BORDERS
▦ All worked with 2¼ needles; they are knitted separately and sewn on for extra firmness. For armhole border cast on 151 (157) sts and work in rib as on welt for 10 rows. Cast off loosely ribwise. Work another border in same way. For back neck border cast on 121 (125) sts and work as for armhole border; work another border in same way for front neck.

MAKING UP
▦ Sew cast-on edge of neck borders to neck edges. Join entire shoulder seams. Sew cast-on edge of armhole borders to armhole edges. Join side seams and ends of borders. Press seams lightly on wrong side with warm iron and damp cloth avoiding ribbing.
▦ Beg at bottom right-hand corner of back, thread ribbon

through holes as shown in sketch No 1; trim front in same way.

STYLE 2
Work exactly as for No 1 but thread the ribbons through as shown in sketch No 2 forming knots where the ribbons cross each other.

STYLE 3
BACK
▦ Work as given for No 1 as far as ✲✲ then change to 3 mm needles and p 1 row on wrong side working 4 incs evenly spaced. 121 (129) sts. Now work in vertical lace patt and cont without shaping until work measures 32 (34 cm), 12⅝ (13⅜) in from beg, ending with a 2nd patt row.

▦ **Armhole Shaping** Cast off 4 sts at beg of next 6 rows. 97 (105) sts. The 1st patt row will now begin k 7 and end k 8; 2nd patt row will begin p 7 and end p 8. Cont without shaping until work measures 40 (43) cm, 15¾ (17) in from beg, ending with a 2nd patt row.

▦ **Neck Shaping** *1st row* Patt 43 (45) and leave these sts on a spare needle for one side of neck, cast off next 11 (15) sts, patt to end. Cont on 43 (45) sts now rem on needle and work 1 row straight. Complete as for No 1 from ✲✲✲ to ✲✲✲. Rejoin yarn to neck edge of other group of sts and complete as for No 1 from ✲✲✲ to ✲✲✲

FRONT
▦ Work exactly as for back.

BORDERS
▦ Work these as for No 1.

MAKING UP
▦ As for No 1; thread the ribbon through vertical lines; on one line pass alternately over 2 threads and under 2 threads and for the next line pass under 2 threads then over 8 threads.

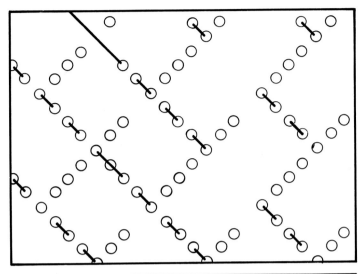

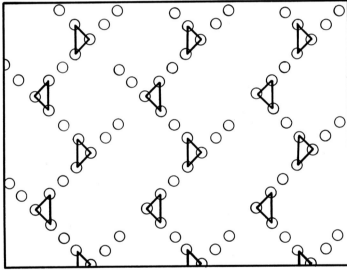

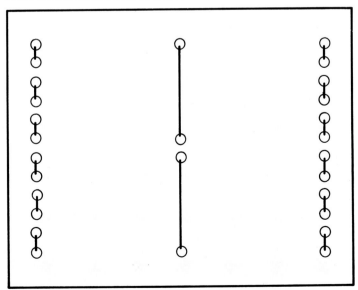

Ribbon weaving patterns: top, style 1; middle, style 2, and bottom, style 3.

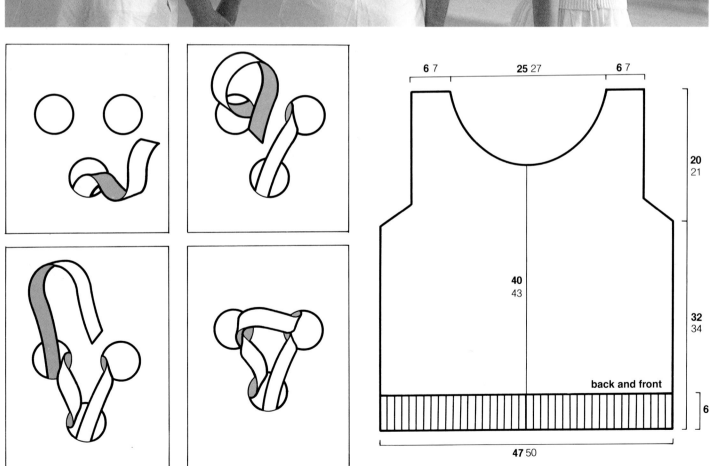

PAINTBOX CARDIGAN

A glorious palette of subtly matched colours. You can achieve the sophisticated gradation of shades without vast expense by using small skeins of tapestry wools for the squares. Fronts and sleeves are patterned all over with the little boxes, while the back has a simpler arrangement of just seven. For the perfect finishing touch, find buttons in various colours to match the samples in the nearby rows.

CHECKLIST

Materials

*Berger du Nord 4-ply: 10 (11) balls ecru (**E**) (if this yarn is unobtainable refer to page 192).*
Laine Colbert DMC: one 8 m (9 yd) skein in each of the foll colours:
7102 7103 7104 7106 7107 7132 7136 7137 7138 7139
7151 7153 7155 7157 7194 7204 7205 7212 7241 7243
7245 7247 7253 7255 7257 7259 7296 7340 7341 7342
7344 7361 7362 7363 7369 7370 7371 7386 7399 7423
7425 7431 7433 7435 7436 7437 7493 7512 7540 7544
7548 7549 7595 7596 7597 7598 7600 7602 7604 7606
7666 7678 7679 7680 7681 7740 7741 7791 7797 7798
7800 7807 7860 7861 7905 7909 7912 7943 7946 7971
7973 7988
For the larger size you will also need a skein each of 7314, 7316, 7318, 7820. Pair each of needles size 3 mm and 3¾ mm; 6 buttons.
Note on colours You can if you prefer use fewer colours; each square only needs approx 3.5 metres – about 4 yards and each skein is sufficient for 2 squares. You can work out a different arrangement of colours using our charts as a guide.

Sizes

Two sizes, to fit bust 82/87 (92/97) cm; 32/34 (36/38) in. Actual measurements shown on diagram in centimetres.

Stitches used

*Single rib; st st. For each square wind off 3.5 metres of the correct colour; wind this onto a piece of cardboard, cut a slit in the card and pass the end through to prevent it becoming tangled. Also use a small ball of **E** for the sections between the squares. Join on the balls as required and always twist the yarns around each other when changing colour. On completion of a square cut off any spare yarn leaving an end for darning in later.*

Tension

Over st st using 3¾ mm needles and either yarn, 23 sts and 30 rows to 10 cm (4 in). Work a sample on 28 sts.

INSTRUCTIONS

BACK

▦ With 3 mm needles and **E** cast on 115 (123) sts and work in rib.
▦ *1st row* (right side). P 1, * k 1, p 1; rep from * to end.
▦ *2nd row* K 1, * p 1, k 1; rep from * to end. Rep these 2 rows until work measures 3 cm (1¼ in) from beg, ending with a 2nd rib row but inc 1 st in centre of last row. 116 (124) sts. Change to 3¾ mm needles and beg with a k row work in st st until 48 (54) rows have been worked then begin 1st square at centre.
▦ *1st row* K 52 (56) **E**, join on colour for 1st square as shown on chart, k 12 with this colour, join on another ball of **E**, k 52 (56) **E**. Cont as set for 14 more rows then cut off remainder of the colour and using one ball of **E** only work 9 rows in st st.
▦ *25th row* K 36 (39) **E**, join on colour for next square and k 12 with this, join on another ball of **E** and k 20 (22), join on colour for next square, k 12 with this, join on another ball of **E**, k 36 (39) **E**. Cont with these 2 squares for 14 more rows then work 9 rows in **E**.
▦ *49th row* K 20 (22) **E**, join on colour for next square, k 12 with this, k 52 (56) **E**, join on colour for next square, k 12 with this, join on another ball of **E**, k 20 (22) **E**. Cont with these 2 squares for 14 more rows then work 9 rows in **E**.
▦ *73rd row* K 4 (5) **E**, join on colour for next square and k 12 with this, k 84 (90) **E**, join on colour for next square and k 12 with this, join on another ball of **E**, k 4 (5) **E**. Cont as now set for 5 more rows; 126 (132) rows have been worked in st st.
▦ **Armhole Shaping** Cast off 4 sts at beg of next 2 rows and 2 sts at beg of next 4 rows. 100 (108) sts. Work 3 more rows with the sts rem from each square in correct colour, then using **E** only work 49 (51) rows in **E**; 184 (192) rows have been worked in st st.
▦ **Neck and Shoulder Shaping**
1st row K 42 (45) and leave these sts of right back on needle, cast off next 16 (18) sts, k to end. Cont on 42 (45) sts now rem at end of needle for left back and work 1 row straight. ** Cast off 6 sts at beg of next row.
▦ Now for shoulder cast off 11 sts at beg of next row and 2 sts at neck edge on foll row; rep last 2 rows once. Cast off rem 10 (13) sts to complete shoulder slope. Rejoin yarn to neck edge of right back sts and complete as for left back from ** to end.

LEFT FRONT

▦ With 3 mm needles and **E** cast on 61 (65) sts and work in rib as on back welt for same number of rows and inc 1 st in centre of last row. 62 (66) sts. Change to 3¾ mm needles and working in st

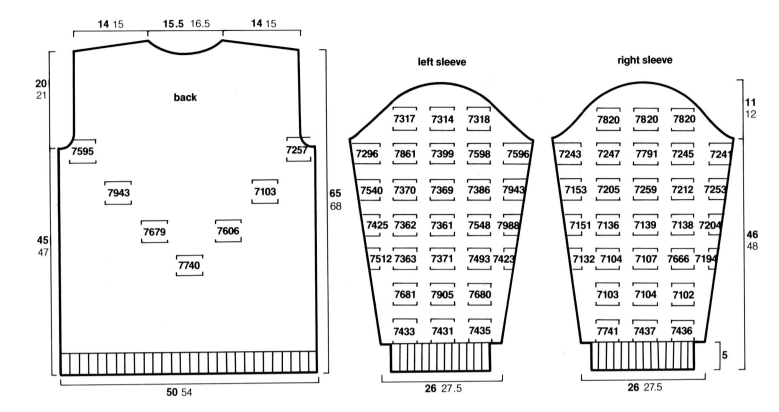

st begin 1st line of squares in the 3 colours indicated, joining on these colours and small balls of **E** as folls:

▦ *1st row* K 7 (8) **E**, work 1st square, k 6 (7) **E**, work 2nd square, k 6 (7) **E**, work 3rd square, k 7 (8) **E**. Work 14 more rows as now set then work 9 rows in **E**. Cont working the lines of squares in the colours shown on chart always placing them above each other and with 9 rows in **E** between each completed line of squares and the next. Cont until 122 (128) rows have been worked in st st thus ending with a p row.

▦ **Front and Armhole Shaping**
1st row K to last 4 sts, SKPO, k 2. Cont to dec in this position on every foll 4th row 3 (4) times. *At same time*, keep side edge straight until 126 (132) rows have been worked then cast off 4 sts at beg of next row and 2 sts at same edge on next 2 alt rows. When the 4 (5) decs at front have been worked, cont to dec at the actual front edge on next 8 alt rows then on every foll 3rd row 10 times. Cont on rem 32 (35) sts until 186 (194) rows have been worked in st

st; for the 1st size 3 rows in **E** have been worked after completing 8th line of squares and for the 2nd size 2 rows of the 9th line of squares have been worked.

▦ **Shoulder Shaping** For 1st size cont with **E** only; for 2nd size cont in patt. Cast off 11 sts at beg of next row and next alt row, work 1 row then cast off rem 10 (13) sts.

RIGHT FRONT
▦ Work as for left front arranging squares in same way but using colours as shown on right front chart. Begin front shaping on same row as for left front and for the first 4 (5) decs work k 2, k 2 tog, k to end, working rem decs at actual front edge as on left front. Begin armhole and shoulder shaping 1 row after those of left front.

RIGHT SLEEVE
▦ With 3 mm needles and **E** cast on 49 (53) sts and work in rib as on back but cont until work measures 5 cm (2 in) from beg, ending with a 1st rib row.
▦ *Inc row* Rib 4 (6), [inc in next st,

rib 3] 10 times, inc in next st, rib 4 (6). 60 (64) sts. Change to 3¾ mm needles and working in st st begin 1st line of squares in the 3 colours indicated.

▦ *1st row* K 6 (7) **E**, k 12 in 1st colour, k 6 (7) **E**, k 12 in 2nd colour, k 6 (7) **E**, k 12 in 3rd colour, k 6 (7) **E**. Cont as now set but inc 1 st at both ends of every foll 10th row 1 (4) times, then every foll 8th row 13 (10) times. Work lines of squares as shown on chart always with 9 rows in **E** between them, beg new squares at sides on 49th row. When incs are completed cont on 88 (92) sts until 122 (128) rows have been worked in st st.

▦ **Top Shaping** Cast off 4 sts at beg of next 2 rows and 2 sts at beg of next 32 (34) rows. Cast off rem 16 sts.

LEFT SLEEVE
▦ Work as for right sleeve but using the colours shown in chart for left sleeve.

FRONT AND NECK BORDERS
▦ With right side facing and using 3 mm needles, pick up and k

113 (118) sts along straight front edge of right front and 66 (69) sts along sloping edge to shoulder. Beg with 2nd row work in rib as on back welt and after working 3 rows make buttonholes.

▦ *Next row* Beg at lower edge, right side facing, rib 6, cast off 3, [rib until there are 17 (18) sts on right needle after previous buttonhole, cast off 3] 5 times, rib to end. On foll row cast on 3 sts over each buttonhole. Work 3 more rows in rib then cast off loosely ribwise. Work similar border on left front picking up sts in reverse order and omitting buttonholes. With right side facing, using 3 mm needles and **E**, pick up and k 41 (43) sts across back neck. Beg with 2nd row work 8 rows in rib then cast off loosely ribwise.

MAKING UP
▦ Join shoulder seams and ends of borders. Sew in sleeves then join side and sleeve seams. Sew on buttons to correspond with buttonholes.

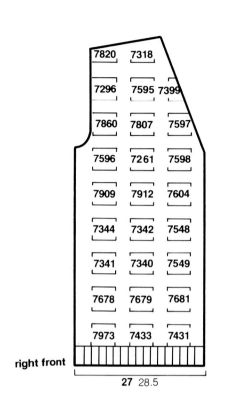

right front

27 28.5

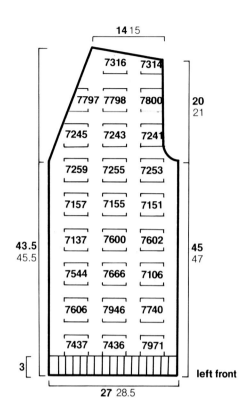

14 15

20 21

43.5 45.5

45 47

3

left front

27 28.5

If you feel that you cannot afford the luxury of using such a wide range of colours, make several copies of these diagrams and colour them in with a more limited range of shades, keeping to the basic arrangement of blocks of reds, blues, greens and yellows.

YARN OPTIONS

Some of the specialty yarns used in this book are not readily available outside France, but this should not deter you from knitting any of the patterns. In all cases, we suggest either acceptable substitutes which will knit to the same tension as the original or, if there is one, list the main stockist for that type of yarn (see below). In some cases, the stockist may not be able to supply the particular yarn used, in which case we give the address of the stockist and at the same time suggest a substitute yarn.

Gemini Gem *See below for stockist.*

Rosa Mundi *See below for stockist.*

Fair Isle Trio *Substitute Pingouin Mohair 50 as follows: azalée (A), fuchsia (B), cobalt (C), persan (D), veronese (E), feu (F), safran (G) and haiphong (H).*

Sleepy Pixie Layette *See below for stockist or use 3 Suisses Suizanyl 4 for the cardigan, sweater, hat and socks, and 3 Suisses Sweet Baby for the trousers.*

Strawberry Ripe *Substitute Pingouin Corrida 3 for DMC Cotonia, but use DMC coton perlé for the embroidery.*

Pastel Perfection *See below for stockist or substitute Pingouin Corrida 3.*

First Best Outfit *Substitute Phildar Luxe 025.*

Mix and Match Set *See below for stockist.*

Stylish Stripes *See below for stockist or substitute Pingouin Pingofine for the sweater and Pingouin Mohair 50, used double, for the cover; match the original shades as follows: lagune (A), opaline (B), poussin (C), flamme (D), porcelaine (E), and griotte (F); for the cover, turquoise (A), azalée (B), cobalt (C), bleu chinois (D), souci (E) and safran (F).*

Calorific Comfort *See below for stockist or substitute Pingouin Pingofrance.*

The Youngest Cabin Boy *See below for stockist.*

Stylish and Practical *See below for stockist or substitute Pingouin Pingolaine for main parts and patches.*

April Twosome *See below for stockist or substitute Pingouin Esprit d'Angora.*

Animal Magic *For Fox and Cat, substitute 3 Suisses New Mohair 3S. For Lamb, substitute 3 Suisses Kalinka, used double. For Mouse, substitute 3 Suisses New Mohair 3S for both yarns.*

Young Shrimpers *See below for stockist.*

Gym Tonic *Substitute Pingouin Sorbet.*

Country Kids *For Style 1 substitute Pingouin Pingofine as follows: giroselle (A), flamme (B), feu (C), aube (D), pouissin (E) and nuage (F). For Style 2, substitute Pingouin Pingofine as follows: dune (A), cuivre (B), flamme (C), feu (D), coralline (E), eucalyptus (F) and griotte (G). For Style 3, substitute Pingouin Pingostar as follows: saigon (A), hawai (B), nuage (C), bleu franc (D) and amiral (E); in the original instructions E is used double as it is a thinner yarn, but there is no need to do this if substituting Pingouin Pingostar for all the colours.*

Heads in the Clouds *Substitute Georges Picaud Feu Vert for Shetland, and Georges Picaud Zig for Orient Express.*

Snow Set *Jacket with Roll Collar, see below for stockist. For Jacket with Revers, substitute Bouton d'Or Pur Mohair 100. For Parka, substitute Anny Blatt Soft'Anny Kid Mohair. Child's jacket, see below for stockist. For scarf and other accessories, substitute Anny Blatt Soft'Anny Mohair.*

Lightning Flash *Substitute either Pingouin Pingofine or Pingouin Pingolaine.*

Scandinavian Snowflakes *For Sleeping Bag, Man's Sweater and Girl's Sweater, substitute 3 Suisses Lanasport Nina Ricci. For Girl's Scarf, substitute 3 Suisses Sweet Lady and size 3¼mm needles. For Woman and Child's Scarf, and Woman and Child's Sweater, substitute 3 Suisses Super Lana Yves St Laurent.*

Paisley Pair *See below for stockist.*

Tweedy Family *Substitute 3 Suisses Morocco and size 3¾mm needles.*

Ming Jersey *Substitute 3 Suisses Shirley as follows: blue no 14 (A) and black no 61 (B).*

Woven Roses *Substitute 3 Suisses Shirley as follows: 9 balls beige no 58 (A) and 8 balls yellow no 36 (B). For the flowers, 3 Suisses Carina Yves St Laurent: 1 ball red no 76 and 1 ball dark wine no 02.*

Silken Shimmer *See below for stockist.*

Wisteria Cardigan *Substitute Pingouin Pingofrance as follows: 9 (10) balls nuage (A), 3 balls lilas (mauve) (B) and 1 ball jade (C).*

Ethnic Africa *Substitute Pingouin Pingofrance as follows: noir (B) and jonquille (Y).*

Cinemascope Jersey *Substitute Pingouin Pingolaine as follows: 10 (11) balls noir (A) and 1 ball brun (5). For the remaining colours only small amounts are needed: vert deau (pale green), giroselle (yellow), lagon (deep blue), glacier (pale blue), nuage (pale grey), orange, citron (yellow), beige rose (pale tan), azalée (dark pink) and eglantine (salmon pink).*

Technicolor Mohair *See below for stockist.*

Japanese Wave *Substitute Pingouin Confort as follows: amiral (1), ecru (7), nuage (4), grège (3), souris (2), dragée (5) giroselle (6), azur (11), glacier (12), givre (13), bleu franc (9), cobalt (8) and cyprés (10).*

Thirties Favourites *For The Waffle, substitute Pingouin fil d'Ecosse no 3.*

At the Russian Ballet *For Berger du Nord Douceur, substitute Pingouin Pingofine as follows: 8 balls noir (1), 3 balls jade (6), 3 balls feu (4), 2 balls azur (5), 3 balls vieux rose (for old rose) and 1 ball poussin (for pale yellow). For Moonlight, substitute Pingouin Luciole as follows: 11 balls Or (2), and to replace the colour champagne (3), use 1 strand of Pingofine vieux rose and 1 strand of Luciole Or (2) together.*

She Sells Scallop Shells *For Scallop Shell Sweater substitute Pingouin Coton Naturel 8 fils as follows: 16 balls ecru (E) and 4 balls white (W); and for shells substitute 3 balls white Pingouin Coton Naturel 4 fils.*

Aran Beauty *See below for stockist.*

Lacy Cotton Tops *See below for stockist.*

Paintbox Cardigan *For main colour, substitute 9 (10) balls of Pingouin Pingofrance ecru; use Laine Colbert DMC colours as listed.*

STOCKISTS

If you have difficulty obtaining the specified yarns in your area, the stockists listed below may be able to help you, either by supplying the yarn directly to you or by giving you the name of your local supplier.

Berger du Nord
Viking Wools Ltd, Rothay Holme, Rothay Road, Ambleside, Cumbria LA22 0HQ. Tel. 0966 32991.

Bouton d'Or
Woolgatherers, 10 Devonshire Road, London W4. Tel. 01-995 6813.

DMC
Dunlicraft Ltd, Pullman Road, Wigston, Leicester LE8 2DY. Tel. 0533 811040.

Georges Picaud Yarns UK
24 Prospect Road, Ossett, West Yorkshire WF5 8AE. Tel. 0924 262137.

Les Filatures de Paris
Woolgatherers, 10 Devonshire Road, London W4. Tel. 01-995 6813.

Phildar UK Ltd
4 Gambrel Road, Westgate Industrial Estate, Northampton NN5 5NF. Tel. 0604 583111.

Pingouin
French Wools Ltd, 7/11 Lexington Street, London W1R 4BU. Tel. 01-439 8891.

Ries Wools Ltd
243 High Holborn, London WC1. Tel. 01-242 7721 (mail order suppliers Pingouin, Phildar and Anny Blatt).

Schaffhousen
Woolgatherers, 10 Devonshire Road, London W4. Tel. 01-995 6813.

Sophie Desroches
Naturally Beautiful (Dent), Broadfield House, Dent, Nr Sedbergh, Cumbria LA10 5TG. Tel. 05875 421.

3 Suisses
Marlborough House, 38 Welford Road, Leicester LE2 7AA. Tel. 0533 554713.